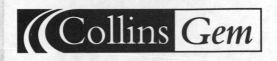

Collins Gem

Portuguese

Phrase Book

CONSULTANT
Edite Vieira

GEM PHRASE BOOKS

DUTCH
FRENCH
GERMAN
GREEK
ITALIAN
PORTUGUESE
SPANISH

*Also available Gem Phrase
Book CD Packs*

First published 1993
This edition published 2003
Copyright © HarperCollins Publishers
Reprint 10 9 8 7 6 5 4 3 2
Printed in Italy by Amadeus S.p.A

www.collins.co.uk

ISBN 0-00-714190-4

Your *Collins Gem Phrase Book* is designed to help you locate the exact phrase you need in any situation, whether for holiday or business. If you want to adapt the phrases, we have made sure that you can easily see where to substitute your own words (you can find them in the dictionary section), and the clear two-colour layout gives you direct access to the different topics.

The *Gem Phrase Book* includes:

■ Over 70 topics arranged thematically. Each phrase is accompanied by a simple pronunciation guide which ensures that there's no problem over pronouncing the foreign words.

■ Practical hints and useful vocabulary highlighted in boxes. Where no article (**o/a/um/uma**) is given, you will generally see the word written on signs and notices. We give the pronunciation for all words.

WORDS APPEARING IN BLACK ARE ENGLISH WORDS	WORDS APPEARING IN BLUE ARE PORTUGUESE WORDS

■ Possible phrases you may hear in reply to your questions. The foreign phrases appear in blue.

■ A clearly laid-out 5000-word dictionary: English words appear in black and Portuguese words appear in blue.

■ A basic grammar section which will enable you to build on your phrases.

It's worth spending time before you embark on your travels just looking through the topics to see what is covered and becoming familiar with what might be said to you.

Whatever the situation, your *Gem Phrase Book* is sure to help!

CONTENTS

PRONOUNCING PORTUGUESE

The Portuguese language is much easier to read than to speak.
However, the pronunciation guide used in this book is as near as
possible to the real sound. The syllable to be stresssed is marked in
heavy italics. Note that in conversation words tend to run together.

■ VOWELS (a, e, i, o, u)

OPEN (LONG) SOUND	CLOSED (SHORT) SOUND
a ie. s<u>a</u>co **sah**-koo	ie. f<u>a</u>ma **fam**uh
e ie. t<u>e</u>rra **terr**uh	ie. de d<u>uh</u>
o ie. c<u>o</u>bra **koh**-bruh	ie. v<u>o</u>ltar vol**tar**

NOTE: The article a sounds like uh (as in **the**), unless stressed, ie. à
e can sound like ay, ie. fecho **fay**shoo, but tends to be silent
at the end of words, ie. pode pod) unless stressed, ie. bebé.
The word e (meaning **and**) always sounds like ee (as in **police**)
o can sound like oo, ie. vaso **vah**-zoo, and the article o always
sounds like oo
i sounds like ee, ie. fica **fee**kuh
u usually sounds like oo, ie. luvas **loo**vush

■ VOWEL COMBINATIONS

ai = y, ie. **mais** = m<u>y</u>sh   **oi** = oy, ie. **coisa** = **koy**-zuh
ei = ay, ie. **peixe** = p<u>ay</u>sh   **ou** = oh, ie. **outro** = **oh**-troo

■ NASAL VOWELS

Vowels with a tilde ~, or followed by m (um) or n (in) should
be pronounced nasally (let air out through nose as well as mouth),
similar to French. We have represented this sound in the
pronunciation by ñ, ie.

tem = tayñ   **com** = koñ   **um** = ooñ
pão = powñ   **manhã** = man-**yañ**   **põe** = poyñ

■ OTHER LETTERS

Try to recognize the sounds of the following:

● **ç** serviço ser**vee**soo ● **nh** tenho **ten**-yoo ● **ch** chá <u>sha</u>
● **r/rr** at the start or middle of word rolled ● **g** gelo jay-loo
(soft like zh) ● **s** (between vowels) coisa koy-zuh; (after vowel and
at end of word) está shta, lápis lah-peesh ● **h** always silent
● **j** loja loj<u>uh</u> (soft like zh) ● **x** caixa ky-<u>shuh</u>
● **lh** mulher mool-**yehr** ● **z** (at end of word) faz fa<u>sh</u>

6

You will find the Portuguese are quite cerimonious and will appreciate reciprocity. The best thing to do is to follow the same approach to them as they have towards yourself.

Please
Por favor / Faz favor
poor fa-**vor** / fash fa-**vor**

Thank you
Obrigado(a)
oh-bree**gah**-doo(-duh)

Thanks very much
Muito obrigado(a)
mweento oh-bree**gah**-doo(-duh)

You're welcome!
De nada!
duh **nah**-duh

Yes
Sim
seeñ

No
Não
nowñ

OK!
Está bem
shta bayñ

Sir / Mr
Senhor / Sr.
sun-**yor**

Madam / Mrs / Ms
Senhora / Sra.
sun-**yo**ruh

Miss
Menina
muh-**nee**nuh

Hello / Hi
Olá
oh-**la**

Goodbye / Bye
Adeus
a**day**-oosh

See you later
Até logo
a**te** **log**oo

See you tomorrow
Até amanhã
a**te** aman-**yañ**

Good morning
Bom dia
bawñ **dee**-uh

Good afternoon/evening
Boa tarde
boh-uh tard

Goodnight
Boa noite
boh-uh noyt

Excuse me! *(to catch attention)*
Por favor!
poor fa-**vor**

Sorry!
Desculpe!
dush**koolp**

How are you?
Como está?
koh-moo shta

Fine, thanks
Bem, obrigado(a)
bayñ oh-bree**gah**-doo(-duh)

And you?
E você?
ee voh-**se**

I don't understand
Não compreendo
nowñ kompree-**en**doo

Do you speak English?
Fala inglês?
fah-luh eenglesh

KEY PHRASES

*The easiest way to ask for something is by naming what you want and adding por favor (poor fa**vor**).*

the (masculine)
o / os
oo / ohsh

glass / glasses
o copo / os copos
*oo **kopo**o / oosh **kop**oosh*

a / one glass
um copo
*ooñ **kopo**o*

the (feminine)
a / as
uh / uhsh

key / keys
a chave / as chaves
*uh shahv / uhsh **shah**-vush*

a / one key
uma chave
***oom**uh shahv*

my (masculine)
o meu
*oo may**oo***

(feminine)
a minha
*uh **meen**-yuh*

my glass
o meu copo
*oo may**oo kopo**o*

my key
a minha chave
*uh **meen**-yuh shahv*

his / your
o seu / a sua
*oo say**oo** / uh **soo**-uh*

his / your glass
o seu copo
*oo say**oo kopo**o*

his / your key
a sua chave
*uh **soo**-uh shahv*

Do you have...?
Tem...?
tayñ...

Do you have a room?
Tem um quarto?
*tayñ ooñ **kwar**too*

Do you have any milk?
Tem leite?
tayñ layt

Do you have stamps
Tem selos?
*tayñ **se**loosh*

I'd like...
Queria...
***kree**-uh...*

I'd like an ice cream
Queria um gelado
***kree**-uh ooñ zhuh-**lah**doo*

I'd like to book a table
Queria reservar uma mesa
***kree**-uh ruh-zer**var oom**uh **may**-zuh*

I'd like pasta
Queria massa
***kree**-uh **mass**uh*

We'd like...
Queríamos...
***kree**-uhmoosh...*

We'd like two cakes
Queríamos dois bolos
***kree**-uhmoosh doysh **boh**loosh*

More...
Mais...
mysh...

More bread
Mais pão
mysh powñ

More water
Mais ágwa
mysh ahg-wuh

Another...
Outro(a)
oh-troo(truh)

Another milky coffee
Outro galão
oh-troo galown

Another lager
Outra cerveja
oh-truh servay-zhuh

How much is it?
Quanto é?
kwantoo e

How much does it cost?
Quanto custa?
kwantoo kooshtuh

large
grande
grond

small
pequeno
puh-kaynoo

with
com
koñ

without
sem
sayñ

Where is...?
Onde é...?
onduh e...

Where are...?
Onde são / estão...?
onduh sowñ / shtowñ...

Where is the toilet?
Onde é a casa de banho?
onduh e uh kahzuh duh ban-yoo

Where are the children?
Onde estão as crianças?
onduh shtowñ uhsh kree-ansush

How do I get ...?
Como se vai...?
koh-moo suh vy paruh

to the station
para a estação
paruh a shtasowñ

to the centre
ao centro
oo sentroo

There is/are...
Há...
a...

There isn't/aren't any...
Não há...
nowñ a...

When...?
Quando...?
kwandoo...

At what time...?
A que hora é...
uh kee oruh e...

today
hoje
ohj

tomorrow
amanhã
aman-yañ

Can I...?
Posso...?
possoo...

Can I smoke?
Posso fumar?
possoo foomar

Can I pay?
Posso pagar?
possoo pagar

How does this work?
Como funciona?
koh-moo foonss-yonuh

What does this mean?
Que quer dizer isto?
kuh kayr deezehr eeshtoo

9

Homens
gentlemen

Senhoras
ladies

auto-serviço
self-service

aberto
open

fechado
closed

EMPURRE
push

água para beber/ água potável
drinking water

CAIXA
cash desk

PUXE
pull

Banco
(hospital) casualty dept.

lavabos
toilets

livre
vacant/free

ocupado
engaged/ occupied

NÃO FUNCIONA
out of order

Primeiros Socorros
first aid

AVARIADO
out of order

CHEIO
full

Liquidação Total
closing down sale

para alugar   for hire / rent

para venda   for sale

saldos   sales

cave ↓	rés-do-chão	entrada
basement	**ground floor**	**entrance**

← BILHETEIRA
ticket office

VAGAS/VAGO
vacancies/vacant

EQUITAÇÃO
horse riding

COMPLETO
no vacancies

Quente
hot

BANHEIRO
lifeguard (beach)

VESTIÁRIOS
changing rooms

casas de banho
bathrooms

Proibido
forbidden/no...

IMPEDIDO
engaged

degustação
tasting

Não mexer/não tocar
do not touch

DESCONTOS
reductions

pagar na caixi
pay at cash desk

INFORMAÇÕES
information

depósito de bagagens
left luggage

Privado
private

PERIGO
danger

fumadores
smoking

11

POLITE EXPRESSIONS

There are three forms of address in Portuguese: formal (senhor/a), semi-formal (você – for both sexes) and informal (tu – for both sexes). Always stick to the formal for older people to be treated in a situation of deference, or the semi-formal for people of one's same age and status, until you are invited to use the informal tu.

The meal was delicious
A refeição estava deliciosa
uh ruhfaysowñ shtavuh duhlees-yohzuh

This is a gift for you
Isto é um presente para si
eeshtoo e ooñ pruh-zent paruh see

This is my husband
Este é o meu marido
esht e oo mayoo muhreedoo

You have a beautiful home
Tem uma linda casa
tayñ oomuh leeñduh kahzuh

Thanks for your hospitality
Gratos pelo convite
grahtoosh pehloo koñveet

Enjoy your holiday!
Boas férias!
boh-ush fehr-yush

It was nice seeing you again
Foi bom encontrá-lo(-la) outra vez
foy boñ ayñ-kontrah-loo(-luh) ohtruh vesh

I enjoyed myself very much
Diverti-me muito
deevehrtee-muh mweentoo

Thank you very much
Muito obrigado(a)
mweentoo oh-breegah-doo(-duh)

Pleased to meet you
Muito prazer
mweentoo prazehr

This is my wife
Esta é a minha mulher
eshtuh e uh meenyuh mool-yehr

You have a beautiful garden
Tem um lindo jardim
tayñ ooñ leeñdoo juhrdeeñ

We'd like to come back
Gostaríamos de voltar
gooshtuhreeamoosh duh voltar

Please come and visit us
Por favor visite-nos
poor favor veezeetnoosh

We must stay in touch
Devemos ficar em contacto
duhvehmoosh feekar ayñ kontaktoo

12

My best wishes for a...
Os meus votos de...
oosh mayoosh votoosh duh...

I'd like to wish you a... *(familiar)*
Desejo que tenhas um...
duh-zay-joo kuh ten-yush ooñ...

Merry Christmas!
Bom Natal!
boñ natal

Happy New Year!
Feliz Ano Novo!
fuh-leesh ah-noo noh-voo

Happy birthday!
Feliz aniversário!
fuh-leesh aneever-sar-yoo

Have a good trip!
Muito boa viagem!
mweentoo boh-uh vee-ah-jayñ

Best wishes!
Felicidades!
feleesee-dah-dush

Welcome!
Bem-vindo(a)!
bayñ-veen-doo(uh)

Enjoy your meal!
Bom apetite!
boñ apuh-teet

Thanks, and you too!
Obrigado(a), igualmente!
oh-breegah-doo(uh) eegwalment

Cheers!
Saúde!
sa-ood

Congratulations! *(having a baby, getting married, etc)*
Parabéns!
paruh-baynsh

see also **MAKING FRIENDS** □ **LETTERS**

MAKING FRIENDS

*In this section we have used the familiar form **tu** for the questions.
Tu is widely used between young people soon after being
introduced and between close friends and relatives – at any age.*

What's your name?
Como te chamas?
*koh-moo tuh **shah**-mush*

My name is...
Chamo-me...
shah-moo-muh...

How old are you?
Quantos anos tens?
***kwan**toosh **ah**-noosh tayñsh*

I'm ... years old
Tenho ... anos
*ten-yoo ... **ah**-noosh*

Where are you from?
De onde és?
*duh **on**duh esh*

I'm English (masc.)
Sou inglês
*soh een**glesh***

I'm English (fem.)
Sou inglesa
*soh een**gle**zuh*

Where do you live?
Onde vives?
***on**duh **vee**vush*

Where do you live? (plural)
Onde vivem?
on**duh vee**vayñ

I live in London
Vivo em Londres
***vee**-voo ayñ **lon**drush*

We live in Glasgow
Vivemos em Glasgow
*vee-**veh**-moosh ayñ **glas**gow*

I'm still studying
Sou estudante
*soh shto**dant***

I work
Trabalho
*tra**bal**-yoo*

I'm retired
Sou reformado(a)
*soh refoor**mah**-doo(uh)*

I'm...
Sou...
soh...

single
solteiro(a)
*sol**tay**-roo(uh)*

married
casado(a)
*ka**zah**-doo(uh)*

divorced
divorciado(a)
*deevoors-**yah**-doo(uh)*

I have...
Tenho...
ten-yoo...

a boyfriend
namorado
*namoo-**rah**-doo*

a girlfriend
namorada
*namoo-**rah**-duh*

a partner
companheiro(a)
*kompan-**yay**-roo(uh)*

I have ... children
Tenho ... filhos
*ten-yoo ... **feel**-yoosh*

I have no children
Não tenho filhos
*nowñ **ten**-yoo **feel**-yoosh*

I'm here...
Estou aqui...
*shtoh a**kee**...*

on holiday
de férias
*duh **fehr**-yush*

for work
por motivo de trabalho
*poor moo**tee**-voo duh tra**bal**-yoo*

see also **WORK** ❑ **LEISURE/INTERESTS** ❑ **SPORT**

What work do you do?
Em que trabalha?
*ayñ kuh tra**bal**-yuh*

Do you enjoy it?
Gosta?
***goosh**tuh*

I'm...
Sou...
soh...

a doctor
médico(a)
*me**di**koo(uh)*

a teacher
professor(a)
*proofuh-**sor**(uh)*

an engineer
engenheiro(a)
*enjun-**ay**roo(uh)*

I work in...
Trabalho em...
*tra**bal**-yoo ayñ...*

a shop
uma loja
***oom**uh **loj**uh*

a factory
uma fábrica
***oom**uh **fab**rikuh*

a bank
um banco
*ooñ **bank**oo*

I work from home
Trabalho em casa
*tra**bal**-yoo ayñ **kah**-zuh*

I'm self-employed
Trabalho por conta própria
*tra**bal**-yoo poor **kon**-tuh **pro**pree-uh*

I am unemployed
Estou desempregado(a)
*shtoh duh-zaympruh-**gah**-doo(uh)*

I don't work
Não trabalho
*nowñ tra**bal**-yoo*

It's very difficult to get a job at the moment
É muito difícil arranjar trabalho agora
*e **mween**too dee**fee**seel arran**jar** tra**bal**-yoo a**gor**uh*

What are your hours?
Qual é teu horário?
*kwal e oo **tay**oo oh-**rar**-yoo*

I work from 9 to 5
Eu trabalho das nove às cinco
*ay-oo tra**bal**-yoo dush nov ash **seen**koo*

from Monday to Friday
de segunda a sexta
*.duh suh**goon**-duh uh **sesh**tuh*

How much holiday do you get?
Quanto tempo tem de férias?
***kwan**too **temp**oo tayñ duh **fehr**-yush*

What do you want to be when you grow up?
Que queres fazer quando cresceres?
*kuh **kehr**ush fa**zehr kwan**doo krush-**sehr**ush*

see also **MAKING FRIENDS** ☐ **BUSINESS**

15

CHUVEIROS / AGUACEIROS *shoovayroosh* / *agwa-sayroosh*		**SHOWERS**
LIMPO *leenpoo*		**CLEAR**
A CHUVA *uh shoovuh*		**RAIN**
A NEBLINA *uh nuhbleenuh*		**MIST**
O NEVOEIRO *oo nuhvooayroo*		**FOG**
NUBLADO *nooblahdoo*		**CLOUDY**

It's sunny
Faz sol
fash sol

It's raining
Está a chover
shta uh shoovehr

It's windy
Está vento
shta ventoo

What a lovely day!
Que lindo dia!
kuh leendoo dee-uh

What awful weather!
Que mau tempo!
kuh maoo tempo

What will the weather be like tomorrow?
Como estará o tempo amanhã?
koh-moo shtuh-rah oo tempoo aman-yañ

Do you think it will rain?
Acha que vai chover?
ashuh kuh vy shoovehr

Do I need an umbrella?
Preciso duma sombrinha?
pre-seezoo doomuh sombreen-ya

When will it stop raining?
Quando parará de chover?
kwandoo parah-rah duh shoovehr

It's very hot
Está muito calor
shta mweento kalor

Do you think there will be a storm?
Acha que haverá uma tempestade?
asha kuh avuhrah oomuh temp-shtahd

What is the temperature?
Qual é a temperatura?
kwal e uh tempratooruh

EM FRENTE *ayñ frent*	**OPPOSITE**
AO LADO DE *ow lah-doo duh*	**NEXT TO**
PERTO DE *pehrtoo duh*	**NEAR TO**
O SEMÁFORO *oo suh-mafooroo*	**TRAFFIC LIGHTS**
NA ESQUINA *nuh shkeenuh*	**AT THE CORNER**

Excuse me, sir / madam!
Por favor, senhor / senhora!
poor favor sun-yor / sun-yoruh

How do I/we get to...?
Como se vai a...?
koh-moo suh vy uh...

to the station
a estação
a shtasowñ

to the Gulbenkian
à Gulbenkian
a gool-ben-kyan

to Rossio
ao Rossio
ow roosyoo

We're looking for...
Estamos à procura de...
shta-moosh a prookooruh duh...

Is it far?
É longe?
e lonzh

Can I walk there?
Pode-se ir a pé?
pod-suh eer uh pay

We're lost
Estamos perdidos
shta-moosh perdee-doosh

Is this the right way to...?
É este o caminho para...?
e esht oo kameen-yoo paruh...

How do I/we get onto the motorway?
Como se entra na auto-estrada?
komo suh entruh nuh owtoo-shtrah-duh

Can you show me where it is on the map?
Por favor indique-me onde está, no mapa?
pod-muh eendeekuh-muh onduh shta noo mah-puh

■ **YOU MAY HEAR**

Depois de passar a ponte
depoysh duh pasar uh pont
After passing the bridge

Volte à esquerda / direita
volt a shkehrduh / deeray-tuh
Turn left / right

Siga em frente até chegar a...
see-guh ayñ frent ate shegar uh...
Keep straight on until you get to...

see also **MAPS & GUIDES**

BUS & COACH

If you intend using buses a lot, it is worth enquiring at the Tourist Office how to get hold of a travel pass – um passe. The word for both bus and coach is o autocarro.

Is there a bus to...?
Há autocarro para...?
*a owtoo-**karr**oo **pa**ruh...*

Which bus goes to...?
Que autocarro vai a...?
*kuh owtoo-**karr**oo vy uh...*

Where do I catch the bus to...?
Onde apanho um autocarro para...?
*onduh apan-**yoo** ooñ owtoo-**karr**oo **pa**ruh...*

We're going to...
Vamos para...
*vuh-moosh **pa**ruh...*

Where do they sell bus tickets?
Onde vendem módulos / bilhetes?
*onduh ven**dayñ moh**-doo-loosh / beel-**yet**sh*

How much is it...?
Quanto é...?
*kwan*too e...*

to the centre	to the beach	to Sintra
para o centro	para a praia	para Sintra
paruh oo sentroo	*paruh uh pry-uh*	*paruh seentra*

How often are the buses to...?
Que frequência têm os autocarros para...?
*kuh fruh-**kwens**yuh tay-**ayñ** oosh owtoo-**karr**oosh **pa**ruh...*

When is the first / the last bus to...?
A que horas é o primeiro / o último autocarro para...?
*uh kee **or**uz e oo pree**may**-roo / oo **ool**timoo owtoo-**karr**oo **pa**ruh...*

Please tell me when to get off
Pode-me dizer quando devo sair?
pod**-muh dee**zehr kwan**doo **deh**-voo suh-**eer

This is my stop
Esta é a minha paragem
***esh**-tuh e uh **meen**-yuh pa**rah**-jayñ*

■ **YOU MAY HEAR**

Este autocarro não pára em...
*aysht owtoo-**karr**oo nowñ **pah**-ruh ayñ...*
This bus doesn't stop in...

Tem que apanhar o...
*tayñ kuh apan-**yar** oo...*
You must catch the...

see also METRO ☐ TAXI ☐ LUGGAGE

*You can buy either **uma caderneta de 10 viagens**, which is valid for 10 journeys (no date limit) or **um passe**, which covers a month's travel on both bus and metro.*

ENTRADA *en**trah**duh*	ENTRANCE
SAÍDA *sa**ee**duh*	WAY OUT / EXIT
A LINHA DE METRO *uh **leen**-yuh duh **me**troo*	METRO LINE

Where is the nearest metro station?
Onde é a estação de metro mais próxima?
*onduh e uh shta**sown** duh **me**troo mysh **pross**imuh*

How does the ticket machine work?
Como funciona a máquina automática?
*koh-moo foonss-**yo**nuh uh **mak**inuh owtoo**ma**tikuh*

Do you have a map of the metro?
Tem um mapa do metro?
*tayñ ooñ **mah**-puh doo **me**troo*

I'm going to...
Vou a...
voh uh...

How do I/we get to...?
Como se vai para...?
*koh-moo suh vy **pa**ruh...*

Do I have to change?
Tenho que mudar?
*ten-yoo kuh moo**dar***

Which line is it for...?
Qual é a linha para...?
*kwal e uh **leen**-yuh **pa**ruh...*

In which direction?
Em que direcção?
*ayñ kuh dee**reh**sowñ*

What is the next stop?
Qual é a próxima paragem?
*kwal e uh **pross**imuh pa**rah**-jayñ*

Excuse me!
Por favor!
*poor fa**vor***

Please let me through
Pode-me deixar passar?
*pod-muh day**shar** pa**ssar***

I'm getting off here
Desço aqui
*desh-soo a**kee***

see also **BUS & COACH** ☐ **TAXI** ☐ **LUGGAGE**

*There are two types of train ticket for all trains: **primeira classe** and **segunda classe** (1st and 2nd class). On longer trips, where it is advisable to book ahead (**reservar lugares**), trains may be called **Rápidos** (fast), **Intercidades** and **Alfa** (both intercity, modern fast trains). These trains depart from the **Santa Apolónia** station in Lisbon and go northwards. To travel south from Lisbon by train you must first cross the Tagus by ferry, making it far easier (and cheaper) to go by coach. Ask for details of departures at the Tourist Office. Commuter trains for the Lisbon area depart from the **Rossio** station (for the Sintra line) and from **Cais do Sodré** (for the Estoril line).*

A ESTAÇÃO *uh shta**sowñ***		**STATION**
PARTIDAS *par**tee**dush*		**DEPARTURES**
CHEGADAS *shuh**gah**dush*		**ARRIVALS**

Where is the station?
Onde é a estação?
*onduh e uh shta**sowñ***

To the station, please
À estação, por favor
*uh shta**sowñ** por fa**vor***

A single ticket
Um bilhete de ida
*ooñ beel-**yet dee**duh*

Two return tickets
Dois bilhetes de ida e volta
*doysh beel-**yetsh dee**duh ee voltuh*

to...
para...
paruh...

First / Second class
Primeira / Segunda classe
*pree**may**ruh / se**goon**duh klas*

Smoking / No smoking
Fumador / Não fumador
*fooma**dor** / nownʹ fooma**dor***

When is the next train to....?
Quando é o próximo comboio para...?
*kwandoo e oo **pross**imoo kom**boy**oo paruh...*

Is there a supplement to pay?
Paga-se suplemento?
*pah-guh-suh soopluh-**men**too*

I want to book a seat on the ALFA to Aveiro
Queria reservar um lugar no ALFA para Aveiro
*kree-uh ruh-zer**var** ooñ loo**gar** noo **alfa** paruh a**vay**roo*

When does it arrive in...?
A que horas chega a...?
*uh kee **or**ush sheh-guh uh...*

Do I have to change?
Tenho que mudar?
ten**-yoo kuh moo**dar

Where?
Onde?
***ond**uh*

How long is there to get the connection?
Que tempo leva para a ligação?
*kuh **tem**poo **lev**uh **par**uh uh leeguh-**sowñ***

Which platform does it leave from?
De que plataforma parte?
*duh kuh platuh**for**muh part*

Is this the right platform for the train to...?
É esta a plataforma do comboio para...?
*e **esht**uh uh platuh**for**muh doo kom**boy**oo **par**uh...*

Is this the train for...?
É este o comboio para...?
*e **aysht** oo kom**boy**oo **par**uh...*

When will it leave?
A que horas parte?
*uh kee **or**ush part*

Why is there a delay?
Porque é o atraso?
*poor**kee** e oo a**trah**-zoo*

Does the train stop at...?
O comboio pára em...?
*oo kom**boy**oo **pah**-ruh ayñ...*

Please let me know when we get to...
Por favor diga-me quando chegarmos a...?
*poor fa**vor** **dee**guh-muh **kwan**doo shuh**gar**-mooz uh...*

Is there a buffet on the train?
Há um vagão restaurante no comboio?
*a ooñ va**gowñ** rushtoh-**rant** noo kom**boy**oo*

Is this free? *(seat)*
Está livre?
*shta **lee**vruh*

Excuse me
Perdão / Desculpe
*puhr**dowñ** / dush**koolp***

see also **LUGGAGE**

TAXI

I need a taxi
Preciso de um táxi
*pre-**see**zoo dooñ **tax**ee*

Where can I/we get a taxi?
Onde se pode arranjar um táxi?
***on**duh suh pod arran**jar** ooñ **tax**ee*

Please order me a taxi
Por favor chame-me um táxi
*poor fa**vor sha**-muh-muh ooñ **tax**ee*

now
agora
*a**gor**uh*

for...*(time)*
para as...
***pa**ruh ush...*

How much will it cost by taxi...?
Quanto custa ir de táxi...?
***kwan**too **koosh**tuh eer duh **tax**ee...*

to the centre
ao centro
*ow **sen**troo*

to the station
à estação
*a shta**sowñ***

to the airport
ao aeroporto
*ow uh-ehroo-**por**too*

to this address
a esta morada
*uh **esh**tuh moo**rah**-duh*

Please take me to...
Por favor leve-me a...
*poor fa**vor** lev-muh uh...*

Please take us to...
Por favor leve-nos a...
*poor fa**vor** lev-noosh uh...*

How much is it?
Quanto é?
***kwan**too e*

Why are you charging me so much?
Porque está a pedir tanto?
***poor**kuh shta uh pe**deer** **tan**too*

It's more than on the meter
É mais do que marca no contador
*e mysh doo kuh **mar**kuh noo kontuh-**dor***

Keep the change
Guarde o troco
*gward oo **tro**koo*

Sorry, I don't have any change
Desculpe, não tenho troco
*dush**koolp** nowñ **ten**-yoo **tro**koo*

I'm in a hurry
Tenho muita pressa
***ten**-yoo **mween**tuh **press**uh*

Is it far?
É longe?
e lonj

I have to catch...
Tenho que apanhar...
***ten**-yoo kuh apan-**yar**...*

the ... o'clock flight to...
o voo das ... horas para...
*oo **voh**-oo dush ... **or**ush **pa**ruh...*

see also **LUGGAGE** ☐ **BUS** ☐ **METRO** ☐ **TAXI**

A TRAVESSIA *uh tra****vess****-yuh*	**CROSSING**
O CRUZEIRO *oo kroo****zay****roo*	**CRUISE**
O CAMAROTE *oo kama****roht***	**CABIN**

When is the next boat to...?
Quando parte o próxima barco para...?
*kwan*doo part oo *pross*imoo **bar**koo *pa*ruh...

Have you a timetable?
Tem um horário?
*tayñ ooñ oh-****rar****-yoo*

Is there a car ferry to...?
Há um ferry-boat para...?
*a ooñ ferry-boat pa*ruh...

How much is a ticket...?
Quanto é o bilhete...?
*kwan*too e oo beel-*yet*...

single
de ida
*dee*duh

return
de ida e volta
*dee*duh ee **vol**tuh

A tourist ticket
Um bilhete de segunda classe
*ooñ beel-****yet*** *duh se****goon****duh klass*

How much is the crossing for a car and ... people?
Quanto é a passagem para ... pessoas e um carro?
*kwan*too e *uh* pa*sah*-jayñ *pa*ruh ... puh-**so**-ush ee ooñ **kar**roo

How long is the journey?
Quanto dura a viagem?
*kwan*to *doo*ruh vee-*ah*-jayñ

What time do we get to...?
A que horas chegamos a...?
*uh kee **o**rush shuh****gah****-moosh uh*...

Where does the boat leave from?
De onde parte o barco?
*dee****on****duh part oo **bar**koo*

When is...?
A que horas é...?
*uh kee **o**ru*z e...

the first boat
o primeiro barco
*oo pree****may****-roo **bar**koo*

the last boat?
o último barco
*oo **ool**timoo **bar**koo*

Is there somewhere to eat on the boat?
O barco tem restaurante?
*oo **bar**koo tayñ rushtoh-****rant***

see also **LUGGAGE**

Most signs are in Portuguese and English and you may go through the airport without having to speak any Portuguese.

How do I get to the airport?
Como se vai para o aeroporto?
koh-moo suh vy paruh oo e-ro-pohrtoo

To the airport, please
Para o aeroporto, por favor
paruh oo e-ro-pohrtoo poor favor

How long does it take to get to the airport?
Quanto tempo leva a chegar ao aeroporto?
kwantoo tempoo lehvuh uh shuhgar aoo e-ro-pohrtoo

What is the best way to get to the airport?
Qual é a melhor maneira de ir para o aeroporto?
kwal e uh mel-yor muh-nayruh duh eer paruh oo e-ro-pohrtoo

How do I/we get to the centre of (name town)**...?**
Como se vai para o centro de...?
koh-moo suh vy paruh oo sentroo duh...

How much is the taxi fare...?
Quanto custa ir de táxi...?
kwantoo kooshtuh eer duh taxee...

into town
para o centro
paruh oo sentroo

to the hotel
para o hotel
pro oh-tel

Is there a bus to the city centre?
Há algum autocarro para o centro?
a algooñ owtoo-karroo paruh oo sentroo

Where do I check in for...(airline)**?**
Onde faço o check-in para...?
onduh fah-soo oo check-in paruh...

Where is the luggage for the flight from...?
Onde está a bagagem do voo de...?
onduh shta uh bagah-jayñ doo voh-oo duh...

■ YOU MAY HEAR

O seu voo está atrasado
oo sayoo voh-oo shta atruh-zah-doo
Your flight is delayed

*With the single European Market, EU citizens are subject only to highly selective spot checks and they can go through the blue customs channel (unless they have goods to declare). There is no restriction, either by quantity or value, on goods purchased by travellers in another EU country provided they are **for their own personal use** (guidelines have been published). If you are unsure of certain items, check with the customs officials as to whether payment of duty is required.*

UE *oo ay*	**EU**
BILHETE DE IDENTIDADE *beel-yet duh eedenteedad*	**IDENTITY CARD**
ALFÂNDEGA *alfanduh-guh*	**CUSTOMS**
NADA A DECLARAR **na**duh uh dekla**rar**	**NOTHING TO DECLARE**
ARTIGOS A DECLARAR ar**tee**goosh uh dekla**rar**	**ARTICLES TO DECLARE**

Do I have to pay duty on this?
É preciso pagar direitos para isto?
*e pre-**see**zoo pa**gar** dee**ray**-toosh **pa**ruh **eesh**too*

I bought this as a gift
Comprei para oferecer
*kom**pray pa**ruh of fuh-ruh-**sehr***

It is for my own personal use
É para meu uso pessoal
*e **pa**ruh **may**oo **oo**zoo puh-**swal***

We are in transit
Estamos aqui em trânsito
*shta**moosh a**kee ayñ **tran**zitoo*

We are going to…
Vamos a…
***vuh**-moosh uh…*

The children are on this passport
As crianças estão neste passaporte
*ush kree-**an**sush shtowñ nesht passuh-**port***

This is the baby's passport
Este é o passaporte do bebé
*esht e oo passuh-**port** doo be-**bay***

SENTIDO ÚNICO
one way

DÊ PRIORIDADE
give way

PERIGO
danger

ESTACIONAMENTO PROIBIDO
no parking

DEVAGAR
slow down

DESVIO
diversion

SEJA PRUDENTE
be careful

zona
P
CARGAS E DESCARGAS
loading and unloading

FIM DE OBRAS
end of roadworks

SAÍDA
exit

INVERSÃO DE MARCHA

300 m

300 m on is a place to do a u-turn

TODAS AS DIRECÇÕES
all routes

PORTAGEM PÉAGE
toll station for motorway

ALFÂNDEGA ADUANA
customs

AUTO-ESTRADA
motorway

north
Norte

Oeste **Leste**
west   east

Sul
south

CIRCUNVALAÇÃO
by-pass

school

post office

town centre

speed limits in Portugal are in km/h

underground

railway station

town hall

disabled

market

A2
A indicates motorway

IP4
IP stands for Itinerário Principal (main trunk road)

IC2
8
IC stands for Itinerário Complementar (complementary trunk road)

Fim de desvio
end of diversion

ÀS 4.ªs FEIRAS
on Wednesdays

DAS 6 às 15h
from 6 to 15h

DIAS ÚTEIS DAS 8 ÀS 20H
weekdays from 8 to 20h

ESTACIONAMENTO
parking

P livre
spaces

P completo
full

27

A CARTA DE CONDUÇÃO *uh kartuh duh kondoosowñ*	DRIVING LICENCE
O SEGURO *oo segooroo*	INSURANCE
A MARCHA ATRÁS *uh marshuh atrash*	REVERSE GEAR

I want to hire a car
Queria alugar um carro
kree-uh aloogar ooñ karroo

for ... days
para ... dias
paruh ... dee-ush

the weekend
o fim-de-semana
oo feeñ du semah-nuh

What are your rates...?
Quais são as tarifas...?
kwaysh sowñ ush tuh-ree-fush...

per day
por dia
poor dee-uh

per week
por semana
poor semah-nuh

How much is the deposit?
Quanto deixo de sinal?
kwantoo day-shoo duh seenal

Is there a kilometre charge?
Paga-se quilometragem?
pah-guh-suh keelometrah-jayñ

Is fully comprehensive insurance included?
Inclui o seguro contra todos os riscos?
een-klwee oo segooroo kontruh toh-duz oosh reeshkoosh

Do I have to return the car here?
Tenho que devolver o carro aqui?
ten-yoo kuh duh-volvehr oo karroo akee

By what time?
A que horas?
uh kuh orush

I'd like to leave it in...
Gostaria de o deixar em...
gooshtuh-ree-uh duh oo dayshar ayñ...

What shall I do if the car breaks down?
Que devo fazer se o carro se avariar?
kuh deh-voo fazehr suh oo karroo suh avuhree-yar

How can I get in touch with you, if needed?
Como devo entrar em contacto, se necessário?
koh-moo deh-voo ayntrar ayñ kontaktoo suh nussuh-sar-yoo

■ **YOU MAY HEAR**

Por favor devolva o carro com o depósito cheio
poor favor duh-volvuh oo karroo koñ oo duh-pozitoo shayoo
Please return the car with a full tank

see also **BREAKDOWN** ❑ **PETROL**

*Parking spaces may be free and car parks vary. You will have to ask about payment and length of stay. A restricted parking area is called a **zona azul**.*

Can I/we park here?
Pode-se estacionar aqui?
pod-suh shtass-yoo**nar** a**kee**

How long for?
Por quanto tempo?
poor **kwan**too **tem**poo

Where is the best place to park?
Onde é o melhor sítio para estacionar?
onduh e oo muhl-**yor** see**ty**oo pa**ruh** shtass-yoo**nar**

How long can I/we park for?
Quanto tempo se pode estacionar aqui?
kwantoo **tem**poo suh pod shtass-yoo**nar** a**kee**

Do I/we need a parking ticket?
É preciso um bilhete?
e pre-**see**zoo oo**ñ** beel-**yet**

How do I get to the motorway?
Como se vai para a auto-estrada?
koh-moo suh vy pa**ruh** uh owto-**shtrah**-duh

Which junction is it for...?
Qual é a junção para...?
kwal e uh zhoon**sowñ** pa**ruh**...

We're going to...
Vamos a...
vuh-moosh uh...

What is the best route?
Qual é o melhor caminho?
kwal e oo muhl-**yor** ka**meen**-yoo

Will the motorway be busy?
Haverá muito tráfego na auto-estrada?
uhv**rah** m**ween**too **trah**-fuh-goo nuh owto-**shtrah**-duh

Is it safe to drive at night?
É seguro conduzir de noite?
e se**goo**roo kondoo**zeer** duh noyt

see also **BREAKDOWN** □ **PETROL**

SUPER soo**pehr**	4 STAR
SEM CHUMBO sayñ **shoom**boo	UNLEADED
GASÓLEO ga**zol**-yoo	DIESEL
A GASOLINA uh gazoo-**lee**nuh	PETROL
A BOMBA DE GASOLINA uh **bom**buh duh gazoo-**lee**nuh	PETROL PUMP

Is there a petrol station near here?
Há alguma garagem aqui perto?
a al**goo**muh ga**rah**-jayñ akee **pehr**too

Fill it up, please
Encha, por favor
enshuh poor fa**vor**

Can you check the oil / the water?
Pode ver o óleo / a água?
pod vehr oo **ol**-yoo / uh **ahg**-wuh

...euros worth of unleaded petrol
...euros de gasolina sem chumbo
...**eur**oosh duh gazoo-**lee**nuh sayñ **shoom**boo

Where is...?	the air line	the water
Onde está...?	o ar	a água
onduh shta...	oo ar	uh **ahg**-wuh

Can you check the tyre pressure, please?
Pode ver a pressão dos pneus, por favor?
pod vehr uh pruh**sowñ** doosh **pnay**-oosh poor fa**vor**

Please fill this can with petrol
Por favor encha esta lata de gasolina
poor fa**vor en**shuh **esh**tuh **lah**-tuh duh gazoo-**lee**nuh

Can I pay with this credit card?
Posso pagar com o cartão de crédito?
possoo pa**gar** koñ oo kar**towñ** duh **kred**itoo

■ **YOU MAY HEAR**

Que bomba usou?
kuh **bom**buh oo**zoh**
Which pump did you use?

see also **BREAKDOWN** □ **CAR**

Can you help me?
Pode-me ajudar?
pod-muh ajoo*dar*

My car has broken down
Tenho o carro avariado
*ten*yoo oo *karr*oo avuh-ree-*ah*-doo

The car won't start
O carro não pega
oo *karr*oo nown*h* *peh*-guh

The battery is flat
A bateria está descarregada
uh batuh-*ree*-uh shta dushkarray-*gah*-duh

I've run out of petrol
Não tenho gasolina
nown*h* *ten*-yoo gazoo-*lee*nuh

Is there a garage near here?
Há alguma garagem por aqui?
a al*goo*muh ga*rah*-jayñ poor a*kee*

The engine is overheating
O motor está a aquecer demais
oo moo*tor* shta akuh-*sehr* duh-*mysh*

I need water
Preciso de água
pre-*see*zoo *dahg*-wuh

It's leaking...
Está a perder...
shta uh per*dehr*...

petrol
gasolina
gazoo-*lee*nuh

oil
óleo
ol-yoo

water
água
ahg-wuh

I've a flat tyre
Tenho um furo
ten-yoo ooñ *foo*roo

I can't get the wheel off
Não consigo tirar a roda
nown*h* kon*see*goo tee*rar* uh *rod*uh

Can you tow me to the nearest garage?
Pode-me rebocar até à oficina mais próxima?
pod-muh ruh-boo*kar* at*e* a ofee-*see*-nuh mysh *pross*imuh

Do you have parts for a (make of car)**...?**
Tem peças para um...?
tayñ *pess*ush *pa*ruh ooñ...

The ... doesn't work properly (see CAR–PARTS)
O/A ... não funciona bem
oo/uh ... nownh foonss-*yo*nuh bayñ

Can you replace the windscreen?
Pode substituir o pára-brisas?
pod soobshtee-*twer* oo *pa*ruh-*bree*zush

see also **CAR PARTS**

CAR PARTS

The ... doesn't work	The ... don't work
O/A ... não funciona	Os/As ... não funcionam
*oo/uh ... nowñ foonss-**yo**nuh*	*oosh/ush ... nowñ foonss-**yo**nowñ*

accelerator	o acelerador *assuh-luh-ra**dor***
battery	a bateria *batuh-**ree**-uh*
bonnet	o capot *kah-**po***
brakes	os travões *tra**voynsh***
choke	o motor de arranque *moo**tor** dee ar**rank***
clutch	a embraiagem *ayñ-bry-**ah**-jayñ*
distributor	o distribuidor *deesh-tree-bwee-**dor***
engine	o motor *moo**tor***
exhaust pipe	o tubo de escape *too*boo dush**kap***
fuse	o fusível *foo**zee**vel*
gears	as mudanças *moo**dan**sush*
handbrake	o travão de mão *tra**vowñ** duh mowñ*
headlights	os farois *fa**roysh***
ignition	a ignição *eegnee-**sowñ***
indicator	o indicador *eendeekuh**dor***
points	os platinados *platee-**nah**-doosh*
radiator	o radiador *radee-uh-**dor***
rear lights	os pilotos traseiros *pee**lo**toosh tra**zay**roosh*
seat belt	o cinto de segurança *seen*too duh segoo**ran**-suh*
spare wheel	a roda sobressalente *rod*uh sobruh-sa**lent***
spark plugs	as velas *vel*ush*
steering	a direcção *deere**sowñ***
steering wheel	o volante *voo**lant***
tyre	o pneu *p**nay**-oo*
wheel	a roda *rod*uh*
windscreen	o pára-brisas *paruh-**bree**zush*
-- washer	o lava pára-brisas *lavuh paruh-**bree**zush*
-- wiper	o limpa pára-brisas *leem*puh paruh-**bree**zush*

see also **BREAKDOWN** □ **PETROL**

If you haven't booked your accommodation, check with the local tourist office to see whether they have a list of hotels and guesthouses. It is also worth checking whether the travel agent through whom you purchased your flight can offer any interesting deals regarding accommodation. They can normally obtain more favourable rates than booking direct. From anywhere in the UK it is possible to get help and advice from the Portuguese Tourist Office, through their Call-Centre 090636 40610 (60p per minute). You can also get information on their website www.portugalinsite.com. You might want to stay in a Pousada luxurious state-run hotels that are often converted palaces, monasteries, or other historic buildings.

I'd like to book a room...
Queria reservar um quarto...
kree-uh ruh-zervar ooñ kwartoo...

single
individual
eendeeveed-wal

double
de casal
duh kazal

We'd like to stay ... nights
Queríamos ficar ... noites
kreeuh-moosh feekar ... noytsh

from ... till...
do dia ... ao dia...
doo dee-uh ... ow dee-uh...

with bath
com casa de banho
koñ kah-zuh duh bahn-yoo

with shower
com chuveiro
koñ shoo-vayroo

with a double bed
com cama de casal
koñ kah-muh duh kazal

twin-bedded
com duas camas
koñ doo-ush kah-mush

with an extra bed for a child
com uma cama extra para uma criança
koñ oomuh kah-muh aysh-truh paruh oomuh kree-ansuh

I'd like a room with three beds
Queria um quarto com três camas
kree-uh ooñ kwartoo kowñ tresh kah-mush

Can I book by e-mail?
Posso fazer a reserva por e-mail?
possoo fazehr uh ruhzervuh poor e-mail

cont...

We'd like two rooms next to each other
Queríamos dois quartos contíguos
*kreeuh-moosh doysh **kwar**toosh kon**teeg**woosh*

I will confirm...	**by e-mail**	**by fax**
Confirmarei...	por e-mail	por fax
*komfeer-ma**ray**...*	*poor e-mail*	*poor fax*
How much is it...?	**per night**	**per week**
Qual é o preço...?	por noite	por semana
*kwal e oo **pray**-soo...*	*poor noyt*	*poor se**mah**-nuh*

for half board	**full board**
com meia-pensão	com pensão completa
*koñ **may**-yuh payn**sowñ***	*koñ payn**sowñ** kom**ple**tuh*

Is breakfast included?
Inclui o pequeno-almoço?
*een-**klwee** oo puh-**kay**noo al**moh**-soo*

Have you anything cheaper?
Tem alguma coisa mais barata?
*tayñ al**goo**muh **koy**-zuh mysh ba**rah**tuh*

Can you suggest somewhere else?
Pode aconselhar outro sítio?
*pod akonsel-**yuhr** oh-troo **seet**yoo*

■ YOU MAY HEAR

Não temos vagas	Estamos cheios
*nowñ **tay**moosh **vah**-gush*	*shta-moosh **shay**oosh*
We've no vacancies	**We're full up**
Para quantas noites?	O seu nome, por favor?
*paruh **kwan**tush noytsh*	*oo **say**oo nom poor fa**vor***
For how many nights?	**Your name, please?**

É favor confirmar...	por escrito	por fax
*e fa**vor** komfeer**mar**...*	*poor sh**kree**-too*	*poor fax*
Please confirm...	**in writing**	**by fax**

On arrival at a hotel the receptionist will ask for your passport to register your stay. This is an official requirement and must not be misinterpreted.

Have you a room for tonight?
Tem um quarto para esta noite?
*tayñ ooñ **kwar**too paruh **esh**tuh noyt*

I booked a room...
Reservei um quarto...
*ruh-zer**vay** ooñ **kwar**too...*

in the name of...
em nome de...
ayñ nom duh...

I'd like to see the room
Queria ver o quarto
***kree**-uh vehr oo **kwar**too*

Have you anything else?
Tem outra coisa?
*tayñ **oh**-truh **koy**-zuh*

Where can I park the car?
Onde posso estacionar o carro?
***on**duh **poss**oo shtass-yoo**nar** oo **karr**oo*

What time is...?   dinner
A que hora é...?   o jantar
*uh kee o**ruh** e...   oo jan**tar***

breakfast
o pequeno-almoço
*oo puh-**kay**noo al**moh**-soo*

We'll be back late tonight
Esta noite voltamos tarde
***esh**tuh noyt vol**tuh**-moosh tard*

Do you lock the door?
Fecham a porta?
*fay-**shown** uh **por**tuh*

The key for room number...
A chave do quarto número...
*uh shahv doo **kwar**too **noo**meroo...*

Can you keep this in the safe, please?
Pode guardar isto no cofre?
*pod gwar**dar** **eesh**too noo **kof**ruh*

Are there any messages for me?
Há algumas mensagens para mim?
*a al**goo**mush men**sah**-jayñsh **pa**ruh meeñ*

I'm leaving tomorrow
Vou-me embora amanhã
voh**-muh em**boh**-ruh aman-**yañ

Please prepare the bill
Por favor faça a conta
*poor fa**vor** **fah**-sa **kon**tuh*

CAMPING

*Local tourist offices should have **uma lista de parques de campismo** with prices.*

Do you have a list of campsites with prices?
Tem uma lista de parques de campismo com os preços?
*tayñ **oom**uh **leesh**tuh duh parksh duh kam**peej**moo koñ oosh **pray**-soosh*

How far is the beach?
A que distância é a praia?
*uh kuh deesh-**tanss**-yuh e uh **pry**-uh*

Is there a restaurant on the campsite?
Há algum restaurante no parque?
*a al**goon** rushtoh-**rant** noo park*

Have you places? | **We'd like to stay for ... nights**
Tem vagas? | Gostaríamos de ficar ... noites
*tayñ **vah**-gush* | *gooshtuh-**ree**-uhmoosh duh fee**kar** ... noytsh*

How much is it per night...? | **for a tent** | **per person**
Quanto é por noite...? | por tenda | por pessoa
***kwan**too e poor noyt...* | *poor **ten**duh* | *poor puh-**so**-uh*

Are showers... | **Is hot water...** | **Is electricity...**
Os duches... | A água quente... | A electricidade...
*oosh **doosh**ush...* | *uh **ahg**-wuh kent...* | *uh eeletree-see**dahd**...*

...included in the price?
...são incluidos no preço?
*...sowñ een-**klwee**doosh noo **pray**-soo*

Can we camp here overnight? *(for tent)*
Podemos acampar aqui para passar a noite?
*poo**deh**-mooz akam**par** a**kee** pa**ruh** pa**ssar** uh noyt*

Can we park the caravan / trailer here?
Podemos estacionar a caravana / roulotte aqui?
*poo**deh**-moosh shtass-yoo**nar** uh karuh-**vah**-nuh / roo**lot** a**kee***

Is good drinking water available?
Há boa água potável?
*a **boh**-uh **ahg**-wuh pootah-vel*

see also **SIGHTSEEING & TOURIST OFFICE**

*If you arrive with no accommodation and want to go self-catering, look for signs **Aluguer de Apartamentos** (apartments for rent).*

Can you give us an extra set of keys?
Pode-nos dar um duplicado das chaves?
*pod-**noosh** dar ooñ dooplee-**kah**doo dush **shah**vesh*

When does the cleaner come?
Quando vem a mulher de limpeza?
***kwan**doo vayñ uh mool-**yer** duh leen-**peh**zuh*

Who do we contact if there are problems?
Quem podemos contactar em caso de problemas?
*kayñ poo**deh**-moosh kontak**tar** ayñ **kah**zoo duh proo**bleh**mush*

How does the heating work?
Como funciona o aquecimento?
***koh**-moo foonss-**yo**nuh oo akehsee**mayñ**too*

Is there always hot water?
Ha sempre água quente?
*a **sayñ**pruh **ahg**-wuh kent*

Where is the nearest supermarket?
Onde é o super-mercado mais perto?
***on**duh e oo sooper-mer**kah**doo mysh **pehr**too*

Where do we leave the rubbish?
Onde pomos o lixo?
***on**duh **poh**moosh oo **lee**shoo*

When is the rubbish collected?
Quando levam o lixo?
***kwan**doo **leh**vowñ oo **lee**shoo*

Where are the recycling containers?
Onde estão os recipientes para reciclagem?
***on**duh shtowñ oosh reseep**yen**tsh **pa**ruh resseek**lah**zhayñ*

What are the neighbours called?
Qual é o nome dos vizinhos?
*kwal e oo nom doosh vee**zeen**-yoosh*

see also **SIGHTSEEING & TOURIST OFFICE**

SHOPPING PHRASES

Many shops still close for lunch between 1 to 3 pm, but the tendency is to remain open throughout the day. Large department stores and food shops generally stay open from 9 am to 7 pm. Shopping centres are now very common and remain open until 10 pm or even 12 midnight.

Where is...?
Onde é...?
onduh e...

Do you have...?
Tem...?
tayñ...?

I'm looking for a present for...
Estou à procura de um presente para...
*shtoh a pro**koo**ruh dooñ pre**zent** paruh...*

a child
uma criança
*oomuh kree-**an**suh*

Where can I buy...?
Onde posso comprar...?
*onduh **poss**oo kom**prar**...*

toys
brinquedos
*breen**kay**-doosh*

gifts
brindes
***breen**-dush*

Can you recommend any good shops?
Pode-me recomendar algumas lojas boas?
***pod**-muh ruh-koomen**dar** al**goo**mush **loj**ush **boh**-ush*

Which floor are shoes on?
Em que andar estão os sapatos?
*ayñ kee an**dar** shtowñ oosh sa**pah**-toosh*

Have you anything else?
Tem alguma outra coisa?
*tayñ al**goo**muh **oh**-truh **koy**-zuh*

It's too expensive for me
É muito caro para mim
*e **mween**too **kah**-roo **par**uh meeñ*

Is there a market?
Há algum mercado?
*a al**gooñ** mer**kah**-doo*

Which day?
Em que dia?
*ayñ kuh **dee**-uh*

■ YOU MAY HEAR

Que deseja?
*kuh de**zay**juh*
Can I help you?

Mais alguma coisa?
*mysh al**goo**muh **koy**-zuh*
Would you like anything else?

SALDO / DESCONTOS **saldoo** / dush**koñ**toosh	**SALE/REDUCTIONS**
LIQUIDAÇÃO leekeeduh**sowñ**	**CLOSING-DOWN SALE**
HOJE, ABERTO ATÉ ÀS... ohj a**behr**too a**tay** ush...	**OPEN TODAY UNTIL...**

baker's	**padaria** paduh-**ree**-uh
bookshop	**livraria** leevruh-**ree**-uh
butcher's	**talho** **tal**-yoo
cake shop	**pastelaria** pashtuh-luh-**ree**-uh
clothes (women's)	**roupa de senhora** **roh**-puh duh sun-**yor**uh
clothes (men's)	**roupa para homem** **roh**-puh paruh **omay**ñ
electrical goods	**electro-domésticos** eeletro-doo-**mesh**tikoosh
fishmonger's	**peixaria** pay-shuh-**ree**-uh
furniture	**mobiliário** moobeel-**ya**-ree-oo
gifts	**brindes** **breen**-dush
glasses	**óculos** **oh**-kooloosh
greengrocer's	**frutaria** frootuh-**ree**-uh
grocer's	**mercearia** mersee-uh-**ree**-uh
hairdresser's	**cabeleireiro(a)** kuh-buh-lay-**ray**-roo(-ruh)
household (goods)	**artigos de ménage** ar**tee**goosh duh may**naj**
ironmonger's	**casa de ferragens** **kah**-zuh duh fe**rah**-jaynsh
jeweller's	**joalharia** jwal-yuh-**ree**-uh
lenses	**lentes** lentsh
market	**mercado** mer**kah**-doo
optician	**oculista** okoo**leesh**-tuh
pharmacy	**farmácia** far**mass**-yuh
self-service	**auto-serviço** owtoo-ser**vee**soo
shoe shop	**sapataria** sapatuh-**ree**-uh
shop	**loja** **lo**juh
stationer's	**papelaria** papuluh-**ree**-uh
supermarket	**super-mercado** sooper-mer**kah**-doo
sweet shop	**confeitaria** konfaytuh-**ree**-uh
tobacconist's	**tabacaria** tabuh-ka**ree**-uh
toy shop	**loja de brinquedos** **lo**juh duh breen**kay**-doosh

FOOD (GENERAL)

beef	a carne de vaca *karn duh **vah**-kuh*
biscuits	as bolachas *bool**ah**-shush*
bread	o pão *powñ*
bread *(brown)*	o pão integral *powñ eentuh-**gral***
bread roll	o papo-seco *pahpoo-**seh**-koo*
butter	a manteiga *man**tay**-guh*
cakes	os bolos *boh-loosh*
cheese	o queijo *kay-joo*
chicken	a galinha *ga**leen**-yuh*
coffee	o café *kuh-**fe***
cream	a nata *nah-tuh*
crisps	as batatas fritas *ba**tah**-tush **free**tush*
eggs	os ovos *oh-voosh*
fish	o peixe *paysh*
flour	a farinha *fa**reen**-yuh*
ham *(cooked)*	o fiambre *fee-**am**-bruh*
ham *(cured)*	o presunto *pruh-**zoon**too*
honey	o mel *mel*
jam	a compota *kom**pot**uh*
lamb	o carneiro *kar**nay**-roo*
margarine	a margarina *marguh-**ree**nuh*
marmalade	a doce de laranja *dohss duh la**ran**juh*
milk	o leite *layt*
olive oil	o azeite *a**zayt***
orange juice	o sumo de laranja *soomoo duh la**ran**juh*
pasta	as massas *mass**ush***
pepper	a pimenta *pee**men**tuh*
pork	a carne de porco *karn duh **por**koo*
rice	o arroz *ar**osh***
salt	o sal *sal*
stock cube	o cubo concentrado *kooboo kon-sayn**trah**-doo*
sugar	o açúcar *a**soo**kar*
tea	o chá *sha*
tin of tomatoes	a lata de tomates *lah*tuh duh to-**matsh***
vinegar	o vinagre *vee**nah**-gruh*

apples	as maçãs *ma***sañsh**
apricots	os damascos *da***mash**koosh
asparagus	os espargos *shpar*goosh
aubergine	a beringela *bereen-je*luh
bananas	as bananas *ba*nah-nush
cabbage	a couve *kohv*
carrots	as cenouras *suh-***noh**-rush
cauliflower	a couve-flor *kohv-***flor**
cherries	as cerejas *suh-***ray**-jush
courgettes	as courgettes *koor***jetsh**
french beans	o feijão verde *fay-jowñ-***vehrd**
garlic	o alho *al*-yoo
grapefruit	a toranja *too***ran**-juh
grapes	as uvas *oo*vush
leeks	os alhos-porros *al-yoosh-***porr**osh
lemon	o limão *lee***mowñ**
lettuce	a alface *al***fass**
melon	o melão *me***lowñ**
mushrooms	os cogumelos *koogoo-***mel**oosh
nectarines	as nectarinas *nek-tuh-***ree**nush
onions	as cebolas *suh-***bol**ush
oranges	as laranjas *la***ran**jush
peaches	os pêssegos *peh-suh-goosh*
pears	as pêras *peh-rush*
peas	as ervilhas *ehr***veel**-yush
peppers	os pimentos *pee***men**toosh
pineapple	o ananás *anuh-***nash**
plums	as ameixas *a***may**-shush
potatoes	as batatas *ba*tah-tush
raspberries	as framboesas *fram-***bway**-zush
spinach	os espinafres *shpee-***na**frush
strawberries	os morangos *moo***rang**oosh
tomatoes	os tomates *too***matsh**
turnips	os nabos *nah*-boosh
watermelon	a melancia *melan-***see**-uh

see also **SHOPPING PHRASES**

CLOTHES

*Size for clothes is **a medida**. Size for shoes is **o número**.*

women			men – suits			shoes			
sizes			**sizes**			**sizes**			
UK	EC		UK	EC		UK	EC	UK	EC
10	36		36	46		2	35	7	41
12	38		38	48		3	36	8	42
14	40		40	50		4	37	9	43
16	42		42	52		5	38	10	44
18	44		44	54		6	39	11	45
20	46		46	56					

May I try this on?
Posso provar isto?
*poss*oo proo*var* eesh*too*

Have you a size...?
Tem uma medida...?
tayñ oomuh muhdee-duh...

Have you this...?
Tem isto...?
tayñ eeshtoo...

That's a shame!
Que pena!
kuh paynuh

I'm just looking
Só estou a ver
so shtoh uh vehr

Where are the changing rooms?
Onde é o gabinete de provas?
onduh e oo gabeenet duh provush

bigger	**smaller**
maior	mais pequena
mayor	*mysh puh-kaynuh*

in my size
na minha medida
nuh meen-yuh muhdee-duh

in other colours
em outras cores
ayñ oh-trush korush

It's too...	**short**	**long**
É muito...	curto	comprido
e mweentoo...	*koortoo*	*kompreedoo*

I'll take it
Quero comprar
kehroo komprar

■ YOU MAY HEAR

De que medida?
duh kuh muhdee-duh
What size?

Quer provar?
kehr proovar
Do you want to try it on?

Fica bem?
feekuh bayñ
Does it fit?

42

belt	o cinto **seen**too
blouse	a blusa **bloo**zuh
bra	o soutien soot-**yañ**
coat	o casaco ka**zah**-koo
dress	o vestido vush**tee**doo
gloves	as luvas **loo**vush
hat	o chapéu sha**pay**-oo
hat (woollen)	a boina **boy**nuh
jacket	o casaco curto ka**zah**-koo **koor**too
knickers	as cuecas **kwe**kush
nightdress	a camisa de dormir ka**mee**zuh duh door**meer**
pyjamas	o pijama pee**jah**-muh
raincoat	o impermeável eempermee-**ah**-vel
sandals	as sandálias san**dahl**-yush
scarf (silk)	o lenço **len**soo
scarf (wool)	o cachecol kashu-**kol**
shirt	a camisa ka**mee**zuh
shorts	os calções kal**soynsh**
skirt	a saia **sy**-uh
slippers	as chinelas shee**ne**lush
socks	as peúgas **pew**-gush
suit	o fato **fah**-too
swimsuit	o fato de banho **fah**-too duh **bahn**-yoo
tie	a gravata gru**vah**-tuh
tights	os collants ko**lansh**
tracksuit	o fato de treino **fah**-too duh **tray**-noo
trousers	as calças **kal**sush
t-shirt	a camisola kuhmee**zoh**-luh
underpants	as cuecas **kwe**kush
zip	o fecho éclair **fay**-shoo ay-**klehr**

see also **SHOPPING** ☐ **SHOPPING PHRASES** ☐ **PAYING**

MAPS & GUIDES

Have you...?
Tem...?
tayñ...

a map of (name town)
um mapa de...
ooñ mah-puh duh...

of the region
da região
duh ruj-yowñ

Can you show me where ... is on the map?
Pode-me mostrar onde fica ... no mapa?
pod-muh moosh-trar onduh feekuh ... noo mah-puh

Do you have a detailed map of the area?
Tem um mapa detalhado da área?
tayñ ooñ mah-puh duhtal-yah-doo duh aree-uh

Can you draw me a map?
Pode-me desenhar um mapa?
pod-muh duhsen-yar ooñ mah-puh

Have you...?
Tem...?
tayñ...

a guide book
algum guia
algooñ ghee-uh

a leaflet
algum folheto
algooñ fool-yetoo

in English?
em inglês?
ayñ eenglesh

I'd like the English language version (of a cassette guide)
Gostaria da versão inglesa (da cassette)
gooshtuh-ree-uh duh versowñ eenglezuh (duh kasset)

Where can I/we buy an English newspaper?
Onde se pode comprar um jornal inglês?
onduh suh pod komprar ooñ joornal eenglesh

Do you have any English newspapers / novels?
Tem jornais / romances ingleses?
tayñ joornaysh / rooman-sush eenglezush

When do the English newspapers arrive?
Quando chegam os jornais ingleses?
kwandoo shehgowñ oosh joornaysh eenglezush

Please reserve (name newspaper) **for me**
Pode-me reservar o ... por favor
pod-muh ruh-zervar oo ... poor favor

see also **ASKING THE WAY** □ **SIGHTSEEING**

Main Post Offices are open from 9 am to 5 pm, Mon. to Fri., and until 1 pm on Saturdays. Check times in small towns.

OS CORREIOS *oosh koorayoosh*	**POST OFFICE**
O MARCO DO CORREIO *oo markoo doo koorayoo*	**POSTBOX**
OS SELOS *oosh seloosh*	**STAMPS**

Is there a post office near here?
Há algum correio aqui perto?
a algooñ koorayoo akee pehrtoo

Which counter sells stamps?
Em que balcão vendem selos?
ayñ kuh balkowñ vendayñ seloosh

I want stamps for ... postcards to Great Britain
Queria selos para ... postais para a Grã-Bretanha
kree-uh seloosh paruh ... poosh-tysh pra grambruh-tahn-yuh

I want to send this letter registered post
Queria mandar esta carta registada
kree-uh mandar eshtuh kartuh rujeesh-tah-duh

How much is it to send this parcel?
Quanto custa mandar este embrulho?
kwantoo kooshtuh mandar aysht aym-brool-yoo

by air	**first class**
por avião	por correio azul
poor av-yowñ	*poor koorayoo azool*
It's a gift	**The value of contents is ... euros**
É um presente	O valor do conteúdo é ... euros
e ooñ pruh-zent	*oo valor doo kont-yoodoo e ... euroosh*

■ YOU MAY HEAR

Preencha este impresso
pree-enshuh aysht eempressoo
Fill in this form

see also **MONEY ▢ PAYING**

Tapes for video cameras and camcorders can be bought in photography shops, department stores and hypermarkets.

Where can I buy tapes for a camcorder?
Onde posso comprar cassettes para a câmara de video?
onduh possoo komprar kasetsh paruh uh ka-maruh duh veed-yoo

A colour film	**with 24 / 36 exposures**
Um rolo a cores	com 24 / 36 fotos
ooñ roh-loo uh korush	*koñ veentee-kwatroo / treentuh-saysh fotosh*

A video tape for this camcorder
Uma cassette para esta câmara de video
oomuh kaset paruh eshtuh ka-maruh duh veed-yoo

Have you batteries...?	**for this camera**
¿Tem pilhas...?	para esta máquina
tayñ peel-yush...	*paruh eshtuh makinuh*

Can you develop this film?	**How much will it be?**
Pode revelar este rolo?	Qual é o preço?
pod ruh-vuh-lar aysht roh-loo	*kwal e oo pray-soo*

I'd like mat / glossy prints
Quero as cópias em mate / com brilho
kehro ush kop-yush ayñ mat / koñ breel-yoo

When will the photos be ready?
Quando estão prontas as fotos?
kwandoo shtowñ prontush ush fotosh

The film is stuck	**Can you take it out for me?**
O rolo não anda	Pode tirá-lo por favor?
oo roh-loo nowñ anduh	*pod teerah-loo poor favor*

Is it OK to take pictures here?
Posso tirar fotos aqui?
possoo teerar fotosh akee

Would you take a picture of us, please?
Pode-nos tirar uma fotografia, por favor?
pod-noosh teerar oomuh footoogruh-fee-uh poor favor

see also **SHOPPING**

*The tourist office is called **Turismo**. If you are looking for somewhere to stay they should have details of hotels, campsites, etc.*

Where is the tourist office?
Onde é o turismo?
onduh e oo tooreej-moo

What can we visit in the area?
Que podemos visitar nesta zona?
kuh poodeh-moosh veezeetar nesh-tuh zoh-nuh

When can we visit the...?
Quando podemos visitar o/a...?
kwandoo poodeh-moosh veezeetar oo/uh...

We'd like to go to...
Gostaríamos de ir a...
gooshtuh-ree-uhmoosh duh eer uh...

Have you any leaflets?
Tem alguns folhetos?
tayñ algoonsh fool-yetoosh

Are there any excursions?
Há algumas excursões?
a algoomush shkoor-soynsh...

When does it leave?
A que horas parte?
uh kee orush part

Where does it leave from?
De onde parte?
dee onduh part

How much does it cost to get in?
Quanto custa a entrada?
kwantoo kooshtuh uh ayntrah-duh

Are there any reductions for...?
Fazem descontos para...?
fahzayñ dushkontoosh paruh...

children
crianças
kree-ansush

students
estudantes
shtoodantsh

unemployed
desempregados
duh-zaympruh-gah-doosh

senior citizens
terceira idade
tersayruh eedahd

---

see also **MAPS & GUIDES** ☐ **LEISURE/INTERESTS**

ENTERTAINMENT

In cities Tourist Offices will give you What's On, a magazine listing events and entertainment. Newspapers carry pages advertising local events.

What is there to do in the evenings?
Que se pode fazer à noite?
kuh suh pod fazehr a noyt

Where do local people go at night?
Onde é que a gente de aqui vai à noite?
onduh e kuh zheñt duhkee vy a noyt

Is there anything for children?
Há alguma coisa para crianças?
a algoomuh koy-zuh paruh kree-ansush

Where can I/we get tickets...?
Onde se arranjam bilhetes?
onduh see arranjowñi beel-yetsh...

for tonight
para esta noite
pra eshtuh noyt

for the show
para o espectáculo
pro shpe-takooloo

for the football match
para o jogo de futebol
pro joh-goo duh footbol

I'd like ... tickets
Queria ... bilhetes
kree-uh ... beel-yetsh

...adults
...para adultos
...pra dooltoosh

...children
...para crianças
...pra kree-ansush

Where can we go dancing?
Onde se pode dançar?
onduh suh pod dansar

What time does it open?
A que horas abre?
uh kee oruz ah-bruh

How much is it to get in?
Quanto é a entrada?
kwantoo e uh ayntrah-duh

Is there a casino?
Há um casino?
a ooñ kazee-noo

■ **YOU MAY HEAR**

A entrada custa ... euros com direito a consumo
uh ayntrah-duh kooshtuh ... euroosh koñ dee-raytoo uh konsoomoo
It costs ... euros to get in including a free drink

see also **MUSIC** ☐ **CINEMA** ☐ **THEATRE/OPERA**

Where can I/we go...?
Onde se pode...?
onduh suh pod...

fishing
pescar
pushkar

riding
andar a cavalo
andar uh kavah-loo

play golf
jogar golfe
joogar golf

play tennis
jogar ténis
joogar tay-neesh

Are there any good beaches near here?
Há algumas praias boas aqui perto?
a algoomush pry-ush boh-ush akee pehrtoo

Is there a swimming pool?
Há piscina?
a peesh-seenuh

Where can I/we hire bikes?
Onde se pode alugar bicicletas?
onduh suh pod aloogar beesee-kletush

Do you have helmets?
Tem capacetes?
tayñ kapuh-setsh

How much is it...?
Quanto é...?
kwantoo e...

per hour
por hora
poor oruh

per day
por dia
poor dee-uh

What do you do in your spare time? *(familiar)*
Que fazes nas horas livres?
kuh fah-zush nuz orush leevrush

I like...
Eu gosto de...
ay-oo goshtoo duh...

painting
pintar
peentar

sunbathing
tomar banhos de sol
toomar bahn-yoosh duh sol

Do you like...? *(formal)*
Gosta de...?
goshtuh duh...

Do you like...? *(familiar)*
Gostas...?
goshtush...

see also **OUTDOOR PURSUITS** ☐ **SPORT** ☐ **WALKING**

MUSIC

Are there any good concerts on?
Há algum bom concerto por aqui?
*a al**goom** boñ kon**sehr**-too poor a**kee***

Where can one get tickets?
Onde se compram os bilhetes?
*on*duh suh kom**prowñ** oosh beel-**yetsh***

Where can we hear some fado / folklore?
Onde podemos ouvir o fado / folclore?
*on*duh poo**deh**-moosh oh-**veer** oo **fah**-doo / folk**lo**ruh*

What sort of music do you like?
De que música gosta?
*duh kuh **mooz**ikuh **gosh**tuh*

I like...
Gosto de...
***gosh**too duh...*

Which is your favourite group?
Qual o seu conjunto preferido?
*kwal oo **say**oo kon**joon**-too pruhfuh-**ree**-doo*

Who is your favourite singer?
De que artista gosta mais?
*duh kuh ar**teesh**tuh **gosh**tuh mysh*

Can you play any musical instruments?
Sabe tocar algum instrumento musical?
*sab too**kar** al**gooñ** eenshtroo-**men**too moozi**kal***

I play...	the guitar	the piano	the clarinet
Toco...	a guitarra	o piano	o clarinete
toh-koo...	*uh ghee**tah**-rruh*	*oo pee-**ah**-noo*	*oo klaree-**net***

Have you been to any good concerts recently?
Esteve em algum concerto bom ultimamente?
*shtehv ayñ al**gooñ** kon**sehr**-too boñ ooltimuh**ment***

Do you like opera?
Gosta de ópera?
***gosh**tuh **do**peruh*

Do you like pop music? *(familiar)*
Gostas de música pop?
***gosh**tush duh **mooz**ikuh pop*

see also **MAKING FRIENDS** ☐ **ENTERTAINMENT**

In Portugal it is customary to show films in their original versions, with sub-titles.

O CINEMA *oo seenay-muh*	**CINEMA**
A SESSÃO *uh suhsowñ*	**PERFORMANCE**

What's on at the cinema?
Qual é o programa no cinema?
kwal e oo proograh-muh noo seenay-muh

When does *(name film)* **start?**
A que horas começa ...?
uh kee orush koomessuh...

How much are the tickets?
Quanto custam os bilhetes?
kwantoo kooshtowñ oosh beel-yetsh

Two for the *(time)* **showing**
Dois para a sessão das...
doysh pra suhsowñ dush...

What films have you seen recently?
Que filmes viu ultimamente?
kuh feelmush vyoo ooltimuhment

What is ... called in Portuguese?
Como se chama ... em português?
koh-moo suh shamah ... ayñ poortoo-gesh

Who is your favourite actor / actress?
De que actor / actriz gosta mais?
duh kee ator / atreesh goshtuh mysh

■ **YOU MAY HEAR**

Para a sala um / dois não temos lugares
paruh uh sah-luh ooñ / doysh nowñ teh-moosh loogarush
For screen 1 / 2 we have no tickets left

see also **ENTERTAINMENT** □ **LEISURE/INTERESTS**

THEATRE/OPERA

Theatre and opera performances generally start quite late, around 9.30 pm and finish around midnight.

What's on at the theatre?
Qual é o programa de teatro?
*kwal e oo proo**grah**-muh duh tee-**ah**-troo*

We'd like to go to the opera
Queremos ir à ópera
***kre**-moosh eer a **o**-puhruh*

What prices are the tickets?
Quais são os preços dos bilhetes?
*kwaysh sown oosh **pray**-soosh doosh beel-**yetsh***

I'd like two tickets...
Queria dois bilhetes...
***kree**-uh doysh beel-**yetsh**...*

for tonight
para esta noite
*paruh **esh**tuh noyt*

for tomorrow night
para amanhã à noite
*paruh aman-**yañ** a noyt*

for 5th August
para cinco de Agosto
*paruh **seen**koo da**gosh**too*

in the stalls
na plateia
*nuh pla**tay**-uh*

in the circle
no balcão
*noo bal**kowñ***

in the upper circle
no segundo balcão
*noo se**goon**doo bal**kowñ***

How long is the interval?
Quanto dura o intervalo?
***kwan**too **doo**-ruh oo eenter-**vah**-loo*

Is there a bar?
Há um bar?
a ooñ bar

When does the performance begin / end?
Quando começa / acaba o espectáculo?
***kwan**doo koo**mess**uh / a**kah**-buh oo shpe-**tak**ooloo*

I enjoyed the play
Gostei muito da peça
*goosh**tay** mweentoo duh **peh**-suh*

It was very good
Foi muito boa
*foy **mween**too **boh**-u*

I didn't like it at all
Não gostei nada
*Nowñ goosh-**tay** nah-duh*

O TELECOMANDO *oo tuh-leh-koo**mañ**-doo*	REMOTE CONTROL
A TELENOVELA *uh tuh-leh-noo-**veh**-luh*	SOAP
O VIDEO *oo **veed**-yoosh*	VIDEO RECORDER
LIGAR *lee**gar***	TO SWITCH ON
DESLIGAR *dush-lee**gar***	TO SWITCH OFF
O PROGRAMA *oo proo**grah**-muh*	PROGRAMME
OS DESENHOS ANIMADOS *oosh duh**zayñ**-yoosh anee**mah**doosh*	CARTOONS

Where is the television?
Onde está o televisor?
*onduh shta oo tuh-luh-vee**zor***

How do you switch it on?
Como se liga?
*koh-**moo** suh **lee**guh*

Which button do I press?
Que botão uso?
*kuh boo**towñ oo**zoo*

Please could you lower the volume?
Por favor pode reduzir o volume?
*poor fa**vor** pod ruhdoo**zeer** oo voo-**loo**-muh*

May I turn the volume up?
Posso aumentar o volume?
***poss**oo owmen**tar** oo voo-**loo**-muh*

What's on television?
Que há na televisão?
*kee a nuh tuh-luh-vee**zowñ***

When is the news?
Quando são as notícias?
***kwan**doo sowñ ush noo-**teess**-yush*

Do you have any English-speaking channels?
Há alguns canais em inglês?
*a al**goonsh** ka**naysh** ayñ een**glesh***

When are the children's programmes?
Quando são os programas para crianças?
***kwan**doo sowñ oosh proo**grah**-mush **pa**ruh kree-**an**sush*

Do you have any English videos?
Tem alguns videos em inglês?
*tayñ al**goonsh veed**-yoosh ayñ een**glesh***

53

O CAMPO *oo kampoo*	PITCH / COURT
EMPATAR *empuhtar*	TO DRAW A MATCH
GANHAR *gañ-yar*	TO WIN

Where can I/we...?	**play tennis**	**play golf**
Onde se pode...?	jogar ténis	jogar golfe
onduh suh pod...	*joogar tay-neesh*	*joogar golf*

go swimming	**go jogging**	**see some football**
nadar	fazer footing	ver futebol
nadar	*fazehr footiñ*	*vehr footbol*

How much is it per hour? **Do you have to be a member?**
Quanto é por hora? É preciso ser sócio?
kwantoo e poor oruh *e pre-seezoo sehr soss-yoo*

Do they hire out...?	**rackets**	**golf clubs**
Alugam ...?	raquetes	tacos de golfe
aloogowñ...	*raketush*	*tah-koosh duh golf*

We'd like to go to see *(name team)* **play**
Queriamos assistir ao jogo de...
kreeuh-moosh aseeshteer ow shoh-goo duh...

Where can we get tickets?
Onde podemos comprar bilhetes?
onduh poodeh-moosh komprar beel-yetsh

How do we get to the stadium?
Como se vai para o estádio?
koh-moo suh vy pro shtad-yoo

Which is your favourite football team? *(familiar)*
Qual é a tua equipa favorita de futebol?
kwal e uh too-uh eekeepuh favooreetuh duh footbol

What sports do you play? *(familiar)*
Que desportos praticas?
kuh dushportoosh prateekush

see also **LEISURE/INTERESTS** ❑ **WALKING**

Portugal is renowned for its many world-class golf courses and golf is one of the main outdoor attractions for visitors. There are, however, many other leisure activities to choose from, such as diving, ballooning, canoeing, skiing, tennis, horse-riding, hunting and fishing (both river and deep sea). Licences for river fishing can be obtained from local town halls. Complete details of all outdoor pursuits can be found on www.portugalinsite.com (the Portuguese Tourism website).

Where is the nearest golf course?
Onde é o campo de golfe mais próximo?
*onduh e oo **kam**poo duh golf mysh **proh**seemoo*

Do you need to be a member to play golf / tennis?
Preciso ser sócio para jogar golfe / ténis?
*pre-**see**zoo ser **soss**-yoo paruh joo**gar** golf / tennis*

Do they hire out...?	**golf clubs**	**racquets**
Alugam...?	tacos de golfe	raquetes
a**loo**gowñ...	**tah**-koosh duh golf	ra**ketsh**

What is your handicap?	**My handicap is...**
Qual é o seu handicap?	O meu handicap é...
kwal e oo **say**-oo handicap	oo **may**oo handicap e...

Where can we go horse-riding?
Onde podemos andar a cavalo?
*onduh poo**deh**-moosh an**dar** uh ka**vah**-loo*

How much is it...?	**per hour**	**per day**
Quanto custa...?	por hora	por dia
kwantoo **koosh**tuh...	por **or**uh	por **dee**-uh

Where's the best place to go fishing?
Qual é o melhor lugar para ir pescar?
*kwal e oo mel-**yor** loogar paruh eer pesh**kar***

A fishing licence, please
Uma licença de pesca, por favor
*oomuh lee**sayñ**sa duh **pesh**-kuh poor fa**vor***

see also **LEISURE/INTERESTS** ❐ **SPORT** ❐ **WALKING**

WALKING

Are there any guided walks?
Há alguns passeios guiados?
*a al**goonsh** pa**say**oosh ghee-**ah**-doosh*

Do you have details?
Pode-me dar informações?
pod**-muh dar eemfoormuh-**soynsh

Do you have a guide to local walks?
Tem algum guia dos passeios locais a pé?
*tayñ al**gooñ** **ghee**-uh doosh pa**say**oosh loo**kysh** uh pe*

How many kilometres is the walk?
De quantos quilómetros é o passeio?
*duh **kwan**toosh kee**lom**etroosh e oo pa**say**oo*

How long will it take?
Que tempo demora?
*kuh tem**poo** duh-**mor**uh*

Is it very steep?
Tem muitas subidas?
*tayñ **mween**tush soo**bee**-dush*

I'd like to go climbing
Queria fazer alpinismo
***kree**-uh fa**zehr** alpee-**neej**moo*

Do we need walking boots?
Precisamos de botas de alpinismo?
*pre-**see**zuhmoosh duh **bot**ush dalpee-**neej**moo*

Should we take...?	**water**	**food**
Devemos levar...	água	comida
duh**veh**-moosh luh**var**...	**ahg**-wuh	ko**mee**duh

waterproofs	**a compass**
impermeáveis	uma bússola
eempermee-**ah**-vaysh	**oom**uh **boos**ooluh

What time does it get dark?
A que horas anoitece?
*uh kee **or**uz anoy**teh**-suh*

*To phone Portugal from the UK, the international code is **00 351** plus the Portuguese number. To phone the UK from Portugal, dial **0044** plus the UK area code less the first **0**, e.g., Glasgow (0)**141**. For calls within Portugal you must use the full area code, even for local calls.*

O CARTÃO TELEFÓNICO	oo kar**town** tuh-luh-**fo**-nee-koo	**PHONECARD**
A LISTA TELEFÓNICA	uh **leesh**tuh tuh-luh-**fon**eekuh	**PHONE DIRECTORY**
AS PÁGINAS AMARELAS	ush **pazh**eenush amuh**rel**ush	**YELLOW PAGES**
ATENDER	uhteñ**der**	**TO PICK UP**
DESLIGAR	dushlee**gar**	**TO HANG UP**

I want to make a phone call
Quero fazer uma chamada telefónica
kehroo fa**zehr oom**uh sha**mah**-duh tuh-luh-**fon**eekuh

What coins do I need?
Que moedas preciso?
kuh **mway**-dush pre-**see**zoo

Where can I buy a phonecard?
Onde posso comprar um cartão telefónico?
onduh **poss**oo kom**prar** ooñ kar**town** tuh-luh-**fo**-nee-koo

Do you have a mobile?
Tem telemóvel?
tayñ tuh-luh-**mo**vel

My mobile number is...
O meu número de telemóvel é...
oo mayoo **noo**meroo duh tuh-luh-**mo**vel e...

What is the number of your mobile?
Qual é o número do seu telemóvel?
kwal e oo **noo**meroo doo **say**oo tuh-luh-**mo**vel

Senhor Lopes, please
O Sr. Lopes, por favor
oo sun-**yor** lopsh poor fa**vor**

Extension...(number)
Extensão...
shten**sowñ**...

Can I speak to...?
Posso falar com...?
possoo fa**lar** koñ...

I would like to speak to...
Queria falar com...
kree-uh fa**lar** koñ...

cont...

This is Jim Brown
Daqui Jim Brown
da**kee** jim brown

Speaking
É o próprio / É a própria *(fem.)*
e oo **prop**ree-oo / e uh **prop**ree-uh

I will call back later
Chamo mais tarde
shamoo mysh tard

I will call back tomorrow
Chamo amanhã
shamoo aman-**yañ**

We were cut off
A chamada caíu
uh sha**mah**-duh ka**yoo**

I can't get through
Não consigo ligar
nowñ kon**see**goo lee**gar**

■ YOU MAY HEAR

Estou / Alô / Sim
shtoh / a**loh** / seeñ
Hello

Quem fala?
kayñ **fah**-luh
Whom am I talking to?

Um momento
ooñ mo**men**-too
Just a moment

Não desligue
nowñ duj-**leeg**
Hold on

Fale, por favor
fah-luh poor favor
Speak now, please

Está impedido
shta eempuh-**dee**doo
It's engaged

Pode chamar mais tarde?
pod sha**mar** mysh tard
Can you try again later?

Quer deixar um recado?
kehr day**shar** ooñ re**kah**-doo
Do you want to leave a message?

...está em reunião
...shta ayñ ree-oo-**nyowñ**
...is in a meeting

É engano
e ayn-**guh**-noo
You've made a mistake

Não é este número
nowñ e aysht **noo**meroo
It's not this number

É favor desligar o telemóvel
e fa**vor** dushlee**gar** oo tuh-luh-**mo**vel
Please turn off mobiles

Este é o gravador de chamadas de...
aysht e oo grava**dor** duh sha**mah**-dush duh...
This is the answering machine of...

see also **E-MAIL** ☐ **INTERNET** ☐ **FAX** ☐ **BUSINESS**

As with most new technology in Portugal, English is widely used for text messaging.

I will text you
Mandarei mensagem por texto
manduh**ray** men**sah**jayñ poor **taysh**too

Can you text me?
Podes mandar mensagem?
pohdush man**dar** men**sah**jayñ

Did you get my text message?
Recebeste a minha mensagem por texto?
ruhssuh**besht** uh **meen**-yuh men**sah**jayñ poor **taysh**too

Can you send me a picture with your mobile?
Podes mandar imagem com o teu telemóvel?
pohdush man**dar** ee**mah**jayñ koñ oo tayoo tuh-luh-**mo**vel

Hello hlo alô	**See You** cu até breve
Tomorrow 2moro amanhã	**Please call me** pcm chama-me
Today 2day hoje	**Too late** 2l8 demasiado tarde
Tonight 2nt esta noite	**Text me** txtme manda-me mensagem
Free to talk? ft2? podes falar?	**Be back later** bbl volto mais tarde
Thanks thx obrigado(a)	**Are you ok?** ruok? estás bem?

*The Portuguese for e-mail is **Correio Electrónico** (koorayoo eletroh-neekoo) although most people use the word e-mail.*

Tem e-mail?
Tem e-mail?
tayñ e-mail

What is your e-mail address?
Qual é o seu endereço de e-mail?
kwal e oo sayoo en-duh-resoo duh e-mail

Do you have a webpage?
Tem uma página Web?
tayñ oomuh pahjeenuh Web

How do you spell it?
Como se soletra?
koh-moo suh soolehtruh

All one word
Tudo uma palavra
too-doo oomuh puhlahvruh

All lower case
Tudo em letras minúsculas
too-doo ayñ lehtrush meenooshkoolush

My e-mail address is...
O meu endereço electrónico é...
oo mayoo en-duh-resoo eletroh-neekoo e...

clare.smith@collins.co.uk
clare.smith@collins.co.uk
clare poontoo smith ar-roh-baya collins poonto co poontoo uk

Can I send an e-mail?
Posso mandar um e-mail?
possoo mandar ooñ e-mail

Did you get my e-mail?
Recebeste o meu e-mail?
ruhsuhbesht oo mayoo e-mail?

Can I book by e-mail?
Posso fazer a reserva por e-mail?
possoo fazehr uh ruhzervuh poor e-mail

English is widely used for both internet and e-mail as most of the instruction books and catalogues are in English with glossaries for other languages. Most Portuguese using the internet are familiar with English.

PÁGINA PRINCIPAL *pah*jeenuh preensee*pal*	HOME
NOME DE USUÁRIO nom doo ooz*wahr*yoo	USERNAME
NAVEGAR nave*gar*	TO BROWSE
PESQUISADOR peshkeeza*dor*	SEARCH ENGINE
SENHA *sen*-yuh	PASSWORD
CONTACTE-NOS kon-*takt*noosh	CONTACT US
VOLTAR AO MENU vol*tar* aoo me*noo*	BACK TO MENU
MAPA DO LOCAL *ma*pa doo loo*kal*	SITEMAP

Are there any internet cafés here?
Há alguns Cafés Internet aqui?
*a al***goonsh** kufesh eenter*net* akee

How much is it to log on for an hour?
Quanto custa ligar à internet por uma hora?
*kwan*too **koosh**tuh lee*gar* ah eenter*net* poor **oo**muh *oruh*

Do you have a website?
Tem uma página de internet?
tayñ **oo**muh *pah*jeenuh duh eenter*net*

The website address is...
O endereço da página é...
oo en-duh-**re**soo duh *pah*jeenuh e...

www.collins.co.uk
www dot collins dot co dot uk
*dub*lyoo *dub*lyoo *dub*lyoo *pon*too collins *pon*too co *pon*too uk

Do you know any good sites?
Conhece algumas páginas interessantes de internet?
koon-**yess** al**goo**mush *pah*jeenush eentere**santsh** duh eenter*net*

see also **E-MAIL** ☐ **FAX** ☐ **BUSINESS**

FAX

To fax Portugal from the UK, the code is **00 351** followed by the Portuguese fax number you require. The code to phone the UK from Portugal is **00 44**. For E-MAIL, see p. 60.

ADDRESSING A FAX	
DE	FROM
À ATENÇÃO DE	FOR THE ATTENTION OF
DATA	DATE
REF.	RE:
ESTE DOCUMENTO CONTEM ...	THIS DOCUMENT CONTAINS ...
PÁGINAS, INCLUINDO ESTA	PAGES INCLUDING THIS

Do you have a fax?
Tem fax?
tayñ fax

I want to send a fax
Queria mandar um fax
***kree**-uh man**dar** ooñ fax*

What is your fax number?
Qual é o seu número de fax?
*kwal e oo **say**oo **noo**meroo duh fax*

My fax number is...
O meu número de fax é...
*oo **may**oo **noo**meroo duh fax e...*

Did you get my fax?
Recebeu o meu fax?
*ruh-suh-**bay**oo oo **may**oo fax*

Please resend your fax
Por favor repita o fax
*poor fa**vor** ruh**pee**tuh oo fax*

I can't read it
Não o posso ler
*nowñ oo **poss**oo lehr*

The fax is constantly engaged
O fax está constantemente impedido
*oo fax shta konshtant-**ment** eempuh-**dee**doo*

Can I send a fax from here?
Posso mandar um fax daqui?
poss**oo man**dar** ooñ fax duh**kee

17 May 2003	17 de Maio de 2003
Dear Sirs	Caros Senhores *(commercial letter)*
Dear Sir / Madam	Caro Senhor / Cara Senhora
Yours faithfully	Atentamente
Dear Mr... / Dear Mrs...	Estimado Sr... / Estimada Sra...
Yours sincerely	Com muitos cumprimentos
Dear Paula	Querida Paula
Best regards	Um abraço
Dear Carlos	Querido Carlos
Love	Um grande abraço *or* Beijos

What is your address?
Qual é a sua morada?
kwal é uh soo-uh moorahduh

What is your postcode (zip)?
Qual é o seu código postal?
kwal e oo sayoo kodeegoo pooshtal

Thank you for your letter
Obrigado(a) pela sua carta
oh-breegah-doo(-duh)

Write soon!
Escreva em breve!
shkrehvuh ayñ brehv

Addressing an envelope

Sr. e Sra. Lopes da Silva
R. da Palma, 35- 2º esq.
1700-220 Lisboa
Portugal

Sr. e Sra. = Mr and Mrs
R. = abbrev for **Rua** (street)
2º esq. = 2nd floor, left
postcode and town

---

see also **INTERNET** ☐ **E-MAIL** ☐ **FAX** ☐ **BUSINESS**

63

*Banks are generally open 8.30 am to 3 pm, Monday to Friday. Double-check opening hours when you arrive as these may be different in some towns. The euro is the currency of Portugal. Euro cents are called **cêntimos** (saynتee-**moosh**).*

Where is the bank?
Onde é o banco?
*on*duh e oo **ban**koo

Is there a cash dispenser near here?
Há uma caixa automática aqui perto?
a **oo**muh ky-shuh owtoo**ma**teekuh akee **pehr**too

Where can I/we change some money?
Onde se pode trocar dinheiro?
*on*duh suh pod troo**kar** deen-**yay**-roo

I want to change these traveller's cheques
Quero trocar estes cheques de viagem
kehroo troo**kar esh**tush sheksh duh vee-**ah**-jayñ

When does the bank open?
Quando abre o banco?
*kwan*doo **ah**-bruh oo **ban**koo

When does the bank close?
Quando fecha o banco?
*kwan*doo **fay**shuh oo **ban**koo

Can I pay with pounds / euros?
Posso pagar em libras / euros?
posso pa**gar** ayñ **lee**brush / **eoo**-rosh

Can I use my card with this cash dispenser?
Posso usar o meu cartão nesta caixa?
posso oo**zar** oo **may**oo kar**towñ nesh**tuh ky-shuh

Do you have any loose change?
Tem trocos?
tayñ **tro**koosh

see also **PAYING**

A CONTA *uh* **koñ***tuh*	**BILL**
A CAIXA *uh* **kay***shush*	**CASH DESK**
A FACTURA *uh* fak**too***ruh*	**INVOICE**
PAGUE NA CAIXA **pah**-guh *uh* **kay***shuh*	**PAY AT THE CASH DESK**
O RECIBO *oo* ruh-**see***boo*	**RECEIPT**

How much is it?
Quanto é?
kwantoo e

How much will it be?
Quanto custará?
kwantoo kooshtuh-rah

Can I pay...?
Posso pagar...?
possoo pagar...

by credit card
com cartão de crédito
koñ kartowñ duh kreditoo

by cheque
por cheque
poor shek

Do you take credit cards?
Aceita cartões de crédito?
asaytuh kartoynsh duh kreditoo

Is service included?
O serviço está incluido?
oo serveesoo shta een-klweedoo

Is VAT included?
O IVA está incluido?
oo eevuh shta een-klweedoo

Put it on my bill
Ponha na minha conta
pon-yuh nuh meen-yuh kontuh

Please can I have a receipt
Pode-me dar um recibo por favor
pod-muh dar ooñ ruh-seeboo poor favor

Do I pay in advance?
Paga-se adiantado?
pah-guh-suh adee-an-tah-doo

Where do I pay?
Onde se paga?
onduh suh pah-guh

I'm sorry
Desculpe
dushkoolp

I've nothing smaller
Não tenho troco
nowñ ten-yoo trokoo

see also **SHOPPING** ☐ **MONEY**

LUGGAGE

A RECOLHA DE BAGAGEM uh re**kol**-yuh duh ba**gah**-jayñ	**BAGGAGE RECLAIM**
O CARRINHO oo kar**reen**-yoo	**TROLLEY**

My luggage hasn't arrived
A minha bagagem não chegou
uh **meen**-yuh ba**gah**-jayñ nowñ shuh-**goh**

My suitcase has arrived damaged
A minha mala chegou danificada
uh **meen**-yuh **mah**-luh shuh-**goh** duhneefee-**kah**-duh

What's happened to the luggage on the flight from...?
Que se passa com a bagagem do voo de...?
kuh suh **passu**h koñ uh ba**gah**-jayñ doo **voh**-oo duh...

Can you help me with my luggage, please?
Pode-me ajudar com a bagagem, por favor?
pod-muh ajoo**dar** koñ uh ba**gah**-jayñ poor fa**vor**

When does the left luggage office open / close?
Quando abre / fecha o depósito de bagagens?
kwandoo **ah**-bruh / **fay**shuh oo duh-**poz**eetoo duh ba**gah**-jayñ

I'd like to leave this suitcase...   **until ... o'clock**
Queria deixar esta mala...   até ... horas
kree-uh day**shar esh**tuh **mah**-luh...   **ate** ... **or**ush

overnight	till Saturday	**I'll collect it at...**
durante a noite	até sábado	Venho buscá-la às...
doo**rant** uh noyt	**ate sa**badoo	**ven**-yoo boosh-**ka**-luh ash...

Can I leave my luggage?
Posso deixar a minha bagagem?
possoo day**shar** uh **meen**-yuh ba**gah**-jayñ

■ **YOU MAY HEAR**

Pode deixá-la aqui até às seis
pod day**sha**-luh a**kee ate** ash saysh
You can leave it here until 6 o'clock

see also **TRAIN** ⬜ **AIR TRAVEL**

SAPATEIRO *sapatayroo*   SHOE REPAIR SHOP

REPARAÇÕES RÁPIDAS *reparasoyñsh rahpeedush*   REPAIRS WHILE
YOU WAIT

This is broken
Isto está partido
eeshtoo shta parteedoo

Where can I get this repaired?
Onde posso arranjar isto?
onduh possoo arranjar eeshtoo

Is it worth repairing?
Vale a pena arranjar?
valuh paynuh arranjar

Can you repair...?
Pode-me arranjar...?
pod-muh arranjar...

these shoes
estes sapatos
ayshtush sapah-toosh

my watch
o relógio
oo ruh-loj-yoo

How much will it be?
Quanto vai custar?
kwantoo vy kooshtar

Can you do it straightaway?
Pode fazer imediatamente?
pod fazehr eemudee-ah-tuh-ment

How long will it take to repair?
Quanto tempo leva a arranjar?
kwantoo tempoo lehva arranjar

When will it be ready?
Quando estará pronto?
kwandoo shtuh-rah prontoo

Where can I have my shoes reheeled?
Onde posso pôr capas nos sapatos?
onduh possoo por kahpush noosh sapah-toosh

I need some...
Preciso de...
pre-seezoo duh...

glue
cola
koluh

Sellotape®
fitacola
feetuh-koluh

string
cordel
koordel

Do you have a needle and thread?
Tem uma agulha e linha?
tayñ oomuh agool-yuh ee leen-yuh

The lights have fused
As lâmpadas fundiram-se
ush lahm-padush foondeerowñ-suh

see also **BREAKDOWN**

LAUNDRY

A TINTURARIA *uh teentooruh**ree**-uh*	**DRY-CLEANER'S**
A LIMPEZA A SECO *uh leem**peh**zuh uh **say**koo*	**DRY-CLEANER'S**
O DETERGENTE EM PÓ *oo duhter**zhent** ayñ poh*	**WASHING POWDER**

Where can I do some washing?
Onde posso lavar alguma roupa?
*onduh **poss**oo lavar al**goo**muh roh-puh*

Do you have a laundry service?
Tem serviço de lavandaria?
*tayñ ser**vee**soo duh lavanduh-**ree**-uh*

When will my things be ready?
Quando estão prontas as minhas coisas?
*kwandoo shtowñ **pron**tush ush meen-yush **koy**-zush*

Is there a launderette near here?
Há uma lavandaria automática perto daqui?
*a **oom**uh lavanduh-**ree**-uh owtoo**ma**tikuh **pehr**too duh**kee***

When does it open?	**When does it close?**
Quando abre?	Quando fecha?
*kwandoo **ah**-bruh*	*kwandoo **fay**shuh*
Does it work with coins?	**Which?**
Trabalha com moedas?	Quais?
*tra**bal**-yuh koñ **mway**-dush*	*kwaysh*

Where can I dry some clothes?
Onde posso secar alguma roupa?
*onduh **poss**oo se**kar** al**goo**muh roh-puh*

Can you iron these clothes?
Pode passar esta roupa a ferro?
*pod pa**sar** esh**tuh** roh-puh uh **fer**roo*

Can I borrow an iron?
Pode-me emprestar um ferro de engomar?
pod**-muh aympresh-**tar** ooñ **fer**roo duh ayngoo-**mar

This doesn't work
Isto não trabalha
eeshto nowñ trabal-yuh

This is out of order
Isto não funciona
eeshto nowñ foonss-yonuh

The ... doesn't work
O/A ... não trabalha
oo/uh ... nowñ trabal-yuh

The ... are out of order
Os/As ... não funcionam
oosh/ush ... nowñ foonss-yonowñ

light
a luz
uh loosh

heating
o aquecimento
oo akuhsee-mentoo

air conditioning
o ar condicionado
oo ar kondeess-yoonah-doo

There's a problem with the room
Há um problema com o quarto
a ooñ proo-blemuh koñ oo kwartoo

It's noisy
Há muito barulho
a mweentoo barool-yoo

It's too hot *(room)*
É muito quente
e mweentoo kent

It's too cold *(room)*
É muito frio
e mweentoo free-oo

It's too hot / cold *(food)*
Está muito quente / frio
shta mweentoo kent / free-oo

The meat is cold
A carne está fria
uh karn shta free uh

It's dirty
Está sujo
shta soojoo

This isn't what I ordered
Isto não é o que eu pedi
eeshtoo nowñ e oo kuh ay-oo puh-dee

To whom should I complain?
A quem me posso queixar?
uh kayñ muh posso kayshar

It's faulty
Tem um defeito
tayñ ooñ duh-fay-too

I want a refund
Quero um reembolso
kehroo ooñ ree-aym-bolsoo

I want to return it
Quero devolver
kehroo duh-volvehr

see also **HOTEL DESK** ☐ **REPAIRS** ☐ **PROBLEMS**

PROBLEMS

Can you help me?
Pode-me ajudar?
pod-muh ajoo*dar*

I only speak a little Portuguese
Só falo um pouco de português
so fah-loo ooñ *poh*koo duh poortoo-*gesh*

Does anyone here speak English?
Há aqui alguém que fale inglês?
a a*kee* al*gayñ* kuh *fah*-luh een*glesh*

What's the matter?
Que se passa?
kuh suh passuh

I would like to speak to whoever is in charge
Queria falar com o encarregado
kree-uh fa*lar* koñ oo aynkuh-ray-*gah*-doo

I'm lost
Perdi-me
perdee-muh

How do I get to...?
Como se vai a...?
koh-moo suh vy uh...

I've missed...
Perdi...
perdee...

my train
o meu comboio
oo mayoo kom*boy*oo

my connection
a minha ligação
uh meen-yuh leeguh-*sowñ*

I've missed my flight because there was a strike
Perdi o meu voo porque havia uma greve
perdee oo *mayoo voh*-oo *poor*kuh a*vee*-uh *oom*uh grev

The coach has left without me
O autocarro partiu sem mim
oo owtoo-*karr*oo part*yoo* sayñ meeñ

Can you show me how this works?
Pode-me mostrar como funciona isto?
pod-muh most*rar koh*-moo foonss-*yo*nuh *eesh*too

I have lost my purse
Perdi o meu porta-moedas
perdee oo *mayoo* portuh-*mway*-dush

I need to get to...
Preciso de ir a...
pre-*see*zoo deer uh...

Leave me alone!
Deixe-me em paz!
day-shu-muh ayñ pash

Go away!
Vá-se embora!
vah-suh aym*boh*-ruh

70   see also **COMPLAINTS** ☐ **EMERGENCIES**

A POLÍCIA *uh poo**leess**-yuh*	POLICE
A AMBULÂNCIA *uh amboo**lanss**-yuh*	AMBULANCE
OS BOMBEIROS *oos bom**bay**-roosh*	FIRE BRIGADE
O BANCO DO HOSPITAL *oo **ban**koo doo oshpee-**tal***	CASUALTY DEPARTMENT

Help!
Socorro!
*soo**korr**oo*

Fire!
Fogo!
foh-goo

Can you help me?
Pode-me ajudar?
pod**-muh ajoo**dar

There's been an accident!
Houve um acidente!
*ohv ooñ asee**dent***

Someone is injured
Há um ferido
*a ooñ fe**ree**doo*

Someone has been knocked down by a car
Alguém foi atropelado
*al**gayñ** foy atroopuh-**lad**oo*

Call...
Chame...
sham...

the police
a polícia
*uh poo**leess**-yuh*

an ambulance
uma ambulância
*oom*uh amboo**lanss**-yuh*

please
por favor
*poor fa**vor***

Where's the police station?
Onde é a esquadra?
*ond*uh e uh shk**wah**-druh

I want to report a theft
Quero participar um roubo
*kehr*oo purteesee**par** ooñ **roh**-boo

I've been robbed
Fui roubado(a)
*fwee roh-**bah**-doo(uh)*

I've been attacked
Fui agredido(a)
*fwee agruh-**dee**-doo(uh)*

Someone's stolen my...
Roubaram-me...
*roh-**bah**-rowñ-muh...*

bag
a mala
*uh **mah**-luh*

passport
o passaporte
*oo passuh-**port***

traveller's cheques
os cheques de viagem
*oosh sheksh duh vee-**ah**-jayñ*

money
o dinheiro
*oo deen-**yay**-roo*

My car's been broken into
Assaltaram-me o carro
*assal-**tah**-rowñ-muh oo **karr**oo*

My car's been stolen
Roubaram-me o carro
*roh-**bah**-rowñ-muh oo **karr**oo*

cont...

EMERGENCIES

I've been raped
Violaram-me
vyolah-rowñ-muh

I am lost
Perdi-me
perdee-muh

I want to speak to a policewoman
Quero falar com uma mulher-polícia
kehroo falar koñ oomuh mool-yehr pooleess-yuh

I need to make an urgent telephone call
Preciso de fazer uma chamada urgente
pre-seezoo duh fazehr oomuh shamah-duh oorjent

I need a report for my insurance
Preciso de um relatório para o meu seguro
pre-seezoo dooñ relatoryoo pro mayoo segooroo

I didn't know the speed limit
Não sabia qual era o limite de velocidade
nowñ sabee-uh kwal eruh oo leemeet duh vuh-loossee-dahd

How much is the fine?
Quanto é a multa?
kwantoo e uh moolta

Where do I pay?
Onde pago?
onduh pahgoo

Do I have to pay straightaway?
Tenho que pagar já?
ten-yoo kuh pagar jah

I'm very sorry
Lamento muito
lamentoo mweentoo

■ **YOU MAY HEAR**

Posso ajudar?
possoo ajoodar
Can I help you?

Passou a luz vermelha
passoh uh loosh vermel-yuh
You went through a red light

A FARMÁCIA uh far**mah** see-uh	**PHARMACY**
A FARMÁCIA DE SERVIÇO uh far**mah**-see-uh duh ser**vee**ssoo	**DUTY CHEMIST**
A RECEITA MÉDICA uh re**say**tuh **meh**deekuh	**PRESCRIPTION**

I don't feel well
Não me sinto bem
nowñ muh **seen**too bayñ

Have you something for...?
Tem alguma coisa para...?
tayñ al**goo**muh **koy**-zuh pa**ruh**...

a headache	**car sickness**	**diarrhoea**
a dor de cabeça	o enjoo	a diarreia
uh dor duh ka**beh**-suh	oo en**joh**-oo	uh dee-uh-**ray**uh

I have a rash
Tenho uma irritação de pele
ten-yoo **oom**uh eer-reetuh-**sowñ** duh pel

Is it safe for children?
Pode-se dar às crianças?
pod-suh dar ash kree-an**sush**

How much should I give?
Quanto devo dar?
kwantoo **deh**-voo dar

■ YOU MAY HEAR

Três vezes por dia antes / com / depois das refeições
tresh **veh**-zush poor **dee**-uh antsh / koñ / duh**poysh** dush ruh-fay-**soynsh**
Three times a day before / with / after meals

■ WORDS YOU MAY NEED

antiseptic	o antiséptico	antee**sep**tikoo
aspirin	a aspirina	ashpeer**een**uh
condoms	os preservativos	pruhzerva**tee**voosh
cotton wool	o algodão	algoo**dowñ**
dental floss	o fio dental	**fee**yoo den**tal**
deodorant	o desodorizante	dez-oh-dooree-**zant**
plasters	os adesivos	aduh-**zee**voosh
sanitary pads	os pensos higiénicos	**pen**soosh eej-**yen**ikoosh
tampons	os tampões	tam**poynsh**
toothpaste	a pasta de dentes	**pash**tuh duh dentsh

see also **BODY** ▢ **DOCTOR**   73

In Portuguese the possessive (my, his, her, etc) is generally not used with parts of the body, e.g.

My head hurts   Doí-me a cabeça
My hands are dirty   Tenho as mãos sujas

ankle	o tornozelo	*toornoo-zeloo*
arm	o braço	*brah-soo*
back	as costas	*koshtush*
bone	o osso	*ossoo*
chin	o queixo	*kay-shoo*
ear	a orelha / o ouvido	*oh-rel-yuh / oh-veedoo*
elbow	o cotovelo	*kootoo-veloo*
eye	o olho	*ohl-yoo*
finger	o dedo	*deh-doo*
foot	o pé	*pe*
hair	o cabelo	*kabay-loo*
hand	a mão	*mowñ*
head	a cabeça	*kabeh-suh*
heart	o coração	*kooruh-sowñ*
hip	a anca	*an-kuh*
joint	a articulação	*arteekoo-lasowñ*
kidney	o rim	*reeñ*
knee	o joelho	*jwel-yoo*
leg	a perna	*pehrnuh*
liver	o fígado	*feeguh-doo*
mouth	a boca	*boh-kuh*
nail	a unha	*oon-yuh*
neck	o pescoço	*push-koh-soo*
nose	o nariz	*nareesh*
stomach	o estômago	*shtoh-magoo*
throat	a garganta	*gargantuh*
thumb	o polegar	*poh-luh-gar*
toe	o dedo do pé	*deh-doo doo pe*
wrist	o pulso	*pool-soo*

see also **DOCTOR** ❑ **PHARMACY**

O HOSPITAL *on oshpeetal*	HOSPITAL
O BANCO (HOSPITAL) *oo bankoo oshpeetahl*	CASUALTY DEPARTMENT
AS HORAS DE CONSULTA *ush orush duh konsooltuh*	SURGERY HOURS

I need a doctor
Preciso de um médico
pre-seezoo dooñ medikoo

My son (daughter) is ill
O meu filho(a) está doente
oo mayoo feel-yoo(yuh) shta doo-ent

I'm diabetic
Sou diabético(a)
soh dee-uh-betikoo(uh)

I'm allergic to penicillin
Sou alérgico(a) a penicilina
soh alehr-jikoo(uh) uh punee-seeleenuh

My blood group is...
O meu grupo sanguíneo é...
oo mayoo groopoo sangeen-yoo e...

Will he / she have to go to hospital?
Tem que ir para o hospital?
tayñ kuh eer pro oshpee-tal

Will I have to pay?
Tenho que pagar?
ten-yoo kuh pagar

I need a receipt for the insurance
Preciso de um recibo para o seguro
pre-seezoo dooñ ruh-seeboo pro segooroo

I have a pain here (point)
Doi-me aqui
doy-muh akee

(s)he has a temperature
ele(a) tem febre
ayl(uh) tayñ februh

I'm pregnant
Estou grávida
shtoh graviduh

I'm on the pill
Tomo a pílula
tomoo uh peeloo-luh

How much will it be?
Quanto será?
kwantoo suh-rah

■ **YOU MAY HEAR**

Tem que entrar no hospital
tayñ kuh ayntrar noo oshpee-tal
You will have to be admitted to hospital

Não é grave
nowñ e grav
It's not serious

see also **EMERGENCIES** ☐ **PHARMACY** ☐ **BODY**   75

DENTIST

O CHUMBO oo **shoom**boo	**FILLING**
A COROA uh koo-**roh**-uh	**CROWN**
A DENTADURA POSTIÇA uh dentuh-**doo**ruh poosh-**tee**suh	**DENTURES**

I need a dentist
Preciso de um dentista
pre-**see**zoo dooñ den**teesh**tuh

I have toothache
Tenho uma dor de dentes
ten-yoo **oom**uh dor duh **dent**sh

Can you do a temporary filling?
Pode pôr um chumbo provisório?
pod por ooñ **shoom**boo provee-**zor**-yoo

It hurts (me)
Doi-me
doy-muh

Can you give me something for the pain?
Pode-me dar alguma coisa para a dor?
pod-muh dar al**goom**uh **koy**-zuh pra dor

I think I have an abscess
Creio que tenho um abcesso
krayoo kuh **ten**-yoo ooñ ab-**seh**-soo

Can you repair my dentures?
Pode reparar a minha dentadura postiça?
pod ruh-pa**rar** uh **meen**-yuh dentuh-**doo**ruh poosh-**tee**suh

How much is it?
Quanto custa?
kwantoo **koosh**tuh

I need a receipt for my insurance
Preciso de um recibo para o seguro
pre-**see**zoo dooñ ruh-**see**boo pro se**goo**roo

■ YOU MAY HEAR

É preciso arrancar
e pre-**see**zoo aran**kar**
It has to come out

Vou-lhe dar uma injecção
vol-yuh dar **oom**uh eenje**sowñ**
I'm going to give you an injection

see also **PHARMACY**

What facilities do you have for disabled people?
Que instalaçãos tem para deficientes?
*kuh eenshtaluh-**soynsh** tayñ paruh duh-feess-**yentsh***

Are there any toilets for the disabled?
Há casas de banho especiais para deficientes?
*a **kah**-zush duh **bahn**-yoo shpussee-**aysh** paruh duh-feess-**yentsh***

Do you have any bedrooms on the ground floor?
Tem alguns quartos no rés-do-chão?
*tayñ al**goonsh** kwar**toosh** noo resh-doo-**showñ***

Is there a lift?
Há elevador?
*a eeluh-vuh-**dor***

Where is the lift?
Onde é o elevador?
*onduh e oo eeluh-vuh-**dor***

How many stairs are there?
Quantas escadas há?
***kwan**tush **shkah**-dush a*

Do you have wheelchairs?
Tem cadeira de rodas?
*tayñ ka**day**-rush duh **rod**ush*

Can I visit ... with a wheelchair?
Posso visitar ... com cadeira de rodas?
***poss**oo veezee**tar** ... koñ ka**day**-rush duh **rod**ush*

Is there a reduction for disabled people?
Há desconto para deficientes?
*a dush**kon**too paruh duh-feess-**yentsh***

Is there somewhere I can sit down?
Há algum sítio para me sentar?
*a al**gooñ seet**yoo paruh muh sen**tar***

Is there an induction loop?
Há auxiliares auditivos?
*a owseelee-**ah**-rush owdee-**tee**-voosh*

see also **HOTEL**

EXCHANGE VISITORS

*We have used the familiar **tu** form for these phrases.*

What would you like for breakfast?
Que queres para o pequeno-almoço?
kuh **keh**-rush paruh oo puh-**kay**noo al**moh**-soo

What would you like to eat?
Que queres comer?
kuh **keh**-rush koo**mehr**

What would you like to drink?
Que queres beber?
kuh **keh**-rush buh**behr**

Did you sleep well?
Dormiste bem?
door**meesht** bayñ

What would you like to do today?
Que queres fazer hoje?
kuh **keh**-rush fa**zehr** ohj

I will pick you up...
Vou-te buscar...
voht boosh**kar**...

at the station
à estação
ah shtuh-**sowñ**

at ... o'clock
às ... horas
ash ... **or**ush

May I phone home?
Posso telefonar para casa?
possoo telefoo**nar** paruh **kah**za

I like...
Gosto...
goshtoo...

I don't like...
Não gosto...
nowñ **gosh**too...

Take care
Passa bem
passuh bayñ

Thanks for everything
Obrigado(a) por tudo
oh-bree**gah**-doo(-duh) poor **too**-doo

Thank you very much
Muito obrigado(a)
mween**too** oh-bree**gah**-doo(-duh)

I've had a great time
Diverti-me muito
deever**tee**muh **mween**too

In Portugal children are always welcome at restaurants and cafés.

A child's ticket
Um bilhete para criança
*ooñ beel-**yet** paruh kree-ansush*

He / She is ... years old
Ele / Ela tem ... anos
*ayl / **ay**luh tayñ ... **ah**-noosh*

Is there a reduction for children?
Há desconto para crianças?
*a dush-**kon**too paruh kree-ansush*

Do you have a children's menu?
Tem uma ementa para crianças?
*tayñ **oo**muh ee**men**tuh paruh kree-ansush*

Is it OK to take children?
É permitido levar crianças?
*e permee**tee**-doo luh**var** kree-ansush*

What is there for children to do?
Há alguma actividade para as crianças?
*a al**goo**muh ateevee**dah**-duh paruh ush kree-**an**sush*

Is there a play park near here?
Há algum parque infantil perto?
*a al**gooñ** park eenfan**teel** pehrtoo*

Is it safe for children?
Não há perigo para as crianças?
*nowñ a **pree**goo paruh ush kree-**an**sush*

Do you have...?
Tem...?
tayñ...

a high chair
uma cadeira alta
*oomuh kuh**day**-ruh **alt**uh*

a cot
um berço
*oon **behr**-soo*

I have two children
Tenho dois filhos
*tayñ-yoo doysh **feel**-yoosh*

He / She is 10 years old
Ele / Ela tem 10 anos
*ayl / **ay**luh tayñ desh **ah**-noosh*

Do you have any children?
Tem filhos?
*tayñ **feel**-yoosh*

79

A SALA DE REUNIÕES *uh* **sah**-luh duh ree-oo-**nyowñ**	MEETING ROOM
O/A DIRECTOR(A) *uh* deerek**tor**(-ruh)	DIRECTOR
A REUNIÃO *uh* ree-oo-**nyowñ**	MEETING
A MOSTRA *uh* **mosh**truh	SAMPLE
A FEIRA DE MOSTRAS *uh* **fay**ruh duh **mosh**trush	TRADE FAIR

I'd like to arrange a meeting with...
Gostaria de ter uma reunião com...
*gooshtuh-**ree**-uh duh tehr **oom**uh ree-oo-**nyowñ** koñ...*

Can we meet...?
Podemos encontrar-nos...?
*poo**deh**-moosh anykon-**trar**-noosh...*

for lunch
para almoçar
*paruh almoo**sar***

for dinner
para jantar
*paruh jan**tar***

on the 4th of May at 1100
no dia quatro de Maio às onze
*noo **dee**-uh **kwa**troo duh **my**-oo ush onz*

I will confirm...
Confirmarei...
*komfeer-ma**ray**...*

by e-mail
por e-mail
poor e-mail

by fax
por fax
poor fax

How do I get to your office?
Como se vai ao seu escritório?
***koh**-moo suh vy ow **say**oo shkree-**tor**-yoo*

I'm staying at Hotel...
Estou no Hotel...
*sh**to** noo oh-**tel**...*

Please let ... know that I will be ... minutes late
Por favor avise ... que chegarei com um atraso de
*poor fa**vor** a-**vee**-zuh ... kuh shuh-ga**ray** koñ ooñ a**trah**-zoo duh ...*

I'm very sorry but I won't be able to see ..., as arranged
Lamento muito mas não posso ver ..., conforme combinado
*la**men**-too **mween**too mush nowñ **poss**oo vehr ... kon**form** kombee-**nah**-doo*

May I leave a message?
Posso deixar um recado?
possoo day**shar** ooñ re**kah**-doo

I have an appointment with...   **at ... o'clock**
Tenho um encontro com...   às ... horas
ten-yoo ooñ ayñ-**kon**troo koñ...   ush ... **or**ush

Here is my card
Aqui tem o meu cartão
a**kee** tayñ oo **may**oo kart**owñ**

I'm delighted to meet you at last
É um prazer encontrá-lo(-la) finalmente
e ooñ pra**zehr** ayñ-kon**trah**-loo(-luh) fee**nal**ment

I don't know much Portuguese   **Can you speak more slowly**
Não sei muito português   Pode falar mais devagar
nowñ say **mween**too poortoo-**gesh**   pod fa**lar** mysh devuh**gar**

I'm sorry I'm late   **My flight was delayed**
Desculpe chegar tarde   O avião veio atrasado
dush**koolp** shuh**gar** tard   oo av-**yowñ** vay**oo** atruh-**zah**-doo

May I introduce you to...
Posso-lhe apresentar...
possoo-lyuh apruhzen-**tar**...

■ **YOU MAY HEAR**

Tem encontro marcado?   **Ele / Ela não vem hoje**
tayñ ayñ-**kon**troo mar**kah**-doo   ayl / **el**uh nowñ vayñ ohj
Do you have an appointment?   **He / She isn't coming in today**

O Senhor... não está   **Está...**   **de férias**   **de viagem**
oo sun-**yor**... nowñ shta   shta...   duh **fehr**-yush   duh vee-**ah**-jayñ
Senhor... isn't in   **He is...**   **on holiday**   **travelling**

Volta dentro de cinco minutos
voltuh **den**troo duh **seen**koo mee**noo**tosh
He / She will be back in five minutes

see also **TELEPHONE** ☐ **E-MAIL** ☐ **INTERNET** ☐ **FAX**   81

ALPHABET

The Portuguese alphabet is the same as the English one, with the exception of the three letters: K, W and Y. These letters are only used in foreign words that have come into use in Portuguese.

How do you spell it?		**C as in Carlos, L as in Lisboa**	
Como se escreve?		**C de Carlos, L de Lisboa**	
koh-moo suh shkrev		*say duh **kar**loosh el duh leej**boh**-uh*	

A	*a*	**Alexandre**	*aluh-**shan**druh*
B	*bay*	**Bastos**	***bash**-toosh*
C	*say*	**Carlos**	***kar**loosh*
D	*day*	**Daniel**	*dan-**yel***
E	*ay*	**Eduardo**	*eed**war**doo*
F	*ef*	**França**	***fran**suh*
G	*jay*	**Gabriel**	*gabree-**el***
H	*a*ga	**Holanda**	*oh-**land**uh*
I	*ee*	**Itália**	*ee**tal**-yuh*
J	***jot**uh*	**José**	*joo**ze***
L	*el*	**Lisboa**	*leej**boh**-uh*
M	*em*	**Maria**	*ma**ree**-uh*
N	*en*	**Nicolau**	*neekoo-**la**-oo*
O	*oh*	**Oscar**	***osh**kar*
P	*pay*	**Paris**	*pa**reesh***
Q	*kay*	**Quarto**	***kwar**too*
R	*err*	**Ricardo**	*ree**kar**doo*
S	*ess*	**Susana**	*soo**zan**uh*
T	*tay*	**Teresa**	*tuh-**ray**-zuh*
U	*oo*	**Ulisses**	*oo**lee**sush*
V	*vay*	**Venezuela**	*vuh-nuh-**zway**-luh*
X	*sheesh*	**Xangai**	*shang-**gye***
Z	*zay*	**Zebra**	***ze**bruh*

■ **LIQUIDS**

1/2 litre...	meio litro de...	*mayoo **leet**roo duh...*
a litre of...	um litro de...	*ooñ **leet**roo duh...*
1/2 bottle of...	meia garrafa de...	*mayuh gar**rah**-fuh duh ...*
a bottle of...	uma garrafa de...	*oomuh gar**rah**-fuh duh...*
a glass of...	um copo de...	*ooñ **kop**oo duh...*

■ **WEIGHTS**

100 grams of...	cem gramas de...	*sayñ **grah**-mush duh...*
1/2 kilo of...	meio quilo de...	*mayoo **keel**oo duh...*
1 kilo of...	um quilo de...	*ooñ **keel**oo duh...*

■ **FOOD**

a slice of...	uma fatia de...	*oomuh fa**tee**-uh duh...*
a portion of...	uma porção de...	*oomuh poor**sowñ** duh...*
a dozen...	uma dúzia de...	*oomuh **doo**zee-uh duh...*
a box of...	uma caixa de...	*oomuh **ky**-shuh duh...*
a packet of...	um pacote de...	*ooñ pa**kot** duh...*
a tin of...	uma lata de...	*oomuh **lah**-tuh duh...*
a jar of...	um boião de...	*ooñ boy-**owñ** duh...*

■ **MISCELLANEOUS**

10 euros of...	dez euros de...	*desh **eur**oosh duh...*
a half	metade	*muh-**tahd***
a quarter	um quarto	*ooñ **kwart**oo*
ten per cent	dez por cento	*desh poor **sent**oo*
more...	mais...	*mysh...*
less...	menos...	*meh-**noosh**...*
enough	chega	*sheh-guh*
double	o dobro	*oo **doh**-broo*
twice	duas vezes	*doo-ush **veh**-zush*
three times	três vezes	*tresh **veh**-zush*

NUMBERS

0	zero *zehr*-oo		1st	primeiro *preemayroo*
1	um (uma) *ooñ* (*oom*uh)			
2	dois (duas) *doysh* (*doo*-uz)		2nd	segundo *segoon*doo
3	três *tresh*			
4	quatro *kwa*troo		3rd	terceiro *tersayroo*
5	cinco *seen*koo			
6	seis *saysh*		4th	quarto *kwar*too
7	sete *set*			
8	oito *oy*too		5th	quinto *keen*too
9	nove *nov*			
10	dez *desh*		6th	sexto *sesh*-too
11	onze *onz*			
12	doze *dohz*		7th	sétimo *set*imo
13	treze *trezh*			
14	catorze *ka*torz		8th	oitavo *oytah*-voo
15	quinze *keenz*			
16	dezasseis *dezuh*-**saysh**		9th	nono *noh*-noo
17	dezassete *dezuh*-**set**			
18	dezoito *dezoy*too		10th	décimo *dess*imoo
19	dezanove *dezuh*-**nov**			
20	vinte *veent*			
21	vinte e um *veentee*-**ooñ**			
22	vinte e dois *veentee*-**doysh**			
23	vinte e três *veentee*-**tresh**			
24	vinte e quatro *veentee*-**kwa**troo			
25	vinte e cinco *veentee*-**seen**koo			
26	vinte e seis *veentee*-**saysh**			
27	vinte e sete *veentee*-**set**			
28	vinte e oito *veentee*-**oy**too			
29	vinte e nove *veentee*-**nov**			
30	trinta *treen*tuh			
40	quarenta *kwaren*tuh			
50	cinquenta *seenkwen*tuh			
60	sessenta *sesen*tuh			
70	setenta *seten*tuh			
80	oitenta *oyten*tuh			
90	noventa *nooven*tuh			
100	cem / cento *sayñ* / *sen*too			
110	cento e dez *sen*too ee *desh*			
500	quinhentos *keen-yen*toosh			
1,000	mil *meel*			
2,000	dois mil *doysh meel*			
1 million	um milhão *ooñ meel-***yowñ**			

days

SEGUNDA-FEIRA *segoonduh fayruh*		MON
TERÇA-FEIRA *tersuh-fayruh*		TUES
QUARTA-FEIRA *kwartuh-fayruh*		WED
QUINTA-FEIRA *keentuh-fayruh*		THURS
SEXTA-FEIRA *seshtuh-fayruh*		FRI
SÁBADO *sabadoo*		SAT
DOMINGO *domeengoo*		SUN

seasons

A PRIMAVERA *uh preema**veh**ruh*	SPRING
O VERÃO *oo vuh-**rowñ***	SUMMER
O OUTONO *oo ohtohnoo*	AUTUMN
O INVERNO *oo een**vehr**noo*	WINTER

months

JANEIRO *juh**nay**roo*		JAN
FEVEREIRO *fuh-**vray**oo*		FEB
MARÇO *mahrsoo*		MAR
ABRIL *abreel*		APRIL
MAIO *my-oo*		MAY
JUNHO *joon-yoo*		JUNE
JULHO *jool-yoo*		JULY
AGOSTO *agoshtoo*		AUG
SETEMBRO *suh**tem**broo*		SEP
OUTUBRO *ohtoobroo*		OCT
NOVEMBRO *nova**yñ**-broo*		NOV
DEZEMBRO *duh**zayñ**-broo*		DEC

What is today's date?
Qual é a data hoje?
*kwal e uh **dah**-tuh ohjkuh dee-uh e ohj*

What day is it today?
Que dia é hoje?

It's the 5th of May 2003
É cinco de Maio de dois mil e três
*e **seen**koo duh **my**-oo duh doysh meel ee tresh*

on Saturday
no sábado
*noo **sa**badoo*

on Saturdays
aos sábados
*awsh **sa**badoosh*

every Saturday
todos os sábados
*toh-**doosh** oosh sabadoosh*

this Saturday
este sábado
esht sabadoo

next Saturday
o próximo sábado
*oo **pross**imoo sabadoo*

last Saturday
o sábado passado
*oo sabadoo puh-**sah**doo*

in June
em Junho
*ayñ **joon**-yoo*

at the beginning of...
no princípio de...
*noo preen-**seep**-yoo duh...*

at the end of...
no fim de...
noo feeñ duh...

before the summer
antes do verão
*antsh doo vuh-**rowñ***

during the summer
durante o verão
*doo**rant** oo vuh-**rowñ***

after the summer
depois do verão
*duh-**poysh** doo vuh-**rowñ***

see also **NUMBERS**

TIME

> The 24-hour clock is used a lot more than in Britain. After 1200 midday, it continues: **1300**– treze horas, **1400**– catorze horas, **1500**– quinze horas, etc, until **2400**– vinte e quatro horas (**meia-noite**). With the 24-hour clock, the words **quarto** (quarter) and **meia** (half) aren't used:
>
> **1315** (1.15 pm)   *treze e quinze*
> **1930** (7.30 pm)   *dezanove e trinta*
> **2245** (10.45 pm)   *vinte e duas e quarenta e cinco*

What time is it?	**am**	**pm**
Que horas são?	da manhã	da tarde
kee **o**rush sowñ	duh man-**yañ**	duh tard

It's …	**2 o'clock**	**3 o'clock**	**6 o'clock** (etc.)
São…	duas horas	três horas	seis horas
sowñ…	**doo**-uz **o**rush	trez **o**rush	sayz **o**rush

It's 1 o'clock	**It's 1200 midday**	**At midnight**
É uma hora	É meio-dia	À meia-noite
e **oom**uh **o**ruh	e **may**oo **dee**-uh	a **may**uh noyt

9	nove horas
	no**vee o**rush
9.10	nove e dez
	no**vee** desh
9.15	nove e um quarto
	no**vee** ooñ **kwar**too
9.20	nove e vinte
	no**vee** veent
9.30	nove e trinta / nove e meia
	no**vee treen**tuh / no**vee may**uh
9.35	nove e trinta e cinco / vinte e cinco para as dez
	no**vee treen**tuh ee **seen**koo / veen**tee seen**koo **par**uh ush desh
9.45	dez menos um quarto / nove e quarenta e cinco
	desh **may**-nooz ooñ **kwar**too / no**vee** kwa**ren**tuh ee **seen**koo
9.50	dez para as dez / nove e cinquenta
	desh **par**uh ush desh / no**vee** seenk**wen**tuh

When does it open / close?
Quando abre / fecha?
*kwandoo ah-bruh / fay*shuh

When does it begin / finish?
Quando começa / acaba?
*kwandoo koomess*uh / a*kah*-buh

at 3 o'clock
às três horas
*ash trez or*ush

before 3 o'clock
antes das três
antsh dush tresh

after 3 o'clock
depois das três
de*poysh dush tresh*

today
hoje
ohj

tonight
esta noite
eshtuh noyt

tomorrow
amanhã
aman-yañ

yesterday
ontem
ontayñ

the day before yesterday
anteontem
antee-ontayñ

the day after tomorrow
depois de amanhã
duh-poysh daman-yañ

in the morning
de manhã
duh man-yañ

this morning
esta manhã
eshtuh man-yañ

in the afternoon (until dusk)
de tarde
duh tard

in the evening (after dusk)
à noite
a noyt

at half past 7
às sete e meia
ash setee mayuh

at about 10 o'clock
à volta das dez horas
a voltuh dush dez orush

in an hour's time
dentro de uma hora
dentroo doomuh oruh

in a while
daqui a bocado
duhkee uh bookah-doo

two hours ago
há duas horas
a doo-ush orush

soon
em breve
ayñ brev

early
cedo
sedoo

late
tarde
tard

later
mais tarde
mysh tard

I'll do it...
vou fazer...
voh fazehr...

as soon as possible
o mais depressa possível
oo mysh duh-pressuh poo-see-vel

...at the latest
...o mais tardar
...oo mysh tardar

see also **NUMBERS**

EATING PLACES

BAR

*Serves drinks, coffee and snacks. Generally open all day. Look out for **pastéis de bacalhau** (cod cakes), **rissóis de camarão** (prawn rissoles) and **um prego** (a steak roll).*

Cafetaria

A cross between a bar and cake shop, serve hot or cold drinks, cakes and light meals.

Casa de Chá

*Literally a tea house, an elegant pâtisserie which serves a variety of drinks. Look out for **bolos**, mouthwatering Portuguese cakes, **torradas** (toast) and **sandes** (sandwiches made with white bread and often **queijo** (cheese), **fiambre** (ham) or **presunto** (cured ham).*

Pastelaria

Pâtisserie or cake shop. Popular for snacks, soups and light meals. Lovely cakes.

Restaurante

At restaurants, lunch is usually between 12.30 and 2.30 pm. Dinner starts at 7 or 7.30 pm and goes on until 9.30 or 10 pm.

MARISQUERIA

Serves seafood as well as drinks

CHURRASCARIA

Restaurant serving barbecued food, mainly chicken. Most are take-away places.

Cervejaria

Beer house, serving good lager and savouries, it generally offers a good menu, often specializing in seafood.

Tasca

A small local tavern – once cheap eating places they are becoming gentrified.

casa de pasto

Simple, old-fashioned, cheap restaurant usually offers good value meals at lunchtime.

If you want a small, strong black coffee ask for um café *(also known as* uma bica*). A small, white coffee is* um garoto. *An ordinary white coffee is* um café com leite. *A large (mug-sized) coffee is* um galão *served in a tall glass. Tea is normally served in a teapot, weak and without any milk.*

a coffee	a large milky coffee	a lager
um café	um galão	uma cerveja
ooñ kuh-**fe**	ooñ ga**lowñ**	**oom**uh ser**vay**-juh

a (strong) tea...	with milk / lemon	with toast
um chá (forte)...	com leite / limão	com torradas
ooñ sha (fort)...	koñ layt / lee**mowñ**	koñ too**rah**-dush

for two	for me	for him / her	for us
para dois	para mim	para ele / ela	para nós
paruh doysh	**paruh** meeñ	**paruh** ayl / **el**uh	**paruh** nosh

with ice, please	very hot, please
com gelo, por favor	muito quente, por favor
koñ **jay**-loo poor fa**vor**	**mween**too kent poor fa**vor**

a bottle of mineral water	sparkling	still
uma garrafa de água mineral	com gás	sem gás
oomuh gar**rah**-fuh **dahg**-wuh meenuh-**ral**	koñ gas	sayñ gas

Would you like a drink?	What will you have?
Quer uma bebida?	Que quer tomar?
kehr **oom**uh buh-**bee**duh	kuh kehr too**mar**

I'm very thirsty	It's my round
Tenho muita sede	É a minha vez
ten-yoo **mween**tuh sed	e uh **meen**-yuh vesh

■ OTHER DRINKS TO TRY

um chocolate *a chocolate, served hot* quente *or cold* frio

um chá de limão *boiling water poured over fresh lemon peel. A refreshing drink after a meal or at any time*

um batido de fruta *fruit milkshake: try strawberry –* morango

see also **IN A BAR/CAFÉ** ▢ **IN A RESTAURANT**

READING THE MENU

*Restaurants will have the menu displayed next to the entrance. If you don't want a full meal it is better to go to a snack bar, **Pastelaria** (cake shop), **Cafetaria**, **Casa de Chá** (tea house) or **Cervejaria** (beer house).*

Pratos Combinados	These are likely to consist of ham, egg, chips, fresh salad, perhaps, sausage and/or cheese and bread. It will be explained in the menu.
Pratos do Dia	Literally, dishes of the day, these are generally more economical and readily served than the à la carte menu.
Ementa do Dia	Set-price menu, with 3 courses (starter, meat or fish and dessert). May include wine.
Ementa Turística	Set-price menu, as above, offering traditional dishes. The set-price menus may only be available for lunch.

Ementa	**Menu (à la carte)**	Note that main
Entradas	*Starters*	dishes (fish/meat)
Acepipes	*Appetisers*	always include
Sopas	*Soups*	their own
Peixe e Marisco	*Fish and Shellfish*	accompaniments
Pratos de Carne	*Meat dishes*	of potatoes/rice,
Ovos	*Eggs*	vegetables/
Acompanhamentos	*Side dishes*	salads.
Legumes	*Vegetables*	Ask before
Saladas	*Salads*	ordering extra
Sobremesa	*Desserts*	side dishes.
Queijos	*Cheeses*	

In Portugal lunch at restaurants is usually between 12.30 and 2 pm. Dinner starts at 7 or 7.30 pm and goes on until 9.30 or 10 pm.

Where can I/we have a snack?
Onde se pode comer alguma coisa?
onduh suh pod koomehr algoomuh koy-zuh

not too expensive
não muito cara
nown mweentoo kah-ruh

Can you recommend a good local restaurant?
Pode recomendar um bom restaurante local?
pod ruh-koomendar ooñ boñ rushtoh-rant lookal

I'd like to book a table for ... people
Queria reservar uma mesa para ... pessoas
kree-uh ruh-zervar oomuh may-zuh paruh ... puh-so-ush

for tonight...
para esta noite...
paruh eshtuh noyt...

for tomorrow night...
para amanhã à noite...
paruh aman-yañ a noyt...

at 8 pm
às 8 horas
ash oytoo orush

The menu, please
A ementa, por favor
uh eementuh poor favor

What is the dish of the day?
Qual é o prato do dia?
kwal e oo prah-too doo dee-uh

Do you have a set-price menu?
Tem a ementa do dia?
tayñ a eementuh doo dee-uh

I'll have this
Quero isto
kehroo eeshtoo

Can you recommend a local dish?
Pode recomendar uma especialidade local?
pod ruh-koomendar oomuh shpuss-yalee-dahd lookal

Excuse me!
Faz favor!
fash favor

Please bring...
Traga...
trah-guh...

more bread
mais pão
mysh powñ

more water
mais água
mysh ahg-wuh

more butter
mais manteiga
mysh mantay-guh

a half portion
meia dose
mayuh doh-zuh

another bottle
outra garrafa
oh-truh garrah-fuh

the bill
a conta
a kontuh

Is service included?
O serviço está incluído?
oo serveesoo shta een-klweedoo

see also **EATING PLACES** ☐ **WINES & SPIRITS**

VEGETARIAN

There are very few vegetarian restaurants in Portugal, and those that do exist are located in the capital or Oporto and in some towns within the Algarve.

Are there any vegetarian restaurants here?
Há algum restaurante vegetariano aqui?
*a al**goon** rushtoh-**rant** vejuh-tuh-ree-**ah**-noo a**kee***

Do you have any vegetarian dishes?
Tem algum prato vegetariano?
*tayñ al**goon prah**-too vejuh-tuh-ree-**ah**-noo*

Do you have any dishes without meat / fish?
Tem pratos sem carne / peixe?
*tayñ **prah**-toosh sayñ karn / paysh*

What fish dishes do you have?
Que pratos de peixe tem?
*kuh **prah**-toosh duh paysh tayñ*

I'd like pasta / rice...	**without meat**	**without fish**
Queria massa / arroz...	sem carne	sem peixe
*kree-uh **massa**h / ar**osh**...*	*sayñ karn*	*sayñ paysh*

I don't like meat / fish
Não gosto de carne / peixe
*nowñ **gosh**too duh karn / paysh*

What do you recommend?
Que recomenda?
*kuh ruh-koo**men**duh*

Is it made with vegetable stock?
É feito com caldo vegetal?
*e **fay**-too koñ **kal**doo vejuh-**tahl***

■ POSSIBLE DISHES

omeleta (simples / com queijo / com cogumelos) *omelette (plain / with cheese / with mushrooms)*

ovos (estrelados / mexidos com batatas fritas) *eggs (fried / scrambled with chips)*

salada (simples / mista) *salad (green / mixed)*

tortilha à espanhola *Spanish-style omelette usuallly made with cooked vegetables rather than potato and onion*

see also EATING PLACES ❑ WINES & SPIRITS

*If you want a reasonably-priced wine, the **vinho de casa** (house wine) is normally quite good and inexpensive.*

The wine list, please
A lista de vinhos, por favor
uh **leesh**tuh duh **veen**-yoosh poor fa**vor**

Can you recommend a good wine?
Pode recomendar um bom vinho?
pod ruh-koomen**dar** ooñ boñ **veen**-yoo

A bottle...	**A carafe...**	**of the house wine**
Uma garrafa...	Um jarro...	de vinho da casa
oomuh gar**rah**-fuh...	ooñ **jarr**oo...	duh **veen**-yoo duh **kah**-zuh

of red wine
de vinho tinto
duh **veen**-yoo **teen**too

of white wine
de vinho branco
duh **veen**-yoo **bran**koo

of rosé wine
de vinho rosé
duh **veen**-yoo roh-**zay**

of 'green' wine
de vinho verde
duh **veen**-yoo vehrd

of dry wine
de vinho seco
duh **veen**-yoo **seh**-koo

of sweet wine
de vinho doce
duh **veen**-yoo dohss

of a local wine
de vinho da região
duh **veen**-yoo duh ruj-**yowñ**

What liqueurs do you have?
Que licores tem?
kuh lee-**korsh** tayñ

A glass of port
Um cálice de Porto
ooñ **kah**-leesuh duh **por**too

A glass of Boal (madeira)
Um cálice de Boal
ooñ **kah**-leesuh duh boo-**al**

cont...

■ **TYPES OF PORT**   PORTO

Port wines offer a wide variety of styles, making them suitable for all sorts of occasions and also to serve with some foods. The main varieties are:

White *(which can be sweet or dry, so check the label). Good on its own or as an aperitif. It should be chilled and can be made into a long drink with a little ice and a twist of lemon.*

Ruby *is a blend of young ports, ready to drink, spicy and fruity. Sweet and ruby in colour. No need to decant.*

Tawny *is a blend from various harvests. It has a rich amber colour, a long finish and complex aroma. Look for labels indicating its age (10, 20, 30 years old). It is ready to drink and does not need decanting. This is the most popular style.*

Vintage Port *is a wine from an exceptional declared harvest. Matured in wood for two or three years, it is bottled and continues to mature, for at least 10 years, or much longer. It must be decanted. It is dark and rich, becoming softer and more complex as it ages. There are intermediate styles (LBV, for example). The label should help.*

■ **TYPES OF MADEIRA**   MADEIRA

Madeira wines fall into four categories and, like the ports, are served as an aperitif or for dessert, or any other occasion, according to their sweetness and personal taste. The four categories are:

Sercial *quite dry and pale*

Verdelho *less dry and slightly darker than* **Sercial**

Boal *richer-coloured and sweeter*

Malvasia *dark, very perfumed, full-bodied and very sweet*

Whatever category, these wines are always very aromatic and complex. The drier styles should be served chilled.

A

...**à caçadora** hunter-style (poultry or game marinated in wine and garlic)

...**à jardineira** garden-style with vegetables like green beans and carrots

...**à lagareiro** baked dish made with lots of olive oil

...**à marinheira** with white wine, onions and parsley

...**à portuguesa** Portuguese fashion, i.e. with tomato sauce

abacate avocado

abacaxi pineapple

abóbora pumpkin
  sopa de abóbora pumpkin soup

açafrão saffron

acelga swiss chard

acepipes appetisers

acompanhamentos side dishes

açorda typical Portuguese dish with bread

açorda com peixe frito thick bread soup accompanying fried fish

açorda de alho thick bread soup with garlic and beaten egg (generally served with fried fish in traditional restaurants)

açorda de marisco thick bread soup with shellfish and a beaten egg, typical of the Lisbon area

açorda de sável thick bread soup with shad

açorda de Sesimbra thick bread soup with fish, garlic and coriander

açúcar sugar

adocicado slightly sweet

agrião watercress

água water

água mineral com gás sparkling mineral water

água mineral sem gás still mineral water

água tónica tonic water

aguardente brandy
  velha old or **velhíssima** very old

aipo celery

albardado in batter

alcachofra artichoke
  fundo de alcachofra artichoke heart

alcaparra caper

alcatra braised beef, typical of the Azores

alecrim rosemary

aletria fine noodles

alface lettuce

alfenim moulded sugar, a speciality of the Azores

alheiras chicken and garlic sausage from Trás-os-Montes

alho garlic

alho francês leek

almoço lunch

almôndegas meatballs

alperces apricots

amargo bitter

amarguinha bitter-almond liqueur made in the Algarve region

amêijoas clams

amêijoas à Bulhão Pato clams with garlic and coriander

amêijoas ao natural steamed clams with herbs and lemon butter

amêijoas na cataplana clams cooked in a 'cataplan' pot, with *chouriço* and herbs

ameixa plum

ameixas de Elvas preserved greengages from Elvas (Alentejo)

ameixa seca prune

amêndoas almonds

amêndoas doces sugared almonds

amendoim peanut

amora blackberry

ananás pineapple

anchovas anchovies

aniz aniseed liqueur

ao in the style of

aperitivo aperitif

areias de Cascais small cookies from Cascais

arenque herring

arjamolho kind of gazpacho soup, typical of the Algarve

arroz branco plain rice

arroz de Cabidela chicken or rabbit highly seasoned risotto

arroz de ervilhas pea rice

arroz de frango chicken with rice

arroz de lampreia lamprey with rice

arroz de lapas limpets with rice (typical of the Azores)

arroz de manteiga rice with butter

arroz de marisco shellfish with rice

arroz de pato rice with duck

arroz de polvo octopus with rice

arroz de tomate tomato rice

arroz doce rice pudding Portuguese-style made on top of the stove with lemon rind, vanilla and topped with cinnamon

arroz no forno rice cooked in the oven

arrufadas de Coimbra sweet buns from Coimbra

assado roasted

assado no forno oven-roasted

assado no espeto spit roasted

atum tuna fish

atum assado braised tuna with onions and tomatoes

atum de cebolada tuna steak with onions and tomato sauce

atum de conserva canned tuna

atum salpresado salted tuna dish often eaten during festivities in Madeira

aveia oats

avelã hazelnut

aves fowl

azeda sorrel

azedas sharp Azorean soups, containing a little vinegar

azedo sour

azeite olive oil

azeitonas olives
preta black
verde green

azevias half-moon shaped cakes

B

bacalhau salt cod

bacalhau à Brás traditional dish with salt cod, onion and potatoes all bound with scrambled eggs

bacalhau à Gomes de Sá good salt cod dish with layers of potatoes, onions and boiled eggs, laced with olive oil and baked

bacalhau à lagareiro salt cod baked with lots of olive oil

bacalhau com natas salt cod in cream sauce au gratin

bacalhau com todos salt cod poached with potatoes and vegetables

bacalhau assado charcoal-grilled cod

bacalhau na brasa salt cod grilled on charcoal, served with olive oil

bagaceira brandy similar to eau-de-vie

banana banana

banha lard

barriga de freira a sweet made with yolks and sugar, slightly caramelised

batata potato

batata doce sweet potato

batata doce assada baked sweet potato

batatas a murro potatoes baked in their own skins then soaked in olive oil

batatas assadas baked potatoes

batatas fritas chips

batatas cozidas boiled potatoes

batido de fruta fruit milkshake

batido de morango strawberry milkshake

baunilha vanilla

bebida drink

bebida sem álcool/não alcoólica non-alcoholic drink

bem passado well done

berbigão cockle

beringela aubergine

besugo sea bream

beterraba beetroot

bica strong small black coffee

bifana pork tenderloin in a roll

bife steak (and chips and perhaps fried egg)

   ...bem passado well done

   ...mal passado medium

   ...muito mal passado rare

bife à café steak in cream sauce topped with a fried egg (with chips)

bife à Portuguesa steak in mustard sauce topped with a fried egg (with chips)

bife do lombo sirloin steak

bifes de atum tuna steaks

bifes de perú turkey steaks

bifinhos de vitela veal fillet served with Madeira sauce

biscoitos cookies

biscoitos de azeite olive oil biscuits

bitoque small steak with fried egg and chips

bola layered bread and cured meat pie

bola de Berlim doughnut

bolachas biscuits

bolachas de água e sal water biscuits (crackers)

boleimas cakes with a bread dough base with olive oil, sugar, eggs and spices

bolinhos de bacalhau cod croquettes

bolo caseiro homemade cake

bolo de chocolate chocolate cake

bolo de mel honey cake

bolo de mel da Madeira Madeira molasses cake made with lots of spices and eaten traditionally at Christmas

bolo de Natal Christmas fruitcake

bolo podre delicious dark cake made with honey, olive oil and spices

bolo rei a cake-ring made with a sweet dough with dried and crystallised fruits, eaten on Epiphany

bolos cakes

bolos de D. Rodrigo cakes made with egg yolks, sugar, almonds and cinnamon, and sold in little pointed foil parcels to keep the syrup inside

bolos de ovos egg cakes

borracho young pigeon

borrego lamb

branco white

    cerveja branca white beer

    vinho branco white wine

broa a crusty rustic maize bread

broas de mel small honey cakes eaten at Christmas

broas podres de Natal small spicy cakes eaten at Christmas

brócolos broccoli

Bucelas a type of wine from the Estremadura region

bucho pork haggis

C

cabrito kid

cabrito assado roast kid with a spiced marinade

cabrito frito fried kid

cabrito montês roebuck

cabrito à ribatejana marinated roast kid with paprika typical of Ribatejo

caça game

cacau cocoa

cachorro hotdog

cachucho small sea bream

café coffee
bica small, strong black coffee (espresso)
carioca small but slightly weaker black coffee
com leite white coffee
duplo large cup of coffee
frio iced coffee
galão large white coffee served in a tall glass
garoto small white coffee
meia de leite ordinary size cup of half coffee, half milk
sem cafeína decaffeinated

caipirinha rum and lemon

caju cashew nut

caldeirada fish stew

caldeirada à fragateira seafood stew, as prepared by fishermen

caldeirada de enguias eel stew

caldeirada de peixe fish stew

caldo broth
caldo de carne beef broth
caldo de galinha chicken broth
caldo verde green broth, made with shredded kale and potatoes with a little *chouriço* and olive oil

camarões shrimps

caneca medium-sized beer glass

canela cinnamon

canja chicken soup, thickened with rice or small pasta and chicken pieces

capão capon

capilé drink made with iced coffee, lemon rind and sugar

caracóis snails (small, cooked in a tasty broth and served with a toothpick)

caranguejo crab

carapau horse mackerel, served whole, fried or grilled

cardápio menu

caril curry

carioca small weak coffee

carioca de limão lemon infusion

carne meat

carne assada roast meat (generally beef, sometimes pork)

carne de porco à alentejana highly seasoned pork dish with clams, typical of the Alentejo

carne de vaca beef

carne de vaca assada roast beef

carne de vaca à antiga marinated roast beef, served with new potatoes (speciality from the Azores)

carne de vinha d'alhos popular festive Madeiran dish, with marinated pork, bread, sweet and new potatoes

carneiro mutton

carnes frias cold meats

carta dos vinhos winelist

casa de chá tea-house

casa de pasto restaurant serving cheap, homely meals

castanha chestnut
  castanhas assadas roasted chestnuts

castanhas cozidas boiled chestnuts with aniseed

cataplana shellfish dish made with pork, pepper, garlic and onion, and cooked in a cataplana pot

cavala mackerel

cavalas com molho de vilão marinated and fried mackerel, served with a reduced marinade (Madeiran speciality)

cebola onion

cebolada fried onion garnish

cenoura carrot
  sopa de puré de cenoura carrot purée soup

cereja cherry

cerveja beer/lager

cerveja à pressão draught beer

cerveja em garrafa bottled beer

cerveja preta dark ale

cervejaria beer house, serving food

chá tea
  chá com leite tea with milk

101

chá com limão tea with lemon

chá forte strong tea

chá de ervas/ tisana herb tea

chanfana rich lamb/ kid stew

chanfana da Bairrada kid stew

cherne species of grouper with dark skin, a very prized fish normally served grilled

chicória endive

chila or **gila** type of pumpkin (spaghetti squash) made into jam, used as a filling for many cakes and desserts all over Portugal

chispalhada pig's trotters stew

chispe com feijão trotters with beans, cured meats and vegetables

chocolate chocolate

chocolate frio cold chocolate

chocolate quente hot chocolate

chocos com tinta cuttlefish in its own ink

choquinhos squid

choquinhos com tinta squid in its ink

chouriço spicy smoked sausage

chuchu marrow

churrasco barbecued/ cooked on charcoal

churrasqueira restaurant specialising in **frango à piri-piri** (chicken with piri-piri)

clarete light red wine

coco coconut

codorniz quail

coelho rabbit

coelho à caçadora hunter's rabbit or hare, cooked in wine and herbs

coentrada with fresh coriander

coentros fresh coriander

cogumelos mushrooms

colares a type of wine from the Estremadura region

colorau sweet paprika

comidas meals

cominho cumin seed

compota jam or compote

congro conger eel

conhaque cognac

conta bill

copo glass

coração heart

cordeiro lamb

costeletas de porco pork chops

costeletas de porco grelhadas grilled pork chops

couve cabbage

couve-de-bruxelas brussels sprouts

couve-flor cauliflower

couve-lombarda savoy cabbage

couve portuguesa Portuguese cabbage (a large and very tender cabbage), commonly used to accompany poached fish, when in season

couve-roxa red cabbage

covilhetes de leite custard tarts from the Azores

cozido boiled or poached

cozido à Madeirense boiled Madeira-style pork and vegetables, with pumpkin and couscous

cozido à portuguesa boiled assorted meats, vegetables and rice, served in a large platter

cravinhos cloves

creme custard

creme de leite milk custard

criação fowl

croissants com fiambre ham-filled croissants

croissants recheados filled croissants

croquetes de carne meat croquettes

cru raw

cuba livre rum and coke

D

damasco apricot

digestivo digestive e.g. brandy

dobrada tripe
  dobrada à moda do Porto tripe Oporto fashion in a bean stew

DOC (denominação de origem controlada) denotes a very good wine

doce sweet

doces de amêndoa marzipan sweets

doce de fruta jam

doce de laranja marmalade

dourada sea bream

E

eirós large eel generally fried and served with an *escabeche* sauce

ementa menu

empadão de batata shepherd's pie

empadas small chicken or veal pies

endívia endive

enguias de caldeirada eel stew, typical of Aveiro

enguias fritas fried eels

ensopado fish or meat stew served on bread slices

ensopado de borrego rich lamb stew served on bread slices

entradas starters

entrecosto entrecôte steak

erva-doce aniseed

ervilhas peas

ervilhas com paio e ovos peas with garlic sausage and poached eggs

escabeche a special sauce containing vinegar, normally served with cold fried fish

escalfado poached
  ovo escalfado poached egg

espada the name given in Madeira to *peixe espada* (scabbard fish)

espadarte swordfish

espadarte fumado smoked swordfish

esparguete spaghetti

espargos asparagus

esparregado spinach purée with garlic

especiarias spices

esperanças delicate cakes from the Azores, filled with almonds

espetada kebab

esplanada open-air restaurant/café

espinafre spinach

espumante sparkling wine (champagne type)

estragão tarragon

estufado braised
  carne estufada braised meat

esturjão sturgeon

extra-seco extra-dry

F

farinha flour

farinheira sausage made with flour and pork fat

farófias 'floating islands' made with egg whites and custard sauce

fartes de batata square cakes of sweet potato purée with spices and almonds

fataça grey mullet

fatias de Tomar sponge slices served in a light syrup

fatias douradas slices of bread dipped in egg, fried and covered with sugar and cinnamon

favada à portuguesa broad beans cooked with smoked meats, onions and coriander

favas broad beans

febras thin slices of roast pork

febras de porco à alentejana pork fillet with onions, chouriço and bacon

feijão beans

feijão encarnado red beans

feijão frade black-eyed beans

feijão guisado beans stewed with bacon in a tomato sauce

feijão preto black beans

feijão verde cozido boiled French beans

feijoada bean stew with pork meat and *chouriço*

fiambre ham

fígado liver

fígado de coentrada pork liver with coriander

fígado de galinha chicken liver

fígado de porco de cebolada pork liver with onions

figos figs

figos cheios dried figs stuffed with almonds

figos secos dried figs

filetes de pescada hake fillet in batter

filhós fritters eaten at Christmas

filhós de abóbora pumpkin purée fritters eaten at Christmas

filhoses festive fried cakes sprinkled with sugar and cinnamon or dipped into honey or syrup

fofas do Faial choux-type pastry filled with cream or custard, typical of the Azores

folar a sweet loaf with spices, topped with boiled eggs and eaten at Easter

folhados de carne meat puff-pastries

framboesa raspberry

frango young chicken

frango à piri-piri barbecued tender chicken with chilli

frango assado roast tender chicken

frango no churrasco barbecued tender chicken in a hot sauce (piri-piri)

fresca/o cold or fresh
uma cerveja muito fresca a very cool beer

fressura de porco guisada pork offal casserole

fricassé meat or fish (generally chicken) served with an egg and lemon sauce

frio cold

fritada de peixe deep-fried mixed fish

frito fried

fruta fruit

fruta cristalizada candied fruit

fruta da época fruit in season

fruta em calda fruit in syrup

fumado smoked
salmão fumado smoked salmon

fundo de alcachofra artichoke heart

G

galheteiro cruet stand

galinha chicken

galinhola woodcock

galinhola à Alentejana Alentejo woodcock, cooked with wine, garlic and seasonings, with a tasty filling

galão milky coffee served in a large glass

gambas large prawns

gambas na chapa large prawns cooked on the hot plate

ganso goose

garoto small white coffee

garoupa grouper

garoupa recheada stuffed and baked grouper, a typical dish from the Azores

garrafa bottle

gasosa soft drink with gas

gaspacho cold soup with finely cut vegetables

gelado ice-cream

geleia jelly

gelo ice

gengibre ginger

gim gin

ginjinha morello-cherry liqueur typical of Portugal

girafa beer glass (equivalent to a pint)

goiaba guava

granizado de café iced coffee

grão chickpeas
bacalhau com grão poached salt cod with boiled chickpeas, seasonings, olive oil and boiled egg

gratinado au gratin

grelhado grilled

grelhado misto mixed grill

groselha red currant

guisado stewed

H

hortaliça generic name given to vegetables
sopa de hortaliça vegetable soup

hortelã mint
chá de hortelã mint tea

hortelã-pimenta peppermint

I

imperial small beer glass

incluído included

inhame yam, very popular on some of the Azores islands

iscas traditional pork liver dish made with wine and garlic

iscas com elas well-seasoned liver dish served with boiled potatoes, a Lisbon speciality

J

jantar dinner

jardineira mixed vegetables

jarro carafe

javali wild boar

jeropiga fortified dessert wine

Joaquinzinhos small horse-mackerel fried whole (like whitebait), very popular in some restaurants

L

lagosta lobster

lagostim-do-rio freshwater crayfish

lagostins king prawns

lampreia lamprey (an eel-like fish)

lampreia de ovos egg lamprey, a rich dessert

lanche afternoon snack consisting of tea and cakes or buttered toast

lapas limpets, popular in Madeira and the Azores

lapas Afonso limpets served with a tasty onion sauce

laranja orange

laranja descascada peeled orange, normally served with a sprinkle of sugar

laranjada engarrafada bottled orange juice

laranjada natural fresh orange juice

lavagante lobster

lebre hare

legumes vegetables

leitão assado à moda da Bairrada crisply roasted suckling pig from the Bairrada region

leite milk

leite-creme crème brûlée

leite frio/quente cold/hot milk

lentilha lentil

licor de leite milk liqueur

licor de tangerina mandarin liqueur

lima lime

limão lemon

limonada lemonade

língua tongue

língua estufada braised tongue

linguado sole

linguado frito fried sole

linguado grelhado grilled sole

linguiça pork sausage with paprika

lista dos vinhos wine list

lombinho de porco pork loin

lombo de porco pork fillet

louro bay leaf

lulas squid

lulas à Algarvia squid in garlic, Algarve style

lulas cheias local name in the Algarve for *lulas recheadas* (stuffed squid)

lulas guisadas stewed squid

lulas recheadas small squid stuffed with rice and seasonings

M

maçã apple

maçã assada large baked russet apple

maçapão marzipan

macarrão macaroni

macedónia de frutas mixed fruit salad

madeira wine from Madeira

maduro mature

maionese mayonnaise

malagueta hot pepper

mal passado rare

mandioca cassava root

manga mango

manjar celeste sweet made with eggs, bread crumbs, almonds and sugar

manjericão basil

manteiga butter

mãozinhas de vitela guisadas stewed calves' trotters

maracujá passion fruit

marinado/a marinated

marisco shellfish

marisqueira a restaurant or bar specialising solely in shellfish

marmelada quince jam – excellent with cheese

marmelo quince, a popular fruit, often baked

massa pasta

medalhão medallion

medronheira strawberry-tree fruit liqueur

meia-dose half-portion

meia garrafa half bottle

meio-doce medium-sweet

meio-seco medium-dry

mel honey

mel de cana molasses

melancia watermelon

melão melon

melão com presunto melon with cured ham slices, a starter

menu turístico budget tourists' menu, good value menu based on local dishes

merenda afternoon snack consisting of tea and cakes or buttered toast

merendinha pastry filled with *chouriço* or *presunto* (ham)

merengue meringue

mero red grouper fish

mexilhões mussels

migas bread cooked with well-seasoned ingredients to form a kind of omelette

migas à alentejana thick bread soup with pork meat and garlic

migas à lagareiro bread cooked with cabbage, salt cod and olive oil

migas de pão de milho thick maize bread soup with olive oil and garlic

mil-folhas millefeuille (custard pastry)

milho corn (maize)

milho doce sweetcorn

milho frito polenta fried in cubes, popular in Madeira

miolos brains

misto mixed

molho sauce

molho béchamel béchamel sauce

molho de caril curry sauce

molho de escabeche a special sauce containing vinegar, normally served with cold fried fish

molho de tomate tomato sauce

molho tártaro piquant mayonnaise with capers, gherkins and olives

morangos strawberries

morcela spicy black pudding

morgado de figo dried pressed figs with spices

moscatel de Setúbal medium-sweet muscat wine

mostarda mustard

mousse de chocolate chocolate mousse

N

nabiça turnip greens

nabo turnip

...na brasa char-grilled

...na cataplana stewed on cataplana vessel (typical double-wok pot used in the Alentejo and Algarve)

...na frigideira sautéed or fried

natas cream

nata batida whipped cream

natural plain, without dressing or served at room temperature (usually wine or water)

...no espeto kebab/on the spit

...no forno roasted or cooked in the oven

nozes walnuts

nozes de Cascais caramelised walnuts, from Cascais

O

óleo vegetable oil

omeleta de cogumelos mushroom omelette

omeleta de fiambre ham omelette

omeleta de queijo cheese omelette

omeleta simples plain omelette

ostras oysters

ouriço-do-mar sea-urchin

ovas fish roe

ovos eggs

ovos cozidos boiled eggs

ovos escalfados poached eggs

ovos estrelados fried eggs

ovos mexidos scrambled eggs

ovos moles soft egg sweet

ovos quentes soft-boiled eggs

P

paio thick smoked sausage made with lean meat

palha de Abrantes sweet made with eggs, looking like straw

panados slices of meat coated in egg and breadcrumbs and fried

pão bread

pão de centeio rye bread

pão de forma sliced bread for toast

pão-de-ló light sponge cake

pão de milho maize bread

pão saloio country-style bread

pãozinho roll
papaia papaya
papas polenta soup
papas de milho doces sweet polenta
papo seco bread roll
papos de anjo small egg cakes with syrup
pargo red bream
parrilhada grilled fish
passas de uva raisins
pastéis de arroz rice tarts from the Azores
pastéis de bacalhau salt cod cakes
pastéis de carne meat pasties
pastéis de feijão tarts made with beans, eggs and almonds
pastéis de nata de Belém egg custard tarts from Belém (Lisbon)
pastéis de Santa Clara pastries with a filling of almonds, egg yolk and sugar
pastéis de Tentugal small pastries with an egg filling
pastelaria pâtisserie/pastry shop

pastel de massa tenra meat pasty
pataniscas (de bacalhau) salt cod fritters
paté de fígado liver pâté
pato duck
pato assado com arroz roast duck with rice
pé de porco com feijão pigs' trotters with beans
peito breast
peixe fish
peixe assado/cozido/frito/grelhado baked/poached/fried/grilled fish
peixe e marisco fish and shellfish
peixe espada scabbard fish
peixe espada frito fried scabbard fish
peixe espada grelhado grilled scabbard fish
peixe-galo John Dory
peixinhos da horta French beans fried in batter
pepino cucumber
pequeno almoço breakfast
pêra pear
percebes barnacles, highly prized shellfish
perdiz partridge

112

perdiz à Montemor Montemor-style partridge, cooked with wine and spices

perdiz com couve lombarda partridge with cabbage

perna leg

pernil ham

perú turkey

pescada hake

pescada com todos hake poached with potatoes and vegetables

pescadinhas de rabo na boca whole rolled-up small fried hake

pêssego peach

pêssego careca nectarine

pezinhos de porco de coentrada pork trotters with coriander and garlic

picante spicy

pimenta pepper (spice)

pimentos peppers

pimentos assados grilled peppers

pinhão pine kernel

pinhoada pinenut brittle

pinhões peanuts

piri-piri chilli sauce

polvo octopus

polvo grelhado grilled octopus

polvo guisado stewed octopus

pombo pigeon

porco pork

porco à alentejana traditional dish with pork, clams and herbs

porco assado roast pork

posta à mirandesa spit-roasted veal, Miranda-style

pouco picante mild

prato dish

prato do dia dish of the day

prato principal main dish

pratos de carne meat dishes

preço price

pregado turbot

prego steak in a roll

prego com fiambre steak with sliced ham

prego no pão steak roll

prego no prato steak with fried egg and chips served on a plate

presunto cured ham

preta dark

cerveja preta dark beer

pudim Abade de Priscos rich egg pudding flavoured with port and lemon

pudim de bacalhau salt cod loaf served with tomato sauce

pudim da casa restaurant's own dessert (often crème caramel)

pudim de coalhada popular Azorean rich, fresh cheese pudding

pudim de pão bread pudding

pudim de queijo cheese pudding

pudim de requeijão ricotta-type cheese pudding

pudim flan crème caramel

pudim Molotov egg-white pudding with egg sauce or caramel

puré de batata mashed potato

Q

queijadas de Évora cheese tarts made with cheese from ewes' milk

queijadas da Madeira small Madeiran cheese cakes

queijadas de requeijão ricotta-type cheese tarts

queijadas de Sintra little cheese cakes with cinnamon made in Sintra

quejinhos de amêndoa little almond cheeses

queijinhos do céu egg yolk and sugar sweets

queijinhos frescos small fresh cheeses (cows', ewes' or goats' milk)

queijinhos secos small dried cheeses

queijo cheese

queijo de Alverca small cheese from Alverca, near Lisbon

queijo cabreiro goats' cheese

queijo cardiga cheese made from ewes' and goats' milk

queijo da Ilha cheddar-type cheese from the Azores, also known as *queijo de S. Jorge*

queijo de Évora small ewes' cheese from Évora

queijo da Serra buttery cheese from Estrela Mountain, a soft, runny cheese made with ewes' milk

queijo de Azeitão hard or soft cheese made with ewes' milk

queijo de cabra goats' cheese

queijo de Nisa a rich ewe's cheese from Nisa (Alentejo)

queijo de ovelha small, dried ewes' milk cheeses

queijo fresco fresh cheese

queijo saloio small cheese made with ewes' milk or a mixture of goats' and ewes' milk

quente hot

quiabo okra

R

rabaçal mild cheese from the Coimbra region

rabanada french toast

rabanete radish

raia skate

rancho a substantial soup

recheado com... stuffed/filled with...

recheio stuffing

regiões demarcadas demarcated wine regions

repolho cabbage

requeijão fresh curd cheese resembling ricotta

rim (rins) kidney

rins à Madeira kidneys served in Madeira wine sauce

rins com vinho do Porto kidneys in port wine sauce

rissóis de camarão/peixe shrimp or fish rissoles

robalo sea bass

rojões crisp pieces of marinated pork

S

sal salt

salada salad

salada de feijão frade black-eyed bean salad, with boiled egg, olive oil and seasonings

salada de fruta fruit salad

salada de polvo a starter with cold octopus, seasoned with olive oil, coriander, onion and vinegar

salada mista mixed salad (tomato, lettuce, cucumber, onion)

salada russa Russian salad

salgados savouries (snacks)

salmão salmon

salmão fumado smoked salmon

salmonetes grel-hados grilled red mullet in a butter and lemon sauce

saloio small cheese made from ewes' or goats' milk, often served as a pre-starter to a meal in the Lisbon region

salpicão slices of large *chouriço*

salsa parsley

salsichas sausages

salteado sautéed

salva sage

sandes sandwich

sandes de fiambre cooked ham sandwich

sandes de lombo steak sandwich

sandes de presunto cured ham sandwich

sandes de queijo cheese sandwich

santola spider crab

sapateira crab (generally dressed)

sarapatel a highly seasoned Madeiran dish made with pork blood and liver

sarda mackerel

sardinhas assadas char-grilled sardines

sardinhas na telha oven-baked sardines cooked on a roof tile with olive oil and seasoning

sável shad

seco dry

sericaia baked custard with cinnamon

serpa a type of ewes' milk cheese from the Alentejo region

serra a creamy cheese made from ewes' milk, from the Serra de Estrela region

serviço incluído service included

sidra cider

simples neat (as in 'neat whisky')

sobremesas desserts

solha plaice

sonho doughnut-type small fried cake, dipped in sugar and cinnamon

sopa soup
sopa à alentejana soup Alentejo-style, made with

chunks of bread, olive oil, fresh coriander and garlic, topped with poached egg

sopa azeda de feijão bean soup with vegetables and bread, sweet potatoes, cinnamon and a spoonful of vinegar (Azores)

sopa de cabeça de peixe fish head soup, using the head of a large fish, tomatoes, potatoes, stale bread and seasonings (Algarve)

sopa de camarão prawn soup

sopa de castanhas piladas hearty soup made with chestnuts, beans and rice

sopa de ervilhas pea soup

sopa de espinafres spinach soup

sopa de feijão bean soup with vegetables

sopa de feijão frade black-eyed bean soup

sopa de feijão verde green bean soup

sopa de funcho fennel soup with beans and bacon fat (Azores)

sopa de grão chickpea soup

sopa de legumes vegetable soup

sopa de marisco shellfish soup

sopa de moganga Madeiran pumpkin soup

sopa de pedra a rich soup with lots of meat, beans and vegetables

sopa de peixe fish soup

sopa de poejos penny-royal soup with eggs (Alentejo)

sopa de rabo de boi oxtail soup

sopa de tomate tomato soup

sopa do dia soup of the day

sopa do Espírito Santo 'Holy Spirit' soup made with meats, vegetables, bread, herbs and spices (Azores)

sopa dos campinos salt cod and tomato soup

sopa dourada dessert made with egg yolks

sopa e um papo-seco soup and roll

sopa seca thick bread soup with meats

sorvete ice-cream

sumo de fruta fruit juice
ananás pineapple
laranja orange
maçã apple
pêra pear
pêssego peach
tomate tomato
uva grape

suspiros meringues

T

tainha grey mullet

tâmara date

tamboril monkfish

tangerina mandarin

tarte de amêndoa almond tart

tarte de limão lemon tart

tarte de maçã apple tart

tasca small taverna serving cheap food and drink

tasquinha small taverna serving cheap food and drink

tempero seasoning

tenro tender

tibornas slices of freshly baked bread sprinkled with coarse sea salt and olive oil

tigeladas de Abrantes individually baked custards in special cups

tinto red wine

tisana herbal tea

tisana de camomila camomile tea

tisana de Lúcia-Lima vervaine tea

tomate tomato

toranja grapefruit

tornedó prime cut of beef

torradas toast

torres Vedras red wine from the Estremadura region

torta swiss roll

torta de laranja orange sponge roll

torta de Viana a sponge roll filled with a rich egg sweet

tosta toasted sandwich

tosta mista ham and cheese toasted sandwich

toucinho bacon

toucinho do céu 'bacon from heaven', an egg and almond pudding

tremoços lupin seeds, commonly consumed with beer

tripas à moda do Porto
tripe stew with beans and
various meats, Oporto-
style

trufa truffle

truta trout

trutas à moda do Minho
trout cooked in wine and
rich seasonings

truta de Barroso traditional
northern dish of fried trout
stuffed with ham

tutano marrow

U

uísque whisky

uvas grapes

V

vaca beef

vagens runner beans

variado assorted

verdelho local Azorean wine

vermute vermouth

vieira scallop

vinagre vinegar

vinha d'alhos marinated in
wine and garlic

vinho abafado
locally made
fortified wine

vinho adamado
sweet wine

vinho branco
white wine

vinho branco seco dry
white wine

vinho branco meio-seco
medium-dry white wine

vinho da casa house wine

vinho espumante sparkling
wine

vinho generoso fortified
wine

vinho Moscatel muscat
wine

vinho regional/da região
local wine

vinho tinto red wine

vinho tinto encorpado
full-bodied red wine, ideal
with red meats

**vinho tinto meio-
encorpado** medium-
bodied red wine, ideal
with salted fish dishes or
light meats

vinho tinto velho mature
red wine, ideal with red
meats

119

vinho verde dry, sparkling 'green' wine made with slightly unripe grapes from the Minho region

vinhos espumantes sparkling wines

vinhos da Madeira madeira wines

vinhos do Porto port wines

vitela veal

vitela no espeto veal cooked on the spit

X

xarope syrup

xarope de groselha blackcurrant syrup

xarope de morango strawberry syrup

xerez sherry

A

a um (uma)
abbey a abadia
able: to be able (to) poder
abortion o aborto
about *(roughly)* mais ou menos
  a book about... um livro
  acerca de...
  about ten o'clock por volta
  das dez
above acima de
abroad *adv* no estrangeiro
  to go abroad ir ao
  estrangeiro
abscess um abcesso
accelerator o acelerador
accent o acento
  (pronunciation) a pronúncia
to accept aceitar
  (approve of) aprovar
access o acesso
  wheelchair access
  o acesso para cadeiras
  de rodas
accident o acidente
accommodation
  o alojamento
to accompany acompanhar
account *(bill)* a conta
  (in bank) a conta (bancária)
account number o número
  da conta
accountant o/a contabilista
to ache doer
  my head aches dói-me
  a cabeça

it aches dói-me
acid o ácido
actor/actress o actor/
  a actriz
to adapt adaptar
adaptor *(electrical)*
  o adaptador
adder a cobra
address a morada
  what is your address?
  qual é a sua morada?
address book a agenda
admission charge/fee
  o preço de entrada
admit: to admit to hospital
  ingresar no hospital
adult o/a adulto(a)
  for adults para adultos
advance: in advance
  antecipadamente
advertisement o anúncio
to advise aconselhar
aerial a antena
aeroplane o avião
aerosol o aerossol
afraid: to be afraid of
  ter medo de
after depois
  after lunch depois do
  almoço
afternoon a tarde
  this afternoon esta tarde
  in the afternoon à tarde
  tomorrow afternoon
  amanhã à tarde
aftershave o aftershave

A

again outra vez

against prep contra
I am against that sou contra isso

age a idade
old age a idade avançada

agency a agência

ago: 2 days ago há 2 dias

to agree concordar

agreement o acordo

AIDS a SIDA

air bag o airbag

air bed o colchão de ar

air conditioning o ar condicionado
is there air conditioning? tem ar condicionado?

air freshener o purificador do ambiente

airline a linha aérea

airmail a via aérea

airplane o avião

airport o aeroporto

airport bus o autocarro do aeroporto

air ticket o bilhete de avião

aisle (plane, theatre, etc) a coxia

alarm o alarme

alarm clock o despertador

alcohol o álcool

alcohol-free sem álcool

alcoholic adj alcoólico(a)

all todo(a), todos(as)

allergic alérgico(a)

I'm allergic to sou alérgico(a) a

allergy a alergia

alley a travessa

to allow permitir
to be allowed estar permitido

all right está bem
are you all right? você está bem?

almond a amêndoa

almost quase

alone sozinho(a)

alphabet o alfabeto

already já

also também

altar o altar

aluminium foil a folha de alumínio

always sempre

a.m. da manhã

am see (to be) **GRAMMAR**

amber (light) amarelo(a)

ambulance a ambulância

America os Estados Unidos

American estado-unidense

amount: total amount o total

anaesthetic a anestesia
general anaesthetic a anestesia geral
local anaesthetic a anestesia local

anchor a âncora

anchovy a anchova

ancient antigo(a)

and e

angel o anjo

angina a angina de peito

angry zangado(a)

animal um animal

aniseed a erva-doce

ankle o tornozelo

anniversary o aniversário

to announce anunciar

announcement o anúncio

annual anual

another um(a) outro(a)
  another beer? mais uma
  cerveja?

answer *n* a resposta

to answer responder

answerphone o gravador
  de chamadas

ant a formiga

antacid o antiácido

antibiotic o antibiótico

antifreeze o anticongelante

antihistamine o anti-
  histamínico

anti-inflammatory o anti-
  inflamatório

antiques as antiguidades

antique shop a loja de
  antiguidades

antiseptic o antiséptico

any *(some)* algum(a)
  (negative) nenhum(a)
  I haven't any money
  não tenho dinheiro

have you any apples?
tem maçãs?

anyone *(in questions)* alguém
  (negative) ninguém

anything *(in questions)*
  alguma coisa
  (negative) nada
  I haven't got anything
  não tenho nada

anywhere *(in any place at all)*
  em qualquer parte
  (negative) em nenhuma
  parte
  *I haven't seen him
  anywhere* não o vi em
  nenhuma parte

apartment o apartamento

aperitif o aperitivo

appendicitis a apendicite

apple a maçã

application form
  o formulário de
  requerimento

appointment *(meeting)*
  o encontro
  (doctor) a consulta
  (hairdresser) a hora marcada
  I have an appointment
  tenho un encontro

approximately
  aproximadamente

apricot o damasco

April o Abril

architect o/a arquitecto(a)

architecture a arquitectura

are see (to be) **GRAMMAR**

arm o braço
armbands *(to swim)* as braçadeiras
armchair a poltrona
aromatherapy a aromaterapia
to arrange organizar
to arrest prender
arrival a chegada
to arrive chegar
art a arte
art gallery a galeria de arte
arthritis a artrite
artichoke a alcachofra
artificial artificial
artist o/a artista
ashtray o cinzeiro
to ask *(question)* perguntar
(to ask for something) pedir
asparagus o espargo
asleep: he/she is asleep está adormecido(a)
aspirin a aspirina
soluble aspirin aspirina efervescente
asthma a asma
I have asthma tenho asma
at em
at home em casa
at 8 o'clock às oito
at once imediatamente
at night à noite
Atlantic Ocean o oceano Atlântico
to attack atacar
attractive *(person)* atraente

aubergine a beringela
auction o leilão
audience a audiência
August o Agosto
aunt a tia
au pair o/a au pair
Australia a Austrália
Australian australiano(a)
author o/a autor(a)
automatic automático(a)
automatic car o carro automático
autumn o outono
available disponível
avalanche a avalancha
avenue a avenida
average a média
(adj) médio(a)
avocado o abacate
to avoid evitar
awake: to be awake estar acordado(a)
awful terrível
axle o eixo

B

baby o bebé
baby food a comida de bebé
baby milk o leite infantil
baby's bottle o biberão
baby seat *(in car)* o assento do bebé
baby-sitter o/a babysitter

baby-sitting service serviço de baby-sitting

baby wipes as toalhitas

bachelor o solteiro

back *(of body)* as costas

backache a dor de costas

backpack a mochila

back seat o assento traseiro

bacon o toucinho

bad *(weather, news)* má (mau) *(fruit, vegetables)* podre

badminton o badminton

bag o saco *(handbag)* o saco de mão *(case)* a mala

baggage a bagagem

baggage allowance o peso limite da bagagem

baggage reclaim a recolha de bagagem

bait *(for fishing)* a isca

baked assado

baker's a padaria

balcony a varanda

bald *(person)* calvo(a) *(tyre)* careca

ball a bola

ballet o ballet

balloon o balão

banana a banana

band *(music)* a banda musical

bandage a ligadura

bank o banco *(river)* a margem

bank account a conta bancária

banknote a nota (bancária)

bankrupt falido(a)

bar o bar

bar of chocolate a barra de chocolate

barbecue o churrasco *to have a barbecue* fazer um churrasco

barber o barbeiro

to bark ladrar

barn o celeiro

barrel o barril

basement a cave

basil o manjericão

basket o cesto

basketball o basquete(bol)

basketwork os artigos de vime

bat *(animal)* o morcego *(for table tennis)* a raqueta

bath o banho *to have a bath* tomar banho

bathing cap a touca de banho

bathroom a casa de banho *with bathroom* com casa de banho

battery *(for car)* a bateria *(for torch, radio, etc)* a pilha

bay a baía

bayleaf a folha de louro

B&B o quarto com pequeno-almoço *(place)* a pensão

B to be see (to be) **GRAMMAR**

beach a praia
  private beach a praia particular
  sandy beach a praia arenosa
  nudist beach a praia naturista

beach hut a barraca

bean o feijão
  broad bean a fava
  French/green bean o feijão verde
  kidney bean o feijão encarnado
  soya bean o feijão de soja

bear *(animal)* o urso

beard a barba

beautiful belo(a)

beauty salon o salão de beleza

because porque

to become tornar-se

bed a cama
  double bed a cama de casal
  single bed a cama de solteiro
  sofa bed o sofá-cama
  twin beds as camas separadas

bedding a roupa de cama

bedclothes a roupa de cama

bedroom o quarto

bee a abelha

beef a carne de vaca

beer a cerveja

beetroot a beterraba

before antes de
  before breakfast antes do pequeno-almoço

beggar o/a mendigo(a)

to begin começar

behind atrás
  behind the bank atrás do banco

beige bege

to believe acreditar

bell *(door)* a campainha *(church)* o sino

to belong to pertencer a

below debaixo de *(less than)* abaixo de

belt o cinto

bend *(in road)* a curva

berth *(in ship)* o beliche

beside *(next to)* ao lado de
  beside the bank ao lado do banco

best: the best o/a melhor

to bet on apostar em

better (than) melhor (do que)

between entre

bib o bibe

bicycle a bicicleta
  by bicycle de bicicleta

bicycle lock o cadeado da bicicleta

bicycle repair kit o estojo de ferramentas

bidet o bidé
big grande
bigger (than) maior que
bike *(motorbike)* a moto
(pushbike) a bicicleta
mountain bike a bicicleta
de montanha
bikini o bikini
bill *(in hotel, restaurant)*
a conta
(for work done) a factura
(gas, telephone) a conta
bin o caixote do lixo
bin liner o saco do lixo
binoculars os binóculos
bird o pássaro
biro a esferográfica
birth o nascimento
birth certificate a certidão
de nascimento
birthday o aniversário
happy birthday parabéns
my birthday is on... faço
anos no...
birthday card o cartão de
aniversário
birthday present a prenda
de anos
biscuits as bolachas
bit: a bit of um bocado (de)
bite *(snack)* a merenda;
o lanche
(of animal) a mordedura
(of insect) a picada
let's have a bite to eat
vamos comer algo

to bite *(animal)* morder
(insect) picar
bitten *(by animal)* mordido(a)
(by insect) picado(a)
bitter amargo(a)
black preto(a)
blackberry a amora
silvestre
blackcurrant a groselha
blank o espaço em branco
blanket o cobertor
bleach a lixívia
to bleed sangrar
blender *(for food)*
o liquidificador
blind *(person)* cego(a)
blind *(for window)* a persiana
blister a bolha
block of flats o prédio de
apartamentos
blocked *(pipe, sink)*
entupido(a)
(road) cortada ao trânsito
blond *(person)* louro(a)
blood o sangue
blood group o grupo
sanguíneo
blood pressure a tensão
arterial
blood test a análise ao
sangue
blouse a blusa
blow-dry o brushing
to blow-dry fazer um
brushing

B

blue azul
dark blue azul escuro
light blue azul claro
blunt *(knife, etc)* embotado(a)
boar o javali
boarding card o cartão de embarque
boarding house a pensão
boat o barco
boat trip a viagem de barco
body o corpo
to boil ferver
boiler a caldeira
boiled cozido(a)
bomb a bomba
bone o osso
fish bone a espinha
bonfire a fogueira
bonnet *(of car)* o capot
book o livro
book of tickets a caderneta de bilhetes
to book reservar
booking a marcação
booking office a bilheteira
bookshop a livraria
boot *(of car)* o porta-bagagem
boots as botas
border a fronteira
boring aborrecido(a)
boss o/a chefe
(employer) o patrão/a patroa
both ambos(as)

bottle a garrafa
a bottle of wine uma garrafa de vinho
a half bottle uma meia-garrafa
bottle opener o abre-garrafas
bowl *(for washing)* a bacia
(for food) a tigela
bow tie o laço
box a caixa
box office a bilheteira
boxer shorts os boxers
boy o rapaz
boyfriend o namorado
bra o soutien
bracelet a pulseira
brain o cérebro
to brake travar
brake fluid o óleo dos travões
brake light a luz de travagem
brake shoes sapata
brakes os travões
branch *(of tree)* o ramo
(of business, etc) a sucursal
brand *(make)* a marca
brandy o conhaque
brass o latão
bread o pão
French bread o cacete
sliced bread o pão em fatias
wholemeal bread o pão integral

128

breadcrumbs o pão ralado
bread roll o papo-seco
to break quebrar
breakable frágil
breakdown *(car)* a avaria
  (nervous) o colapso nervoso
breakdown service
  o pronto-socorro
breakdown van o pronto-
  socorro
breakfast o pequeno-
  almoço
breast *(chicken)* o peito
to breastfeed amamentar
to breathe respirar
brick o tijolo
bride a noiva
bridegroom o noivo
bridge a ponte
  (game) o brídege
briefcase a pasta
bright brilhante
Brillo pad® a esponja
  de aço
brine a salmoura
to bring trazer
Britain a Grã-Bretanha
British britânico(a)
broad largo(a)
broccoli os brócolos
brochure a brochura
broken partido(a)
broken down *(car, etc)*
  avariado(a)
bronchitis a bronquite

bronze o bronze
brooch o broche
broom a vassoura
brother o irmão
brother-in-law o cunhado
brown castanho(a)
bruise a nódoa negra
brush a escova
Brussels sprouts as couves-
  de-Bruxelas
bubble bath a espuma para
  o banho
bucket o balde
buffet car o vagão
  restaurante
to build construir
building o edifício
building site o terreno
  de construção
bulb *(light)* a lâmpada
bull o touro
bullfight a tourada
bullfighter o toureiro
bullring a praça de touros
bumbag a carteira de
  cintura
bumper *(on car)* o pára-
  choques
bunch *(of flowers)* o ramo
  (of grapes) o cacho
bungee jumping o bungee
  jumping
bureau de change a casa
  de câmbio
burger um hambúrger

B

burglar o ladrão/a ladra
burglar alarm o alarme de roubo
burglary o roubo
to burn queimar
burnt *(food)* queimado(a)
burst rebentado(a)
bus o autocarro
bus pass o passe de autocarro
bus station a estação de autocarros
bus stop a paragem de autocarros
bus ticket o bilhete de autocarro
bus tour a excursão de autocarro
business os negócios
  on business de negócios
business card o cartão-de-visita
business class a classe executiva
businessman/woman o homem/a mulher de negócios
business trip a viagem de negócios
busy ocupado(a)
but mas
butcher's o talho
butter a manteiga
button o botão
to buy comprar
by por

130

(near) perto de
(next to) ao lado de
by bus de autocarro
by car de carro
by ship de barco
by train de comboio
bypass *(road)* o desvio

C

cab *(taxi)* o táxi
cabaret o cabaré
cabbage a couve
cabin *(on boat)* o camarote
cabin crew os tripulantes de cabine
cable car o teleférico
cable TV a televisão por cabo
café o café
  internet café o cibercafé
cafetière a cafeteira
cake o bolo
cake shop a pastelaria
calamine lotion a loção de calamina
calculator a calculadora
calendar o calendário
calf *(young cow)* o vitelo
to call chamar
call *(telephone)* uma chamada
  a long-distance call uma chamada interurbana
calm calmo(a); tranquilo(a)
camcorder o camcorder
camera a máquina fotográfica

camera case o estojo da máquina fotográfica

to camp acampar

camping gas o gás para campismo

camping stove o fogão portátil; o fogão de campismo

campsite o parque de campismo

can *(verb - to be able)* poder
I/we can posso/podemos
I/we cannot nao posso
can I...? posso ...?
can we...? podemos ...?

can *n* a lata

canned goods as conservas

can opener o abre-latas

Canada o Canadá

Canadian canadiano(a)

canal o canal

to cancel cancelar

cancellation o cancelamento

cancer o cancro

candle a vela

canoe a canoa

to go canoeing fazer canoagem

cap *(hat)* o boné
(diaphragm) o diafragma

capital *(city)* a capital

cappuccino o cappuccino

car o carro
car alarm o alarme do carro

car ferry o barco de passagem

car hire o aluguer de automóveis

car insurance o seguro de automóveis

car keys as chaves do carro

car park o parque de estacionamento

car parts as peças sobressalentes

car radio o rádio do carro

car seat (for children) o banco para crianças

car wash a lavagem automática

carafe a garrafa

caravan a caravana

carburettor o carburador

card *(business)* o cartão (de visita)
(greetings) o cartão
(playing) a carta de jogar

cardboard o cartão

cardigan o casaco de lã

careful cuidadoso(a)
to be careful ter cuidado
be careful! cuidado!

carnation o cravo

carpet a carpete
(rug) o tapete

carriage a carruagem

carrot a cenoura

to carry transportar

carton o pacote

case *(suitcase)* a mala

cash o dinheiro

C

to cash (cheque) levantar
cash desk a caixa
cash dispenser a caixa automática
cashier o/a caixa
cash machine a caixa automática
cashpoint a caixa automática
casino o casino
casserole (dish) o tacho
(meal) o guisado (no forno)
cassette a cassette
cassette player o toca-fitas
castle o castelo
casualty department o Serviço de Urgências
cat o gato
cat food comida para gatos
catacombs as catacumbas
catalogue o catálogo
to catch (bus, train, etc) apanhar
cathedral a catedral
Catholic católico(a)
cauliflower a couve-flor
cave a caverna
cavity (in tooth) a cárie dentária
CD o disco compacto
CD player o leitor de discos compactos
ceiling o tecto
celery o aipo
cellar a cave
cellphone o telefone celular

cemetery o cemitério
centimetre o centímetro
central central
central heating o aquecimento central
central locking o fecho centralizado
cent o cêntimo (i.e. 1/100th of a euro)
centre o centro
century o século
19th century o século dezanove
21st century o século vinte e um
ceramics a cerâmica
cereal (for breakfast) os cereais
certain certo(a)
certificate o certificado
chain a corrente
chair a cadeira
chairlift o teleférico
chalet o chalé
challenge o desafio
chambermaid a empregada de quarto
Champagne o champanhe
change (loose coins) o dinheiro trocado
(money returned) o troco
to change trocar ; mudar
to change money trocar dinheiro
to change (clothes) mudar de roupa
to change (train, etc) mudar

changing room o gabinete de provas
Channel: the English Channel o Canal da Mancha
chapel a capela
charcoal o carvão
charge o custo
 cover charge o couvert
 please charge it to my account por favor ponha na minha conta
charger (for battery) o carregador
charter flight o voo charter
cheap barato(a)
cheaper mais barato(a)
to check verificar
to check in (at airport) fazer o check-in
 (at hotel) apresentar-se
check-in desk o balcão do check-in
cheek a bochecha
cheerful alegre
cheers saúde!
cheese o queijo
cheeseburger um hambúrger com queijo
chef o cozinheiro-chefe/ a cozinheira-chefe
chemist's a farmácia
cheque o cheque
chequebook o livro de cheques
cheque card o cartão de cheques

cherry a cereja
chess o xadrez
chest (of body) o peito
chestnut a castanha
chewing gum a pastilha elástica
chicken a galinha ; o frango
chicken breast o peito de galinha
chickenpox a varicela
child a criança
child safety seat (car) o banco de segurança para crianças
children as crianças
chilli a malagueta
chimney a chaminé
chin o queixo
china a porcelana
chips as batatas fritas
chocolate o chocolate
chocolates os chocolates
choice a escolha
choir o coro
to choose escolher
chop (meat) a costeleta
chopping board a tábua da cozinha
christening o baptizado
Christian name o nome próprio
Christmas o Natal
 merry Christmas! feliz Natal!
Christmas card o cartão de Boas Festas

Christmas Eve a véspera de Natal

Christmas present a prenda de Natal

church a igreja

cider a cidra

cigar o charuto

cigarette o cigarro

cigarette lighter o isqueiro

cigarette papers as mortalhas

cinema o cinema

circle *(theatre)* o balcão

circuit breaker o disjuntor

circus o circo

cistern a cisterna

citizen o cidadão/a cidadã

city a cidade

city centre o centro (da cidade)

claim a reclamação

to clap bater palmas

class: *first class* primeira classe

second class segunda classe

clean limpo(a)

to clean limpar

cleaner *(person)* o/a empregado (a) de limpeza *(product)* produto de limpeza

cleanser o leite de limpeza

clear claro(a)

client o/a cliente

cliff o rochedo

to climb subir

climbing o alpinismo

climbing boots as botas de alpinismo

clingfilm® a película aderente

clinic a clínica

cloakroom o vestiário

clock o relógio

to close fechar

closed fechado(a)

cloth *(fabric)* o tecido *(rag)* o trapo

clothes as roupas

clothes line o estendal

clothes peg a mola da roupa

clothes shop as roupas

cloudy nublado(a)

clove *(spice)* o cravinho

club o clube

clutch a embraiagem

coach o autocarro

coach station a rodoviária

coach trip a viagem de autocarro

coal o carvão

coast a costa

coastguard a polícia marítima

coat o casaco

coat hanger o cabide

Coca Cola® a Coca-Cola®

cockroach a barata

cocktail o cocktail

cocoa o cacau

coconut o coco
cod o bacalhau
code o código
coffee o café
  white coffee o café com leite
  large white coffee o galão
  small black coffee a bica
  decaffeinated coffee o café descafeinado
coil *(contraceptive)* o DIU
coin a moeda
Coke® a Coca-Cola®
colander o coador
cold frio(a)
  I'm cold tenho frio
  it's cold está frio
  cold water a água fria
cold *(illness)* a constipação
  I have a cold tenho uma constipação
cold sore a herpes labial
collar *(of dress)* a gola
  (of shirt) o colarinho
collarbone a clavícula
colleague o/a colega
to collect coleccionar
  (to collect someone) ir buscar
collection a colecção
colour a cor
colour-blind daltónico(a)
colour film *(for camera)* o rolo a cores
comb o pente
to come vir
  (arrive) chegar

to come back voltar
to come in entrar
  come in! entre!
comedy a comédia
comfortable confortável
company *(firm)* a companhia
compartment o compartimento
compass a bússola
to complain queixar-se (de)
  I want to complain of... Quero queixar-me de...
complaint uma queixa
  complaints book livro de reclamações
  I wish to make a complaint quero fazer uma reclamação
complete completo(a)
to complete completar
composer o/a compositor(a)
compulsory obrigatório(a)
computer o computador
computer disk *(floppy)* uma disquete
computer game o jogo de computador
computer program o programa de computador
computer software o software
concert o concerto
concert hall a sala de concertos
concession o desconto

concussion o traumatismo craniano

condensed milk o leite condensado

condition *(requirement)* a condição
(state) o estado

conditioner o amaciador

condom o preservativo

conductor *(of orchestra)* o maestro/a maestrina

cone o cone

conference a conferência

confession a confissão

to confirm confirmar
please confirm é favor confirmar

confirmation *(of booking)* a confirmação

confused confuso(a)

congratulations! parabéns!

connection *(flight, etc)* a ligação

constipated com prisão de ventre

constipation a prisão de ventre

consulate o consulado

to consult consultar

to contact pôr-se em contacto com

contact lens cleaner o líquido para as lentes de contacto

contact lenses as lentes de contacto

to continue continuar

contraception a anticoncepção

contraceptive o preservativo ; o anticoncepcional

contract o contrato

convenient: is it convenient? é conveniente?

convulsions as convulsões

to cook cozinhar

cooked cozinhado(a)

cooker o fogão

cookies os biscoitos

cool fresco(a)

cool box *(for picnics)* a caixa refrigerada

copper cobre

copy a cópia

to copy copiar

coriander os coentros

cork *(in bottle)* a rolha

corkscrew o saca-rolhas

corner o canto

corridor o corredor

cortisone a cortisona

cost o custo

to cost custar
how much does it cost? quanto é que custa?

costume o traje
(swimming – men) os calções de banho
(swimming – women) o fato de banho

cot o berço

cottage a casa de campo

cotton o algodão

cotton buds os cotonetes

cotton wool o algodão (hidrófilo)

couchette a couchette

to cough tossir

cough a tosse

cough mixture o xarope para a tosse

cough sweets as pastilhas para a tosse

counter (shop, bar etc) o balcão

country o país

countryside o campo

couple (two people) o casal
    a couple of... um par

courgettes as courgettes

courier (tour guide) o guia turístico/a guia turística

courier service o mensageiro

course (of meal) o prato
    (of study) o curso

cousin o/a primo(a)

cover charge o couvert

cow a vaca

crab o caranguejo

crafts artesanato

craftsman/woman o artesão/ a artesã

cramps as cãibras

crash (car) o choque

to crash colidir

crash helmet o capacete

cream (for face, etc) o creme
    (on milk) a nata
    soured cream as natas azedas
    whipped cream o chantilly

creche a creche

credit card o cartão de crédito

crime o crime

crisps as batatinhas fritas

crop a colheita

croissant o croissant

to cross (road) cruzar

cross a cruz

crossed lines as linhas cruzadas

crossing (sea) a travessia

crossroads a encruzilhada

crossword puzzle as palavras cruzadas

crowd a multidão

crowded cheio(a) de gente

crown a coroa

cruise o cruzeiro

crutches as muletas

to cry (weep) chorar

crystal o cristal

cucumber o pepino

cufflinks os botões de punho

cul-de-sac o beco sem saída

cumin o cominho

cup a chávena

cupboard o armário

c

curlers os rolos
currant a passa de corinto
currency a moeda
current a corrente
curtain a cortina
cushion a almofada
custard o leite-creme
custom *(tradition)* o costume
customer o freguês/
a freguesa
customs *(at airport etc)*
a alfândega
customs declaration
declaração alfandegária
customs officer o/a
funcionário(a) aduaneiro(a)
to cut cortar
we've been cut off foi
interrompida a ligação
cut o corte
cut and blow-dry cortar
e secar
cutlery os talheres
to cycle andar de bicicleta
cycle track a pista para
ciclistas
cycling o ciclismo
cyst o quisto
cystitis a cistite

D

daily cada dia
dairy produce os lacticínios
daisy a margarida

dam a barragem
damage os danos
damp húmido(a)
dance o baile
to dance dançar
danger o perigo
dangerous perigoso(a)
dark o escuro
(adj) escuro
after dark depois do
anoitecer
date a data
date of birth a data de
nascimento
daughter a filha
daughter-in-law a nora
dawn o amanhecer
day o dia
every day todos os dias
per day ao dia
dead morto(a)
deaf surdo(a)
dear *(on letter)* querido(a)
(expensive) caro(a)
death a morte
debt a dívida
decaff o café descafeinado
have you decaff? tem café
descafeinado?
decaffeinated coffee o café
descafeinado
December o Dezembro
deckchair a cadeira de lona
to declare: *nothing to
declare* nada a declarar

deep fundo(a)

deep freeze o congelador

deer o veado

to defrost descongelar

to de-ice descongelar

delay a demora
how long is the delay? quanto é o atraso?

delayed atrasado(a)

delicatessen a charcutaria

delicious delicioso(a)

demonstration *(political)* a manifestação

dental floss o fio dental

dentist o/a dentista

dentures a dentadura postiça

deodorant o desodorizante

to depart partir

department o departamento

department store o grande armazém

departure lounge a sala de embarque

departures as partidas

deposit o depósito

to describe descrever

description a descrição

desk a secretária
(in hotel, airport) o balcão

dessert a sobremesa

details os pormenores

detergent o detergente

detour o desvio

to develop desenvolver

diabetes a diabetes

diabetic *(person)* diabético(a *(food)* para diabéticos
I'm diabetic sou diabético(a)

to dial marcar

dialect o dialecto

dialling code o código

dialling tone o sinal

diamond o diamante

diaper a fralda

diaphragm *(in body)* o diafragma
(contraceptive) o diafragma

diarrhoea a diarreia

diary o diário

dice os dados

dictionary o dicionário

to die morrer

diesel o gasóleo

diet a dieta
I'm on a diet estou de dieta
special diet o regime especial

different diferente

difficult difícil

to dilute diluir

dinghy o bote

dining room a sala de jantar

dinner o jantar
to have dinner jantar

dinner jacket o smoking

diplomat o/a diplomata

D **direct** directo(a)

directions (instructions) instrucções
to ask for directions pedir indicações

directory (phone) a lista telefónica

directory enquiries as informações telefónicas

dirty sujo(a)

disability a incapacidade

disabled deficiente
disabled person o/a deficiente

to disagree discordar

to disappear desaparecer

disappointed desiludido(a)

disaster o desastre

disco a discoteca

discount o desconto

to discover descobrir

disease a doença

dish o prato

dishtowel o pano de cozinha

dishwasher a máquina de lavar louça

dishwasher powder o detergente em pó

disinfectant o desinfectante

disk (computer) o disco
floppy disk a disquete
hard disk o disco duro

to dislocate (joint) deslocar

disposable descartável

distance a distância

distant distante

distilled water a água destilada

district o distrito

to disturb incomodar

to dive mergulhar

diver o/a mergulhador(a)

diversion o desvio

diving mergulhar

divorced divorciado(a)
I'm divorced sou divorciado(a)

DIY shop a loja de bricolaje

dizzy tonto(a)

to do fazer; see GRAMMAR

doctor o/a médico(a)

documents os documentos

dog (male) o cão
(female) a cadela

dog food comida para cães

dog lead a correia

doll a boneca

dollar o dólar

domestic doméstico(a)

domestic flight o voo doméstico

dominoes o dominó

donor card o cartão de dador

donkey o burro

door a porta

doorbell a campainha

double o dobro

double bed a cama de casal

double room o quarto de casal

doughnut a bola de Berlim

down: *to go down* descer

downstairs em baixo

dragonfly a libélula

drain *(sewer)* o esgoto

draught *(of air)* a corrente de ar

  there's a draught há uma corrente de ar

draught lager a imperial

drawer a gaveta

drawing o desenho

dress o vestido

to dress (oneself) vestir-se

dressing *(for food)* o tempero ; o molho

  (for wound) o penso

dressing gown o roupão

drill *(tool)* a broca

drink a bebida

to drink beber

drinking chocolate o chocolate

drinking water a água potável

to drive conduzir

driver o/a condutor(a)

driving licence a carta de condução

drizzle o chuvisco

drought a seca

to drown afogar

drug *(medicine)* o medicamento

  (narcotic) a droga

drunk bêbedo(a)

dry seco(a)

to dry secar

dry-cleaner's a limpeza a seco

dryer o secador

duck o pato

due: *when is it due?* está previsto para quando?

dummy *(for baby)* a chupeta

during durante

dust o pó

to dust limpar o pó

duster o pano do pó

dustpan and brush pá e vassoura

duty *(tax)* o imposto

duty-free livre de impostos

duvet o edredão

duvet cover o saco do edredão

dye a tinta

dynamo o dínamo

E

each cada

eagle a águia

ear a orelha

earache a dor de ouvidos

  I have earache doem-me os ouvidos

earlier mais cedo

early cedo

earphones os auscultadores

E

earplugs as borrachinhas
(de ouvido)

earrings os brincos

earth *(planet)* a terra

earthquake o terramoto

east o leste

Easter a Páscoa
   Happy Easter! feliz Páscoa!

easy fácil

to eat comer

ebony o ébano

echo o eco

economy a economia

edge a beira ; a aresta

eel a enguia

effective eficaz

egg o ovo
   fried egg o ovo estrelado
   hard-boiled egg o ovo
   cozido
   scrambled eggs os ovos
   mexidos
   soft-boiled egg o ovo
   quente

egg white a clara de ovo

egg yolk a gema de ovo

either... or... ou... ou...

elastic band o elástico

Elastoplast® o penso

elbow o cotovelo

electric eléctrico(a)

electric blanket o cobertor
eléctrico

electrician o/a electricista

electricity a electricidade

electricity meter o contador
de electricidade

electric razor a máquina de
barbear

electric shock o choque
eléctrico

elevator o elevador

elegant elegante

e-mail o correio electrónico;
e-mail
   to e-mail someone mandar
   um e-mail

e-mail address o endereço
de e-mail

embarrassing embaraçoso(a)

embassy a embaixada

emergency a emergência

emergency exit a saída de
emergência

emery board a lixa de unhas

empty vazio(a)

end o fim

engaged comprometido(a)
(phone, toilet, etc)
ocupado(a)

engine o motor

engineer o/a engenheiro(a)

England a Inglaterra

English inglês (inglesa)
(language) o inglês

Englishman o inglês

Englishwoman a inglesa

enjoy oneself divertir-se
   I enjoy swimming gosto
   de nadar

I enjoy dancing gosto de dançar
enjoy yourself! diverte-te!
enjoy your meal! bom apetite!
to enlarge aumentar
enormous enorme
enough bastante
that's enough chega
enquiries informações
enquiry desk o balcão de informações
to enter entrar
entertainment a diversão
enthusiastic entusiástico(a)
entrance a entrada
entrance fee o bilhete de entrada
envelope o envelope
epileptic epiléptico(a)
epileptic fit o ataque epiléptico
equipment o equipamento
eraser a borracha
error o erro
eruption a erupção
escalator a escada rolante
to escape escapar
escape ladder a escada de salvação
espadrilles as alpercatas
espresso a bica
essential essencial
estate agent o/a agente imobiliário(a)

estate agent's a imobiliária
establish estabelecer
euro o euro
Eurocheque o Eurocheque
Europe a Europa
European europeu (européia)
European Union a União Européia
eve a véspera
Christmas Eve a véspera de Natal
New Year's Eve a véspera de Ano Novo
even *(number)* par
evening a noite
in the evening à noite
this evening esta noite
tomorrow evening amanhã à noite
evening dress o traje de cerimónia
evening meal o jantar
every cada
everyone toda a gente
everything todas as coisas, tudo
everywhere por todo o lado
examination o exame
example: *for example* por exemplo
excellent excelente
except excepto
excess baggage/luggage o excesso de bagagem
to exchange trocar

exchange rate o câmbio

exciting excitante

excursion a excursão

excuse a desculpa
excuse me! desculpe!

exercise *(physical)* o exercício

exercise book o caderno

exhaust pipe o tubo de escape

exhibition a exposição

exit a saída

expenses as despesas

expensive caro(a)

expert o/a perito(a)

to expire *(ticket, etc)* caducar

expiry date o vencimento

to explain explicar

explosion a explosão

to export exportar

express *(train)* o expresso

express: *to send a letter express* mandar uma carta por correio expresso

extension *(electrical)* a extensão

extra extra
an extra bed uma cama adicional

to extinguish apagar

eye o olho

eyebrows as sobrancelhas

eyedrops as gotas para os olhos

eyelashes as pestanas

eyeliner o lápis para os olhos

eyeshadow a sombra para os olhos

F

fabric o tecido

face a cara

face cloth a toalha de rosto

facial a limpeza facial

facilities as facilidades; instalações

factory a fábrica

to fail fracassar
(engine, brakes) falhar

to faint desmaiar

fainted desmaiado(a)

fair *(hair)* louro(a)

fair *(just)* justo(a)

fair *(funfair)* o parque de diversões
(trade) a feira

fairway *(golf)* o fairway

fake falso(a)

fall *(autumn)* o Outono

to fall cair
he/she has fallen ele/ela caiu

false teeth os dentes postiços

family a família

famous famoso(a)

fan *(hand-held)* o leque
(electric) a ventoínha
(football, jazz) o/a fan

fan belt a correia da ventoínha

fancy dress o traje de Carnaval

far longe
is it far? é longe?
how far is it to...? qual é a distância daqui a...?

fare *(train, bus, etc)* o preço (da passagem)

farm a quinta

farmer o/a agricultor(a)

farmhouse a casa da quinta

fashionable de moda

fast rápido(a)
too fast rápido demais

to fasten *(seatbelt)* apertar

fat gordo(a)
saturated fats gorduras saturadas
unsaturated fats gorduras insaturadas

father o pai

father-in-law o sogro

fault *(defect)* o defeito
it's not my fault a culpa não é minha

favour o favor

favourite favorito(a)

fax o fax
by fax por fax

to fax mandar por fax

fax number o número de fax

feather a pena

February o Fevereiro

to feed alimentar

to feel apalpar ; sentir
I feel sick tenho náuseas
I don't feel well sinto-me mal-disposto(a)

feet os pés

fellow o companheiro

felt-tip pen a caneta de feltro

female mulher

ferry o ferry-boat

festival o festival

to fetch *(to bring)* trazer
(to go and get) ir buscar

fever a febre

few poucos(as)
a few alguns (algumas)

fiancé(e) o/a noivo(a)

field o campo

fig o figo

fight a briga

to fight brigar

file *(computer)* o ficheiro
(nail) a lima
(folder) a pasta

filigree a filigrana

to fill encher
fill it up! encha o depósito!
to fill in (form) preencher

fillet o filete

filling *(in tooth)* a obturação

filling station a estação de serviço

film *(at cinema)* o filme
(for camera) o rolo de películas
colour film rolo a cores

F

black and white film o rolo a preto e branco

Filofax® a agenda

filter o filtro

to find achar

fine *(to be paid)* a multa

fine fino(a)

fine arts as belas-artes

finger o dedo

to finish acabar

finished acabado(a)

fire o fogo

fire alarm o alarme contra incêndios

fire brigade os bombeiros

fire engine o carro dos bombeiros

fire escape a saída de incêndios

fire extinguisher o extintor

fireplace a lareira

fireworks os fogos de artifício

firm *(company)* a firma

first o/a primeiro(a)

first aid os primeiros socorros

first aid kit o estojo de primeiros socorros

first class a primeira classe

first-class de primeira classe

first floor o primeiro andar

first name o próprio nome

fish o peixe

to fish pescar

to go fishing ir pescar

fisherman o pescador

fishing permit a licença de pesca

fishing rod a cana de pesca

fishmonger's a peixaria

to fit: it doesn't fit me não me serve

fit o ataque
he had a fit ele teve um ataque

to fix reparar
can you fix it? pode arranjá-lo?

fizzy gasoso(a)

flag a bandeira

flame a chama

flash *(for camera)* o flash

flashlight a lanterna

flask o termo

flat *(apartment)* o apartamento

flat plano(a)
(battery) descarregado
this drink is flat esta bebida já perdeu o gás

flat tyre o furo

flavour sabor
which flavour? de que sabor?

flaw a falha

fleas as pulgas

fleece *(top/jacket)* de fibra polar

flesh a carne

flex o cabo eléctrico

flight o voo

flip flops os chinelos

flippers as barbatanas

flood a inundação
  flash flood a inundação repentina

floor o chão
  (storey) o andar
  which floor? qual é o andar?
  ground floor o rés-do-chão
  first floor o primeiro andar
  second floor o segundo andar

floorcloth o pano do chão

floppy disk a disquete

florist's shop a florista

flour a farinha

flower a flor

flu a gripe

fly a mosca

to fly voar

fly sheet o duplo-tecto

fog o nevoeiro

foggy enevoado(a)

foil *(silver)* o papel de alumínio

to follow seguir

food a comida

food poisoning a intoxicação alimentar

fool tonto(a)

foot o pé
  on foot a pé

football o futebol

football match o jogo de futebol

football pitch o campo de futebol

football player o jogador de futebol

footpath o caminho

for para
  for me para mim
  for you para si
  for him/her/us para ele/ela/nós
  for them para eles (elas)

forbidden proibido(a)

forecast a previsão
  weather forecast a previsão do tempo

forehead a testa

foreign estrangeiro(a)

foreigner o/a estrangeiro(a)

forest a floresta

forever para sempre

to forget esquecer-se de

to forgive perdoar

fork *(for eating)* o garfo
  (in road) a bifurcação

form *(document)* o formulário

formal dress o traje de cerimónia

fortnight a quinzena

fortress a fortaleza

forward(s) para a frente

foul *(in football)* a falta

fountain a fonte

four-wheel drive o quatro-vezes-quatro

fox a raposa

fracture a fractura

F

fragile frágil
fragrance a fragrância
frame *(picture)* a moldura
France a França
free *(not occupied)* livre
  (costing nothing) grátis
freezer o congelador
French francês (francesa)
  (language) o francês
French beans o feijão-verde
French fries as batatas fritas
frequent frequente
fresh fresco(a)
fresh water a água doce
Friday a sexta-feira
fridge o frigorífico
fried frito(a)
friend o/a amigo(a)
friendly simpático(a)
frog a rã
from de
  from England da Inglaterra
  from Scotland da Escócia
front a frente
  in front of em frente de
front door a porta da frente
frost a geada
frozen congelado(a)
fruit a fruta
  dried fruit os frutos secos
fruit juice o sumo de frutas
fruit salad a salada de
  frutas
to fry fritar
frying pan a frigideira

fuel *(petrol)* a gasolina
fuel gauge o medidor
  de gasolina
fuel pump a bomba de
  gasolina
fuel tank o depósito de
  combustível
full cheio(a)
full board a pensão
  completa
fumes *(of car)* os fumos
  de escape
fun a diversão
funeral o funeral
funfair o parque de
  diversões
funny engraçado(a)
  (strange) estranho(a)
fur a pele
furnished mobilado(a)
furniture a mobília
fuse o fusível
fuse box a caixa de fusíveis
futon o futon
future o futuro

G

gallery *(art)* a galeria de arte
gallon = approx. 4.5 litres
game o jogo
  (animal) a caça
garage *(private)* a garagem
  (for repairs) a oficina
  (for petrol) a estação de
  serviço

garden o jardim
gardener o/a jardineiro(a)
garlic o alho
to garnish guarnecer
gas o gás
gas cooker o fogão a gás
gas cylinder a botija de gás
gastritis a gastrite
gate *(airport)* a porta
gay *(person)* gay
gear a velocidade
  first gear a primeira
  velocidade
  second gear a segunda
  velocidade
  third gear a terceira velocidade
  fourth gear a quarta
  velocidade
  fifth gear a quinta
  velocidade
  neutral o ponto morto
  reverse a marcha atrás
gearbox a caixa de
velocidades
generous generoso(a)
gents' *(toilet)* Homens
  where is the gents'? onde
  é o lavabo do homens?
genuine *(leather, antique etc)*
autêntico(a)
German alemão (alemã)
  (language) o alemão
German measles a rubéola
Germany a Alemanha
to get *(to obtain)* obter

(to receive) receber
(to fetch) ir buscar
to get in *(vehicle)* subir em
to get into entrar
to get off descer de
to get on *(vehicle)* subir para
gift o presente
gift shop a loja de
lembranças
gin and tonic um gim tónico
ginger o gengibre
girl a rapariga
girlfriend a namorada
to give dar
to give back devolver
glacier o glaciar
glass *(substance)* o vidro ;
  o cristal
  (to drink out of) o copo
  a glass of water um copo
  de água
glasses os óculos
glasses case a caixa dos
óculos
gloss o brilho
gloves as luvas
glue a cola
to go ir
  I'm going to... vou para...
  we're going to... vamos
  para...
to go back voltar
to go down descer
to go in entrar
to go out saír

G **goat** a cabra

God o Deus

godchild o/a afilhado(a)

goggles os óculos protectores

gold o ouro

golf o golfe

golf ball a bola de golfe

golf clubs os tacos de golfe

golf course o campo de golfe

good bom (boa)
very good muito bom

good afternoon boa tarde

goodbye adeus

good evening boa noite

good morning bom dia

good night boa noite

goose o ganso

gooseberry a groselha branca

Gothic gótico(a)

graduate o/a licenciado(a)

gram o grama

grandchild o/a neto(a)

granddaughter a neta

grandfather o avô
great grandfather o bisavô

grandmother a avó
great grandmother a bisavó

grandparents os avós

grandson o neto

grapefruit a toranja

grapefruit juice o sumo de toranja

grapes as uvas
green grapes as uvas brancas
black grapes as uvas pretas

grass a erva

grated *(cheese, etc)* ralado(a)

grater *(for cheese, etc)* o ralador

greasy oleoso(a) ; gorduroso(a)

great *(big)* grande
(wonderful) óptimo(a)

Great Britain a Grã-Bretanha

green verde

green card *(car insurance)* o cartão verde

greengrocer's a frutaria

greetings card o cartão de felicitações

grey cinzento(a)

grill a grelha

to grill grelhar

grilled grelhado(a)

grocer's a mercearia

ground *(earth)* a terra
(floor) o chão

ground floor o rés-do-chão
on the ground floor... no rés-do-chão...

groundsheet a cobertura impermeável

group o grupo

to grow crescer

guarantee a garantia

guard o guarda

guest o/a convidado(a)
(in hotel) o/a hóspede
guesthouse a pensão
guide o/a guia
to guide guiar
guidebook a guia
guided tour a excursão
guiada
guitar a guitarra
gun a pistola
gym o ginásio
gym shoes os ténis

H

haberdasher's a retrosaria
haddock o eglefim
haemorrhoids as
hemorróidas
hail o granizo
hair o cabelo
hairbrush a escova de cabelo
haircut o corte de cabelo
hairdresser o/a
cabeleireiro(a)
hairdryer o secador de
cabelo
hair dye a tinta para o
cabelo
hair gel o gel para o cabelo
hairgrip o gancho de cabelo
hair mousse a espuma para
o cabelo
hairspray a laca
hake a pescada

half a metade
a half bottle of meia
garrafa de
half an hour meia hora
half board a meia pensão
half fare meio-bilhete
half-price pela metade do
preço
ham o presunto
hamburger o hambúrger
hammer o martelo
hand a mão
handbag a bolsa
handicapped *(person)*
deficiente
handkerchief o lenço
handle *(of cup)* a asa
(of door) a maçaneta
handlebars os guiadores
hand luggage a bagagem
de mão
hand-made feito(a) à mão
hands-free phone kit de
mãos livres
handsome bonito(a), giro(a)
to hang up *(phone)* desligar
hanger o lcabide
hang gliding a asa-delta
hangover a ressaca
to happen acontecer
what happened? o que
aconteceu?
happy feliz
happy birthday! feliz
aniversário!
harbour o porto

H

hard duro(a)
(difficult) difícil
hard disk o disco duro
hardware shop a loja de ferragens
hare a lebre
harm o mal ; o dano
harvest a colheita
hat o chapéu
to have ter
I have... eu tenho...
I don't have... eu não tenho...
we have... nós temos...
we don't have... nós não temos...
do you have...? tem...?
to have to ter que
hay fever a febre dos fenos
hazelnut a avelã
he ele see GRAMMAR
head a cabeça
headache a dor de cabeça
I have a headache dói-me a cabeça
headlights os faróis
headphones os auscultadores
head waiter o chefe de mesa
health a saúde
health food shop a loja de produtos dietéticos
healthy saudável
to hear ouvir
hearing aid o aparelho auditivo

heart o coração
heart attack o ataque de coração
heartburn a azia
heartstroke a insolação
to heat up aquecer
heater o aquecedor
heating o aquecimento
heaven o Céu
heavy pesado(a)
heel *(of foot)* o calcanhar
(of shoe) o salto
heel bar sapateiro
height a altura
helicopter o helicóptero
hello olá
(on phone) está?
helmet o capacete
help a ajuda
help! socorro!
to help ajudar
can you help me? pode-me ajudar?
hem a bainha
hen a galinha
hepatitis a hepatite
herb a erva aromática
herbal tea a tisana
here aqui
here is... aqui está...
here is my passport aqui está o meu passaporte
hernia a hérnia
hi! olá!
to hide *(something)* esconder

(oneself) esconder-se

high (price, speed, building) alto(a)
  (number) grande
high blood pressure a tensão alta
highchair a cadeira de bebé
high tide a maré alta
hill a colina
hill-walking o alpinismo
him (direct object) o
  (indirect object) lhe
  (after preposition) ele
hip a anca
hip replacement a prótese de anca
hire o aluguer
  car hire o aluguer de carros
  bike hire o aluguer de bicicletas
  boat hire o aluguer de barcos
  ski hire o aluguer de esquis
to hire alugar
historic histórico(a)
history a história
to hit bater
to hitchhike andar à boleia
HIV o vírus da SIDA
HIV positive seropositivo(a)
hobby o passatempo
to hold (to contain) conter
hold-up o engarrafamento
hole o buraco
holiday as férias
  (public holiday) o feriado
  on holiday de férias
holiday rep o/a representante da agência de viagens
hollow oco(a)
holy santo(a)
home a casa
  at home em casa
  to go home voltar para casa
homeopath o/a homeopata
homeopathic homeopático(a)
homeopathy a homeopatia
homesick: to be homesick ter saudades de casa
  I'm homesick tenho saudades de casa
homosexual homossexual
honest honesto(a)
honey o mel
honeymoon a lua-de-mel
hood (of jacket) o capuz
  (of car) a capota
hook (for fishing) o anzol
to hope esperar
  I hope so/not espero que sim/não
horn (of car) a buzina
hors d'œuvre a entrada
horse o cavalo
horse racing as corridas de cavalo
horse riding: to go horse riding montar a cavalo

H

hosepipe a mangueira
hospital o hospital
hostel a pousada
hot quente
  I'm hot tenho calor
  it's hot está calor
hot chocolate o chocolate
  quente
hotel o hotel
hot water a água quente
hot-water bottle o saco
  de água quente
hour a hora
  half an hour meia hora
  1 hour uma hora
  2 hours duas horas
house a casa
housewife/husband
  a/o dona(o) de casa
house wine o vinho da casa
housework a lida da casa
hovercraft o hovercraft
how como
  how much? quanto(a)?
  how many? quantos(as)?
  how are you? como está?
hundred cem
  five hundred quinhentos
hungry: I am hungry tenho
  fome
hunt a caça
to hunt caçar
hunting permit a licença
  de caça
hurry: I'm in a hurry tenho
  pressa

154

to hurt doer
  that hurts isso dói
  my back hurts tenho dor
  de costas
husband o marido
hut a cabana
hydrofoil o hidrofólio
hypodermic needle a agulha
  hipodérmica

I

I eu see **GRAMMAR**
ice o gelo
  (cube) o cubo
  with ice com gelo
  without ice sem gelo
ice box o frigorífico
ice cream o gelado
iced coffee o café gelado
iced tea o chá gelado
ice lolly o gelado
ice rink o rinque de
  patinagem
to ice-skate patinar sobre
  o gelo
ice skates os patins de
  lâmina
idea a idéia
identity card a carteira
  de identidade
if se
ignition a ignição
ignition key a chave de
  ignição
ill doente

I'm ill estou doente
illness a doença
immediately imediatamente
immersion heater o esquentador de imersão
immigration a imigração
immunisation a imunização
to import importar
important importante
impossible impossível
to improve melhorar
in em
 (within) dentro de
 in 10 minutes dentro de dez minutos
 in London em Londres
in front of em frente de
inch = approx. 2.5 cm
included incluído(a)
inconvenient inconveniente
to increase aumentar
indicator *(on car)* o pisca-pisca
indigestion a indigestão
indigestion tablets os comprimidos para indigestão
indoors em casa
inefficient ineficiente
infection a infecção
infectious contagioso(a)
informal *(person)* sem formalidades
 (costume) informal
information a informação

information desk o balcão de informações
information office departamento de informações
ingredient o ingrediente
inhaler *(for medication)* o inalador
injection a injecção
to injure lesionar
injured ferido(a)
injury a lesão
ink a tinta
inn a estalagem
inner tube a câmara-de-ar
inquiries informações
inquiry desk o balcão de informações
insect o insecto
insect bite a picada de insecto
insect repellent o repelente contra insectos
inside dentro
instalment a prestação
instant coffee o café instantâneo
instead of em vez de
instructor o/a instrutor(a)
insulin a insulina
insurance o seguro
insurance certificate a apólice de seguro
to insure pôr no seguro

insured: to be insured estar no seguro
intelligent inteligente
to intend to do tencionar fazer
interesting interessante
internet a internet
internet café o cibercafé
international internacional
interpreter o/a intérprete
interval o intervalo
interview a entrevista
into em
 into the centre ao centro
to introduce someone to someone apresentar alguém a alguém
invitation o convite
to invite convidar
invoice a factura
Ireland a Irlanda
Irish irlandês (irlandesa)
iron (metal) o ferro
 (for clothes) o ferro de engomar
to iron passar a ferro
ironing board a tábua de engomar
ironmonger's a loja de ferragens
is see (to be) GRAMMAR
island a ilha
it o/a see GRAMMAR
Italian italiano(a)
 (language) o italiano

Italy a Itália
itch a comichão
to itch fazer comichão
 it itches faz comichão
item o artigo
itemized bill a factura detalhada
ivory o marfim

J

jack (for car) o macaco
jacket o casaco
 waterproof jacket o casaco impermeável
jackpot o prémio (de lotaria, rifa)
jacuzzi® o jacuzzi
jam a compota
jammed (stuck) bloqueado(a)
January o Janeiro
jar o jarro
jaundice a icterícia
jaw o queixo
jazz o jazz
jealous ciumento(a)
jeans as jeans
jelly a geleia
jellyfish a medusa; a alforreca
jet ski a motonáutica
jetty o quebra-mar
jewel a jóia
jewellery a joalharia
Jewish judeu (judia)

job o emprego
to jog ir fazer jogging
to join (club) associar-se a
to join in participar
joint (of body) a articulação
joke a piada; a anedota
to joke brincar
journalist o/a jornalista
journey a viagem
judge o juiz (a juíza)
jug o jarro
juice o sumo
   apple juice o sumo de maçã
   orange juice o sumo de laranja
   tomato juice o sumo de tomate
   a carton of juice um pacote de sumo
July o Julho
to jump saltar
jump leads os cabos para ligar a bateria
junction o cruzamento
June o Junho
just: *just two* apenas dois
   I've just arrived acabo de chegar

K

karaoke o karaokê
to keep guardar
   (retain) ficar com
   keep the change! guarde o troco!

kennel a casota
kettle a chaleira
key a chave
   card key a chave-cartão
keyboard o teclado
keyring o porta-chaves
to kick (person) dar um pontapé em
   (ball) chutar
kid (young goat) o cabrito
   (child) a criança
kidneys os rins
to kill matar
kilo o quilo
   a kilo of apples um quilo de maçãs
   2 kilos dois quilos
kilogram o quilograma
kilometre o quilómetro
kind (person) amável
kind (sort) a espécie
king o rei
kiosk o quiosque
kiss o beijo
to kiss beijar
kitchen a cozinha
kitchen paper o papel de cozinha
kite o papagaio
kitten o/a gatinho(a)
knee o joelho
knee highs as meias até o joelho
knickers as cuecas
knife a faca

K

to **knit** fazer malha

to **knock** (on door) bater

to **knock down** (with car) atropelar

to **knock over** (vase, glass) derrubar

knot o nó

to **know** (have knowledge of) saber
(person, place) conhecer
I don't know não sei

to **know how to do something** saber fazer alguma coisa
to know how to swim saber nadar

kosher kosher

L

label a etiqueta

lace a renda

laces (for shoes) os atacadores

ladder a escada

ladies' (toilet) Senhoras

lady a senhora

lager a cerveja
bottled lager a cerveja de garrafa
draught lager a imperial

lake o lago

lamb o cordeiro

lame coxo(a)

lamp a lâmpada

lamppost o poste de iluminação

lampshade o abajur

land a terra
(country) o país

to **land** aterrar

landing (of plane) a aterragem

landlady a senhoria

landlord o senhorio

landslide o desabamento

lane (on motorway) a faixa

language a língua

language school a Escola de Línguas

laptop o computador portátil

large grande

last último(a)
the last bus o último autocarro
the last train o último comboio
last night ontem à noite
last week a semana passada
last year o ano passado
the last time a última vez

late tarde
the train is late o comboio está atrasado
sorry we are late desculpe o atraso

later mais tarde

to **laugh** rir

launderette a lavandaria automática

laundry service o serviço de lavandaria

lavatory o lavabo

lavender a alfazema

law a lei

lawn o relvado

lawyer o/a advogado(a)

laxative o laxante

layby a berma

lazy preguiçoso(a)

lead *(electrical)* o cabo
(for dog) a correia

lead *(metal)* o chumbo

lead-free sem chumbo

leaf a folha

leak *(of gas, liquid)* o escape; o derrame

to leak: it's leaking *(pipe)* está a verter
(gas) escape de gás
(roof) infiltração

to learn aprender

lease o arrendamento

least: at least pelo menos

leather o couro

leather goods os cabedais

to leave *(leave behind)* deixar
(train, bus etc) partir
when does it leave? a que horas parte?
when does the bus leave? a que horas parte o auto-carro?
when does the train leave? a que horas parte o comboio?

leek o alho francês

left: on/to the left à esquerda

left-handed canhoto(a)

left luggage *(office)* o depósito de bagagens

left luggage locker o cacifo

leg a perna

legal legal

lemon o limão

lemonade a limonada

lemon tea o carioca de limão

to lend emprestar

length o comprimento

lens *(of glasses)* a lente
(of camera) a objectiva

lenses *(contact lenses)* as lentes de contacto

lesbian a lésbica

less menos
less than menos do que

lesson a lição

let *(allow)* deixar
(lease) alugar

letter a carta
(of alphabet) a letra

letterbox o marco do correio

lettuce a alface

level crossing a passagem de nível

library a biblioteca

licence a licença
(driving) a carta de condução*

L

lid a tampa
lie *(untruth)* a mentira
to lie down deitar-se
life a vida
lifebelt o cinto salva-vidas
lifeboat o salva-vidas
lifeguard o banheiro salva-vidas
life insurance o seguro de vida
life jacket o colete de salvação
life raft a bolsa salva-vidas
lift *(elevator)* o elevador
(in car) a boleia
light a luz
  have you a light? tem lume?
light *(not heavy)* leve
(colour) claro(a)
light bulb a lâmpada
lighter o isqueiro
lighthouse o farol
lightning os relâmpagos
lights out luzes apagadas
like como
  it's like this é assim
to like gostar de
  I like coffee gosto de café
  I don't like... não gosto de...
  I'd like to... gostava de...
  we'd like to... gostávamos de...
lilo o colchão de ar
lime a lima

line *(row, queue)* a fila
(phone) a linha
linen *(cloth)* o linho
(bed linen) a roupa de cama
lingerie a roupa interior
lion o leão
lip reading leitura de lábios
lips os lábios
lip salve a manteiga de cacau
lipstick o bâton
liqueur o licor
list a lista
to listen to ouvir
litre o litro
  a litre of milk um litro de leite
litter *(rubbish)* o lixo
little pequeno(a)
  a little... um pouco de...
to live viver
  I live in Edinburgh moro em Edimburgo
  he lives in London ele vive em Londres
  he lives in a flat ele vive num apartamento; ele mora num apartamento
liver o fígado
living room a sala de estar
lizard o lagarto
loaf *(of bread)* o pão
lobster a lagosta
local local
to lock fechar com chave
lock a fechadura

the lock is broken a fechadura está quebrada

bike lock o cadeado da bicicleta

locker *(luggage)* o depósito de bagagem

locksmith o/a serralheiro(a)

log o tronco

log book *(for car)* a documentação do carro

lollipop o chupa-chupa

London Londres
in London em Londres
to London a Londres

long comprido(a) ; longo(a)
for a long time durante muito tempo

long-sighted presbíope

to look after cuidar de

to look at olhar

to look for procurar

loose solto(a)
it's come loose soltou-se

lorry o camião

to lose perder

lost perdido(a)
I have lost my wallet perdi a minha carteira
I am lost perdi-me

lost property office a secção de perdidos e achados

lot: *a lot (much)* muito(a)
(many) muitos(as)

lotion a loção

lottery a lotaria

loud *(noisy)* ruidoso(a)
(volume) alto(a)

lounge *(in hotel)* a sala de estar
(in house) a sala de estar
(in airport) o salão

to love amar
I love swimming gosto muito de nadar
I love you amo-te

lovely encantador(a)

low baixo(a)

low-fat com baixo teor de gordura

low tide a maré baixa

luck a sorte

lucky: *to be lucky* ter sorte

luggage a bagagem

luggage rack o porta-bagagens

luggage tag a etiqueta de bagagem

luggage trolley o carrinho

lump *(swelling)* o inchaço
(on head) o galo

lunch o almoço

lunch break a hora do almoço

lung o pulmão

luxury o luxo

M

machine a máquina

mad *(insane)* louco(a)
(angry) furioso(a)

madam a senhora

magazine a revista

maggot a larva

magnet o íman

magnifying glass a lupa

magpie a pega

maid a empregada

maiden name o nome de solteira

mail o correio
by mail pelo correio

main principal

main course *(of meal)* o prato principal

main road a estrada principal

mains *(electrical)* a rede eléctrica

to make *(generally)* fazer
(meal) preparar

make-up a maquilhagem

male masculino(a)

mallet o maço

man o homem

to manage *(cope)* arranjar-se

manager o/a gerente

managing director o/a director(a) geral

manual manual

many muitos(as)

map o mapa

marathon a maratona

marble o mármore

March o Março

margarine a margarina

marina a marina

marinated marinado

marjoram o orégão

mark *(stain)* a nódoa

market o mercado
where is the market? onde é que fica o mercado?
when is the market? quando é que há mercado?

marketplace o mercado

marmalade o doce de laranja

married casado(a)
I'm married sou casado(a)
are you married? é casado(a)?

marry: *to get married* casar(-se)

marsh o pântano

marzipan o maçapão

mascara o rímel®

mashed potato o puré de batata

Mass *(church service)* a missa

mast o mastro

masterpiece a obra-prima

match o fósforo
(game) o jogo

matches os fósforos

material o material
(cloth) o tecido

to matter: *it doesn't matter* não tem importância
what is the matter? o que é que se passa?

mattress o colchão

maximum o máximo

May o Maio
mayonnaise a maionese
mayor o presidente do
  município
me me
  (after preposition) mim
meadow o prado
meal a refeição
to mean significar
  what does this mean?
  o que é que isto quer
  dizer?
measles o sarampo
to measure medir
meat a carne
  white meat as carnes
  brancas
  red meat as carnes
  vermelhas
  I don't eat meat não como
  carne
mechanic o/a mecânico(a)
medical insurance seguro
  de doença
medicine o medicamento
medieval medieval
Mediterranean
  o Mediterrâneo
medium médio(a)
  medium rare (meat)
  meio-passado(a)
to meet *(by chance)*
  encontrar
  (by arrangement) encontrar-
  se com
  pleased to meet you
  prazer em conhecê-lo(a)

meeting a reunião
meeting point o ponto de
  encontro
melon o melão
to melt derreter
member *(of club, etc)*
  o/a sócio(a)
membership card o cartão
  de sócio(a)
memory a memória
  (thing remembered)
  a lembrança
men os homens
to mend arranjar
meningitis a meningite
menu a ementa
  set menu a ementa fixa
  à la carte menu a ementa
  a la carte
meringue o merengue
message a mensagem
metal o metal
meter o contador
metre o metro
microwave oven o micro-
  ondas
midday o meio-dia
  at midday ao meio-dia
middle o meio
middle-aged de meia-idade
midge o mosquito
midnight a meia-noite
  at midnight à meia-noite
migraine a enxaqueca
  I've a migraine tenho uma
  enxaqueca

M

mild *(climate)* temperado(a)
(taste) suave
mile a milha
milk o leite
  fresh milk o leite fresco
  full-cream milk o leite
  gordo
  hot milk o leite quente
  long-life milk o leite
  ultrapasteurizado
  powdered milk o leite em
  pó
  semi-skimmed milk o leite
  meio-gordo
  skimmed milk o leite magro
  soya milk o leite de soja
  with milk com leite
  without milk sem leite
milkshake o batido de leite
millenium o milénio
millimetre o milímetro
million o milhão
mince *(meat)* a carne picada
mind *n* a mente
to mind *vb (take care of)*
  ocupar-se de
  (object to) objectar
  do you mind if...? importa-
  se?
  I don't mind não me
  importo
mineral water a água mineral
minibar o minibar
minimum o mínimo
minister *(political)* o ministro
  (church) o pastor
mink o vison

minor road a estrada
  secundária
mint *(herb)* a hortelã
  (sweet) o rebuçado de
  mentol
minute o minuto
mirror o espelho
to misbehave comportar-se
  mal
miscarriage o aborto
  (espontâneo)
Miss... Menina...
to miss *(plane, train, etc)*
  perder
missing *(lost)* perdido(a)
  my son is missing o meu
  filho desapareceu
mistake o erro
misty: *it's misty* há nevoeiro
misunderstanding o mal-
  entendido
to mix misturar
mixer a batedeira
mobile phone o telemóvel
modem o modem
modern moderno(a)
moisturizer o creme
  hidratante
mole *(on skin)* o sinal
moment: *just a moment*
  um momento
monastery o mosteiro
Monday a segunda-feira
money o dinheiro
  I've no money não tenho
  dinheiro

money order o vale postal

monkey o macaco

month o mês
  this month este mês
  last month o mês passado
  next month o mês que
  vem

monthly mensalmente

monument o monumento

moon a lua

mooring o atracadouro

mop a esfregona

moped a motocicleta

more mais
  more than 3 mais de três
  more bread mais pão
  more wine mais vinho

morning a manhã
  in the morning de manhã
  this morning esta manhã
  tomorrow morning
  amanhã de manhã

morning-after pill a pílula
  abortiva

mosque a mesquita

mosquito o mosquito

mosquito net o mosquiteiro

mosquito repellent o
  repelente contra mosquitos

most: *most of* a maioria de

moth a borboleta
  (clothes) a traça

mother a mãe

mother-in-law a sogra

motor o motor

motorbike a moto

motorboat o barco a motor

motorcycle a motocicleta

motorway a auto-estrada

mould *(mildew)* o bolor

mountain a montanha

mountain bike a bicicleta de
  montanha

mountain rescue o socorro
  para alpinistas

mountaineering alpinismo

mouse o rato

mousse *(food)* a mousse
  (hair) a espuma

moustache o bigode

mouth a boca

mouthwash desinfectante
  para a boca

to move mexer ; mover
  it isn't moving não se
  mexe ; não se move

movie o filme

to mow cortar

Mr Senhor

Mrs Senhora

Ms Senhora

much muito(a)
  too much demais

mud a lama

muddy *(road)* lamacento(a)
  (clothes) enlameado(a)

mugging o assalto

mumps a papeira

muscle o músculo

museum o museu

mushroom o cogumelo

music a música
musical o musical
mussel o mexilhão
must *(to have to)* dever
  I must devo
  we must devemos
  I mustn't não devo
  we mustn't não devemos
mustard a mostarda
mutton o carneiro
my meu (minha)

N

nail *(metal)* o prego
  (on finger) a unha
nailbrush a escova das unhas
nail clippers o corta-unhas
nail file a lima para as unhas
nail polish o verniz das unhas
nail polish remover
  a acetona
nail scissors as tesouras
  para as unhas
name o nome
  my name is... o meu nome
  é...
  what's your name? como
  é que te chamas?
nanny a ama
napkin o guardanapo
nappy a fralda
narrow estreito(a)
national nacional
national park o parque
  nacional

nationality a nacionalidade
natural natural
nature a natureza
nature reserve a reserva
  natural
navy blue azul-marinho
near perto
  near the bank perto do
  banco
  is it near? fica perto?
necessary necessário(a)
neck o pescoço
necklace o colar
nectarine a nectarina
to need precisar de
  I need... preciso de
  we need... precisamos de
  I need to go tenho que ir
needle a agulha
  a needle and thread uma
  agulha e a linha
negative *(photo)* a película
neighbour o/a vizinho(a)
nephew o sobrinho
nest o ninho
net a rede
nettle a urtiga
never nunca
  I never drink wine nunca
  bebo vinho
new novo(a)
news a notícia
  (on television) o noticiário
newsagent a tabacaria
newspaper o jornal
newsstand o quiosque

New Year o Ano Novo
   happy New Year! Feliz Ano
   Novo!
New Year's Eve a véspera
   de Ano Novo
New Zealand a Nova
   Zelândia
next próximo(a)
   next to ao lado de
   next week a semana que
   vem
   the next bus o próximo
   autocarro
   the next stop a próxima
   paragem
   the next train o próximo
   comboio
nice *(person, holiday)*
   agradável
   (place) bonito(a)
niece a sobrinha
night a noite
   at night à noite
   last night ontem à noite
   per night por noite
   tomorrow night amanhã
   à noite
nightclub a boite
nightdress a camisa de noite
night porter o porteiro da
   noite
no não
   no entry entrada proibida
   no smoking proibido fumar
   no thanks não, obrigado(a)
   (without) sem
   no sugar sem açúcar
   no ice sem gelo

nobody ninguém
noise o barulho
noisy barulhento(a)
   it's very noisy há muito
   barulho
nonalcoholic não-alcoólico(a)
none nenhum(a)
   there's none left não
   sobrou nada
non-smoker o/a não-
   fumador(a)
non-smoking não-fumador(a)
north o norte
Northern Ireland a Irlanda
   do Norte
North Sea o Mar do Norte
nose o nariz
not não
note *(banknote)* a nota
   (letter) a nota
note pad o bloco-notas
nothing nada
   nothing else mais nada
notice o aviso
noticeboard o placar
novel o romance
November o Novembro
now agora
nowhere *(be)* em nenhum
   lugar
   (go) a lugar nenhum
nuclear nuclear
nudist beach a praia para
   nudistas
number o número

N numberplate *(car)* a matrícula

nurse o/a enfermeiro(a)

nursery *(creche)* a creche

nursery slope a rampa para principiantes

nut *(to eat)* a noz
(for bolt) a porca

nutmeg a noz moscada

O

oak o carvalho

oar o remo

oats a aveia

to obtain obter

obvious óbvio(a)

occasionally às vezes

occupation *(work)* a ocupação

ocean o oceano

October o Outubro

octopus o polvo

odd *(number)* ímpar

of de
a bottle of water uma garrafa de água
a glass of wine um copo de vinho
made of... feito de...

off *(radio, engine, etc)* desligado(a)
(milk, food, etc) estragado(a)
this meat is off esta carne está estragada

to offer oferecer

office o escritório

often muitas vezes
how often? quantas vezes?

oil o óleo

oil filter o filtro do óleo

oil gauge o indicador do óleo

ointment a pomada

OK está bem

old velho(a)
how old are you? que idade tem?
I'm ... years old tenho ... anos

old age pensioner o/a reformado(a)

olive a azeitona

olive oil o azeite

omelette a omeleta

on *(light, TV)* aceso(a)
(engine) a trabalhar

on em
on the table na mesa
on time a horas

once uma vez
at once imediatamente

one um (uma)

one-way de sentido único

onion a cebola

only somente
(adj) único(a)

open *adj* aberto(a)

to open abrir

opera a ópera

opera house o teatro da ópera

operation (surgical) a operação

operator (phone) o/a telefonista

opposite: *opposite (to)* em frente de
opposite the hotel em frente do hotel

optician's o oculista

or ou
tea or coffee? chá ou café?

orange adj cor-de-laranja

orange (fruit) a laranja
(colour) cor-de-laranja

orange juice o sumo de laranja

orchestra a orquestra

order: *out of order* fora de serviço

to order (in restaurant) pedir
can I order? posso pedir?

oregano o orégão

organic biológico(a)

to organize organizar

original original

ornament o ornamento

other: *the other one* o/a outro(a)
have you any others? tem outros(as)?

ounce = approx. 30 g

our nosso(a)

out fora
he's gone out ele saiu
he's out não está

out of order fora de serviço

outdoor ao ar livre

outside: *it's outside* está lá fora

oven o forno

oven gloves as luvas de cozinha

ovenproof refratário(a)

over (on top of) sobre

to be overbooked ter mais reservas que lugares

to overcharge cobrar demais

overcoat o sobretudo

overdone (food) cozido demais

overdose a dose excessiva

to overheat aquecer demasiado

to overload sobrecarregar

to oversleep dormir além da hora

to overtake (in car) ultrapassar

to owe dever
you owe me... deve-me...
I owe you... devo-lhe...

owl o mocho

owner o/a dono(a)

oxygen o oxigénio

oyster a ostra

P

pace o passo

pacemaker o pacemaker

to pack bags fazer as malas

P **package** o embrulho

package tour a viagem organizada

packet o pacote

padded envelope o envelope almofadado

paddling pool a piscina para crianças

padlock o cadeado

page a página

paid pago(a)

pain a dor

painful doloroso(a)

painkiller o analgésico

to paint pintar

paintbrush o pincel

painting a pintura
(picture) o quadro

pair o par

palace o palácio

pale pálido

pan *(frying)* a frigideira
(saucepan) o tacho

pancake a panqueca

panniers *(for bike)* as bolsas para a bicicleta

pants *(briefs)* as cuecas

panty liner os pensos higiénicos

paper o papel
(newspaper) o jornal

paper hankies os lenços de papel

paper napkins os guardanapos de papel

papoose *(for carrying baby)* a mochila para levar o bebé

paracetamol o paracetamol

paraffin o óleo de parafina

paragliding para-pente

paralysed paralisado(a)

parcel a encomenda

pardon desculpe?
I beg your pardon! desculpe-me!

parents os pais

park o parque

to park estacionar

parking disk o disco de estacionamento

parking meter o parquímetro

parking ticket a multa por estacionamento em lugar proibido

parsley a salsa

parsnip a cenoura branca

part a parte

partner *(business)* o/a sócio(a)
(friend) o/a companheiro(a)

party *(celebration)* a festa
(political) o partido

pass *(mountain)* o desfiladeiro
(train, bus) o passe

passenger o/a passageiro(a)

passport o passaporte

passport control o controle de passaportes

pasta as massas

pastry *(dough)* a massa
(cake) o bolo

pâté o paté
path o caminho
patient o/a paciente;
o/a doente
(adj) paciente; doente
pavement o passeio
to pay pagar
I'd like to pay quero pagar
where do I pay? onde é
que se paga?
I've paid já paguei
payment o pagamento
payphone o telefone público
peace a paz
peach o pêssego
peak rate a taxa alta
peanut o amendoim
peanut allergy a alergia a
amendoins
peanut butter a manteiga
de amendoim
pear a pêra
pearls as pérolas
peas as ervilhas
pedal o pedal
pedal boat o barco de
pedáis
pedestrian o/a peão
pedestrian crossing a
passadeira para peões
to pee fazer chichi
to peel *(fruit)* descascar
peg *(clothes)* a mola
(tent) a estaca
pen a caneta

pencil o lápis
penfriend o/a
correspondente
penicillin a penicilina
penis o pénis
penknife o canivete
pension a pensão
pensioner o/a reformado(a)
people as pessoas
pepper *(spice)* a pimenta
(vegetable) o pimento
per por
per day por dia
per hour por hora
per week por semana
per person por pessoa
50 km per hour 50 km por
hora
perch *(fish)* a perca
perfect perfeito(a)
performance a
representação
the next performance
a próxima representação
perfume o perfume
perhaps talvez
period *(menstruation)* a
menstruação
perm a permanente
permit a licença
person a pessoa
per person por pessoa
personal organizer
a agenda
personal stereo
o Walkman®

P

pet o animal doméstico

pet food a comida para animais domésticos

pet shop a loja para animais domésticos

petrol a gasolina
4-star petrol a gasolina super
unleaded petrol a gasolina sem chumbo

petrol cap a tampa do depósito de gasolina

petrol pump a bomba de gasolina

petrol station a estação de serviço

petrol tank o depósito da gasolina

pewter o estanho

pharmacy a farmácia

pheasant o faisão

phone o telefone
mobile telephone o telemóvel

to phone telefonar

phonebook a lista telefónica

phonebox a cabine telefónica

phonecard o credifone

photocopy a fotocópia
I need a photocopy preciso duma fotocópia

photograph a fotografia
to take a photograph tirar uma fotografia

phrase book o guia de conversação

piano o piano

to pick *(fruit, flowers)* colher *(to choose)* escolher

pickled de conserva

pickpocket o/a carteirista

picnic o piquenique
to have a picnic fazer um piquenique

picnic area a zona de piqueniques

picnic hamper o cesto para piqueniques

picnic rug a manta

picnic table a mesa para piqueniques

picture *(painting)* o quadro *(photo)* a foto

pie *(savoury)* a empada *(sweet)* a torta

piece o bocado

pier o cais

pig o porco

pill o comprimido
to be on the Pill tomar a pílula

pillow a almofada

pillowcase a fronha

pilot o/a piloto(a)

pin o alfinete
safety pin o alfinete de segurança

pineapple o ananás

pink cor-de-rosa

pint = approx. 0.5 litre

a pint of beer uma caneca de cerveja

pipe *(for smoking)* o cachimbo
(drain, etc) o tubo ; o cano

pity: *what a pity!* que pena!

pizza a pizza

place o lugar

place of birth o lugar de nascimento

plain *(yoghurt, etc)* natural
(obvious) claro(a)

plait a trança

plan o plano

to plan planear

plane o avião

plant a planta

plaster *(sticking)* o adesivo
(for broken limb) o gesso

plastic o plástico

plastic bag a sacola de plástico

plate o prato

platform *(railway)* a plataforma
which platform? qual é a plataforma?

play *(at theatre)* a peça

to play jogar

playground o pátio de recreio

play park o parque infantil

playroom o quarto de brinquedos

pleasant agradável

please por favor ; faz favor

pleased: *pleased to meet you* prazer em conhecê-lo(a)

plenty: *plenty of (much)* muito(a)
(many) muitos(as)

pliers o alicate

plug *(electric)* a ficha ; a tomada
(for sink) a válvula

to plug in ligar

plum a ameixa

plumber o canalizador

plumbing *(pipes)* a canalização

plunger *(for sink)* o desentupidor

p.m. *(afternoon/evening)* de tarde
(night) de noite

poached *(fish)* cozido(a)
poached egg o ovo escalfado

pocket o bolso

points *(in car)* os platinados

poison veneno

poisonous venenoso(a)

police *(force)* a polícia

police officer o/a polícia

police station a esquadra

polish *(for shoes)* a pomada para o calçado
(for furniture) a cera

pollen o pólen

polluted poluído(a)

pollution a poluição

P **pony** o pónei
pony trekking o passeio a cavalo
pool a piscina
pool attendant o/a empregado(a) da piscina
poor pobre
poorly: he feels poorly ele não se sente bem
pope o papa
poppy a papoila
pop socks as peúgas
popular popular
pork a carne de porco
port *(wine)* o vinho do porto *(seaport)* o porto
porter *(for door)* o porteiro *(for luggage)* o carregador
portion a porção
Portugal Portugal
Portuguese português (portuguesa) *(language)* o português
possible possível
post: by post pelo correio
to post pôr no correio
postbox o marco do correio
postcard o postal
postcode o código postal
poster o póster *(advertising)* o cartaz
postman/woman o/a carteiro(a)
post office os correios
to postpone adiar

pot *(for cooking)* a panela
potato a batata
   baked potato a batata assada
   boiled potatoes as batatas cozidas
   fried potatoes as batatas fritas
   mashed potatoes o puré de batata
   roast potatoes as batatas assadas
   sautéed potatoes as batatas salteadas
potato masher o passe-vite
potato peeler o descascador de batatas
potato salad a salada de batata
pothole o buraco
pottery a cerâmica
pound *(money)* a libra *(weight)* = approx. 0.5 kilo
to pour deitar
powdered: in powdered form em pó
powdered milk o leite em pó
power o poder
power cut o corte de energia
pram o carrinho do bebé
prawn o lagostim
to pray rezar
prayer a oração
to prefer preferir
pregnant grávida

I'm pregnant estou grávida
to prepare preparar
to prescribe receitar
prescription a receita
  médica
present *(gift)* o presente;
  a oferta
preservative o preservativo
president o/a presidente
press *(newspapers)* a imprensa
pressure pressão
  blood pressure a tensão
  arterial
  tyre pressure a pressão
  dos pneus
pretty bonito(a)
price o preço
price list a lista de preços
priest o padre
prince o príncipe
princess a princesa
print *(photo)* a cópia
printer a impressora
prison a prisão
private privado(a)
prize o prémio
probably provavelmente
problem o problema
  no problem não tem
  problema
programme o programa
professor o/a professor(a)
  catedrático(a)
prohibited proibido(a)
promise a promessa

to promise prometer
pronounce pronunciar
  how is this pronounced?
  como se pronuncia isto?
protein a proteína
Protestant protestante
to provide fornecer
prune a ameixa seca
public público(a)
public holiday o feriado
publisher o/a editor(a)
pudding o pudim
to pull puxar
  I've pulled a muscle
  distendi o músculo
to pull over *(car)* encostar
pullover o pulôver
pump a bomba
pumpkin a abóbora
puncture o furo
puncture repair kit o estojo
  de ferramentas
puppet o fantoche
puppet show o teatro de
  marionetes; os fantoches
puppy o cachorro
purple roxo(a)
purpose: *on purpose* de
  propósito
purse o porta-moedas
to push empurrar
pushchair o carrinho
to put pôr
to put back repor
pyjamas o pijama

quail a codorniz
quality a qualidade
quantity a quantidade
quarantine a quarentena
to quarrel discutir
quarter o quarto
quay o cais
queen a rainha
query a pergunta
question a pergunta
queue a fila ; a bicha
to queue fazer fila
quick rápido(a)
quickly depressa
quiet *(place)* sossegado(a)
  a quiet room um quarto
  tranquilo
quilt o edredão
quite: *it's quite good* é
  bastante bom
  quite expensive é muito
  caro
quiz o concurso
quiz show *(TV)* o concurso
  televisivo

R

rabbit o coelho
rabies a raiva
race *(sport)* a corrida
  (human) a raça
race course o hipódromo

rack *(luggage)* o porta-
  bagagens
racket a raqueta
radiator *(car)* o radiador
  (heater) o radiador
radio o rádio
radish o rabanete
raffle a rifa
rag o trapo
railcard o passe do comboio
railway o caminho-de-ferro
railway station a estação
  de comboio
rain a chuva
to rain: *it's raining* está a
  chover
rainbow o arco-íris
raincoat o impermeável ;
  a gabardina
raisin a passa de uva
rake o ancinho
rape a violação
to rape violar
raped: *I've been raped*
  fui violada
rare *(unique)* raro(a)
  (steak) mal passado(a)
rash *(skin)* a urticária
raspberries as framboesas
rat o rato
rate *(price)* a taxa
rate of exchange o câmbio
raw cru(a)
razor a máquina de barbear

razorblades as lâminas de barbear
to read ler
ready pronto(a)
  to get ready preparar-se
real real
to realize perceber
rearview mirror o retrovisor
reason a razão
receipt o recibo
receiver *(phone)* o auscultador
recently recentemente
reception *(desk)* a recepção
receptionist o/a recepcionista
to recharge recarregar
recipe a receita
to recognize reconhecer
to recommend recomendar
record *(music)* o disco
to record *(facts)* registar
  (music) gravar
to recover *(from illness)* recuperar
to recycle reciclar
red vermelho(a)
redcurrants as groselhas
to reduce reduzir
reduction o desconto
reel *(fishing)* o carretel
to refer to referir-se a
referee o/a árbitro(a)
refill *(pen, lighter)* a recarga
refund o reembolso

to refuse recusar
regarding com relação a
region a região
to register *(at hotel)* preencher o registo
registered *(letter)* registado(a)
registration form a folha de registo
regulations os regulamentos
to reimburse reembolsar
relation *(family)* o/a parente
relationship *(personal)* as relações
  (family) o parentesco
relative *(family)* o/a parente
to relax repousar
reliable de confiança
to remain ficar
to remember lembrar-se de
  I don't remember não me lembro
remote control o controlo à distância
removal firm a companhia de mudanças
to remove retirar
rent *(house)* a renda;
  o aluguer
  (car) o aluguer
to rent *(house, car)* alugar
rental o aluguer
repair a reparação
to repair reparar
to repeat repetir

to reply responder
report o relatório
to report *(crime, person)* comunicar
request o pedido
to request pedir
to require precisar de
to rescue salvar
reservation a reserva
to reserve reservar
reserved reservado(a)
resident *(at hotel)* o/a hóspede
resort a estância
rest *(repose)* o descanso
(remainder) o resto
the rest of the wine o resto do vinho
to rest descansar
restaurant o restaurante
restaurant car o vagão restaurante
to retire reformar-se
retired reformado(a)
I'm retired estou reformado(a)
to return *(to go back)* voltar
(to give something back) devolver
return ticket o bilhete de ida e volta
to reverse fazer marcha atrás
to reverse the charges fazer uma chamada pagável no destino

reverse-charge call a chamada pagável no destino
reverse gear a marcha atrás
rheumatism o reumatismo
rhubarb o ruibarbo
rib a costela
ribbon a fita
rice o arroz
rich *(person)* rico(a)
(food) suculento(a)
to ride *(horse)* montar a cavalo
(in a car, bus, etc) viajar
right *(correct)* certo(a)
to be right ter razão
right: on/to the right à direita
right-handed destro(a)
right of way a preferência
ring *(for finger)* o anel
to ring *(bell)* tocar
(phone) telefonar
it's ringing está a tocar
ring road a circunvalação
ripe maduro(a)
river o rio
road a estrada
road map o mapa das estradas
road sign o sinal de trânsito
roadworks as obras na estrada
roast assado(a)
robber o ladrão (a ladra)
robin o pintarroxo

roll *(bread)* o pãozinho
rollerblades os patins em linha
rollers os rolos
roller skates os patins de rodas
rolling pin o rolo da massa
romance *(novel)* o romance
Romanesque românico(a)
romantic romântico(a)
roof o telhado
roof rack o tejadilho
room *(in house, hotel)* o quarto
(space) espaço
  double room o quarto de casal
  family room o quarto de família
  single room o quarto individual
room number o número do quarto
room service o serviço de quarto
root a raiz
rope a corda
rose a rosa
rosemary o alecrim
rosé wine o vinho rosé
rotten *(fruit, etc)* podre ; estragado(a)
rough *(surface)* áspero(a)
(sea) agitado(a)
round *(shape)* redondo(a)
roundabout *(traffic)* a rotunda

route a rota
row *(line)* a fila
to row *(boat)* remar
rowing *(sport)* o remo
rowing boat o barco a remos
royal real
rubber *(eraser)* a borracha
(material) a borracha
rubber band o elástico
rubber gloves as luvas de borracha
rubbish o lixo
rubella a rubéola
rucksack a mochila
rudder o leme
rug o tapete
ruins as ruínas
ruler *(for measuring)* a régua
rum o rum
to run correr
rush hour a hora de ponta
rusty ferrugento(a)
rye o centeio

S

saccharin a sacarina
sad triste
saddle *(bike)* o selim
(horse) a sela
safe *(for valuables)* o cofre
safe seguro(a)
  is it safe? é seguro?
safety belt o cinto de segurança

S

safety pin o alfinete de
  segurança
sage *(herb)* a salva
to sail *(sport, leisure)* velejar
sailboard a prancha
sail(ing) a vela
sailing boat o barco à vela
saint o/a santo(a)
salad a salada
  green salad a salada verde
  mixed salad a salada mista
  potato salad a salada de
  batatas
  tomato salad a salada de
  tomate
salad dressing o tempero
  da salada
salami o salame
salary o salário
sale(s) o saldo
salesman/woman o/a
  vendedor(a)
sales rep o/a representante
  de vendas
salmon o salmão
  smoked salmon o salmão
  fumado
salt o sal
salt water a água salgada
salty salgado(a)
same mesmo(a)
sample a amostra
sand a areia
sandals as sandálias
sandwich a sandes
  toasted sandwich a tosta

sanitary towel o penso
  higiénico
sardine a sardinha
satellite dish a antena
  parabólica
satellite TV a televisão via
  satélite
Saturday o sábado
sauce o molho
  tomato sauce o molho de
  tomate
saucepan a caçarola
saucer o pires
sauna a sauna
sausage a salsicha
to save *(life)* salvar
  (money) poupar
savoury saboroso(a)
savouries os salgados
saw a serra
to say dizer
scales *(weighing)* a balança
scallops as vieiras
scampi as gambas panadas
scarf *(woollen)* o cachecol
  (headscarf) o lenço (de
  pescoço)
scenery a paisagem
schedule o programa
school a escola
  primary school a escola
  primária
  secondary school o colégio
scissors a tesoura
score *(of match)* o resultado

to score marcar
Scot o/a escocês (escocesa)
Scotland a Escócia
Scottish escocês (escocesa)
scouring pad a palha de aço
screen (computer, TV) o ecrã
screenwash o detergente para o pára-brisas
screw o parafuso
screwdriver a chave de parafusos
phillips screwdriver® a chave phillips®
scuba diving mergulhar
sculpture a escultura
sea o mar
seafood o peixe e o marisco
seagull a gaivota
seal a foca
seam (of dress) a costura
to search for procurar
seasick enjoado(a)
I get seasick enjoo
seasickness o enjoo
seaside a praia
at the seaside na praia
season (of year) a estação
(holiday) a temporada
in season da época
season ticket o passe
seasoning o tempero
seat (chair) a cadeira
(on bus, train, etc) o lugar
seatbelt o cinto de segurança

seaweed a alga marinha
second segundo(a)
second class a segunda classe
second-class adj de segunda classe
second-hand em segunda mão ; usado(a)
secretary o/a secretário(a)
security guard o guarda de segurança
sedative o sedativo
to see ver
seed a semente
to seize agarrar
self-catering com cozinha
self-employed que trabalha por conta própria
self-service o auto-serviço
to sell vender
do you sell...? vende...?
sell-by date... usar antes de...
Sellotape ® a fita-cola
semi-skimmed milk o leite meio-gordo
to send mandar
senior citizen o/a reformado(a)
sensible sensato(a)
separated separado(a)
separately: to pay *separately* pagar separadamente
September o Setembro
septic tank a fossa séptica

sequel *(film, book)* a continuação; a sequela

serious sério(a) *(illness)* grave

to serve servir

service *(in church)* o serviço religioso *(in restaurant)* o serviço **is service included?** o serviço está incluído?

service charge o custo do serviço

service station a estação de serviço

serviette o guardanapo

set menu a ementa fixa

settee o sofá

several vários(as)

to sew coser

sewer o esgoto

sex *(gender)* o sexo *(intercourse)* o sexo

shade a sombra **in the shade** à sombra

to shake *(bottle)* sacudir

shallow pouco profundo(a)

shampoo o champô

shampoo and set a lavagem e mise

to share dividir

to share out distribuir

sharp *(razor, knife)* afiado(a)

to shave fazer a barba

shaving cream o creme de barbear

shawl o xaile

she ela see **GRAMMAR**

sheep a ovelha

sheet *(for bed)* o lençol

shelf a prateleira

shell *(seashell)* a concha *(egg, nut)* a casca

shellfish o marisco

sheltered abrigado(a)

shepherd o pastor

sherry o xerez

to shine brilhar

shingles *(illness)* o herpes zóster; a zona

ship o barco

shirt a camisa

shock absorber o amortecedor

shoe o sapato

shoelaces os cordões (de sapato)

shoe polish a graxa

shoe repairer's o sapateiro

shoe shop a sapataria

shop a loja

shop assistant o/a vendedor(a)

shop window a montra

shopping: to go shopping ir às compras

shopping centre o centro comercial

shore a costa

short curto(a)

short circuit o curto-circuito

short cut o atalho

shortage a escassez

shorts os calções

short-sighted míope

shoulder o ombro

to shout gritar

show o espectáculo

to show mostrar

shower o duche; o chuveiro
to have a shower tomar
um duche; tomar um
chuveiro
(rain) o chuveiro ;
o aguaceiro

shower cap a touca de
banho

shower curtain a cortina
do chuveiro

shower gel o gel para
banho

shrimps os camarões

to shrink encolher

shrub o arbusto

shut *(closed)* fechado(a)

to shut fechar

shutters as persianas ;
as gelosias

shuttle service o serviço
de ligação

shy tímido(a)

sick *(ill)* doente
I feel sick sinto-me mal-
disposto(a)

side o lado

side dish o
acompanhamento

sidelight o farolim

sidewalk o passeio

sieve *(for liquids)* o coador
(for flour) a peneira

to sightsee fazer turismo

sightseeing o turismo
to go sightseeing fazer
turismo

sightseeing tour a excursão

sign *(road-, notice, etc)* o sinal

to sign assinar

signature a assinatura

signpost a sinalização

silk a seda

silver a prata

similar: *similar to*
semelhante a

simple simples

since *(time)* desde que
(because) porque
since Saturday desde
sábado

to sing cantar

single *(not married)* solteiro(a)
(not double) simples

single bed a cama de
pessoa só

single room o quarto
individual

single ticket o bilhete de ida

sink o lava-louça

sir senhor

sister a irmã

sister-in-law a cunhada

to sit sentar-se
please, sit down faça o
favor de se sentar

S

size (clothes) o tamanho
(shoes) o número

to skate patinar

skates (ice) os patins de
lâmina
(roller) os patins de rodas

skating rink o rinque de
patinagem

ski o esqui
skis os esquis

to ski esquiar

ski boots as botas de
esquiar

skiing o esqui
to go skiing ir esquiar

ski instructor o/a
instructor(a) de esqui

ski jump a pista para saltos
de esqui

ski lift o ski lift

ski pole a vara de esqui

ski run a pista de esqui

ski stick a vara de esqui

ski suit o traje de esqui

skimmed milk o leite magro

skin a pele

skindiving mergulhar

skirt a saia

sky o céu

slang o calão

sledge o trenó

to sleep dormir

to sleep in dormir até tarde

sleeper (on train) a
carruagem-cama

sleeping bag o saco cama

sleeping car a carruagem-
cama

sleeping pill o comprimido
para dormir

slice a fatia

slide (photograph)
o diapositivo

to slip escorregar

slippers os chinelos

slow lento(a)

small pequeno(a)

smaller mais pequeno(a)

smell o cheiro

smile o sorriso

to smile sorrir

smoke o fumo

to smoke fumar
I don't smoke não fumo
can I smoke? posso fumar?

smoke alarm o alarme
contra incêndios

smoked fumado(a)

smokers os fumadores

smoking: *no smoking*
proibido fumar

smooth liso(a) ; macio(a)

snack o lanche
to have a snack comer
qualquer coisa

snack bar o snack-bar

snake a cobra

snake bite a mordedura de
cobra

to sneeze espirrar

to snore ressonar
snorkel o tubo de ar
snow a neve
to snow nevar
  it's snowing está a nevar
snowboard o snowboard
snowboarding: *to go*
  snowboarding fazer
  snowboarding
snow chains as correntes
  para a neve
snowed up coberto de neve
snowman o boneco-de-neve
snowplough a máquina
  limpa-neve
snow tyres os pneus para
  a neve
so portanto
  so much tanto(a)
soap o sabão
soap powder o sabão em pó
sober sóbrio(a)
socket *(electrical)* a tomada
socks as peúgas
soda water a água com gás
sofa o sofá
sofa bed o sofá-cama
soft macio(a)
soft drink o refrigerante
software o software
soldier o soldado
sole *(fish)* o linguado
  (of shoe) a sola
soluble solúvel
some alguns (algumas)

someone alguém
something alguma coisa
sometimes às vezes
son o filho
son-in-law o genro
song a canção
soon em breve
  as soon as possible
  o antes possível
sore magoado(a)
sore throat: *I have a sore*
  throat dói-me a garganta
sorry: *I'm sorry!* lamento
sort: *what sort of cheese?*
  que tipo de queijo?
sound o som
soup a sopa
sour azedo(a)
soured cream as natas
  azedas
south o sul
souvenir a recordação
spa as termas
space o espaço
spade a enxada
Spain a Espanha
Spanish espanhol(a)
  (language) o espanhol
spanner a chave inglesa
spare parts as peças sobressalentes
spare room o quarto de
  hóspedes
spare tyre o pneu
  sobressalente

spare wheel a roda sobressalente

sparkling espumoso(a)
sparkling water a água com gás
sparkling wine o espumante

spark plug a vela

to speak falar
do you speak English? fala inglês?
I don't speak Portuguese não falo português

special especial

specialist o/a especialista

speciality a especialidade

speech a fala
(address) o discurso

speed a velocidade

speedboat a lancha

speeding o excesso de velocidade

speeding ticket a multa por excesso de velocidade

speed limit o limite de velocidade
to exceed the speed limit ultrapassar o limite de velocidade

speedometer o conta-quilómetros

spell: *how do you spell it?* como se escreve?

to spend *(money)* gastar

spices as especiarias

spicy picante

spider a aranha

to spill entornar

spinach o espinafre

spin-dryer a secadora

spine a coluna

spirits as bebidas espirituosas

splinter a falha ; a lasca

spoke *(wheel)* o raio

sponge a esponja

spoon a colher

sport o desporto

sports centre o centro de desportos; centro desportivo

sports shop a loja de artigos desportivos

spot *(pimple)* a borbulha

to sprain: *to sprain one's ankle* torcer o tornozelo

spring *(season)* a primavera
(coil) a mola

spring onion a cebolinha

square *(in town)* a praça

squash *(drink)* o sumo
(game) o squash

to squeeze apertar

squid as lulas

stadium o estádio

staff o pessoal

stage o palco; a cena

stain a nódoa

stained glass o vitral

stain remover o tira-nódoas

stairs a escada

stale *(bread)* duro(a)

stalls *(in theatre)* a plateia

stamp *(postage)* o selo

to stand estar em pé

to stand up levantar-se

star *(in sky, in films)* a estrela

starfish a estrela-do-mar

to start começar

starter *(in meal)* a entrada *(in car)* o motor de arranque

station a estação

stationer's a papelaria

statue a estátua

stay a estadia; a visita
enjoy your stay! desfrute a sua visita

to stay ficar
I'm staying at a hotel fico num hotel

steak o bife
medium steak o bife ao ponto
well-done steak o bife bem-passado
rare steak o bife mal-passado

to steal roubar

to steam cozer no vapor

steamed cozido(a) a vapor

steel aço

steep: is it steep? custa a subir?

steeple o campanário

steering wheel o volante

step *(stair)* o degrau

stepdaughter a enteada

stepfather o padrasto

stepmother a madrasta

stepson o enteado

stereo o estéreo
personal stereo o Walkman®

sterling *(pounds)* esterlino(a)

stew o guisado

steward *(on plane)* o comissário de bordo

stewardess *(on plane)* a hospedeira de bordo

to stick *(with glue)* colar

sticking plaster o adesivo

still *(not moving)* imóvel
(not sparkling) sem gás
(yet) ainda

sting a picada

to sting picar

stitches *(surgical)* os pontos

stock cube o cubo de caldo

stockings as meias

stolen roubado(a)

stomach o estômago

stomach upset o mal-estar de estômago

stone a pedra
(weight) = approx. 6.5 kg

to stop *(come to a halt)* parar
(stop doing something) deixar de fazer alguma coisa

stop sign o sinal de paragem

store *(shop)* a loja

storey o andar

S

storm a tempestade
story a história
straightaway imediatamente
straight on sempre em frente
strainer o coador
strange estranho(a)
straw *(for drinking)* a palha
strawberry o morango
stream o riacho
street a rua
street map o mapa das ruas
strength a força
stress o stress
strike *(of workers)* a greve
    to be on strike estar em greve
string o cordel
striped às riscas
stroke *(medical)* a trombose
    to have a stroke ter uma trombose
strong forte
    strong coffee o café forte
    strong tea o chá forte
stuck: *it's stuck* está preso(a)
student o/a estudante
student discount o desconto para estudantes
stuffed recheado(a)
stung picado(a)
stupid estúpido(a)
subscription a assinatura
subtitles as legendas

subway *(underpass)* a passagem subterrânea
suddenly de repente
suede a camurça
sugar o açúcar
    icing sugar o açúcar em pó
sugar-free sem açúcar
to suggest sugerir
suit *(men's and women's)* o fato
suitcase a mala
sum a soma
summer o verão
summer holidays as férias de verão
summit o cume
sun o sol
to sunbathe tomar banhos de sol
sunblock o protector solar
sunburn a queimadura de sol
Sunday o domingo
sunflower o girassol
sunflower oil o óleo de girassol
sunglasses os óculos de sol
sunny: *it's sunny* está sol
sunrise o nascer do sol
sunroof o tecto de abrir
sunscreen o filtro solar
sunset o pôr do sol
sunshade o guarda-sol; a sombra; o toldo

sunstroke a insolação
suntan o bronzeado
suntan lotion a loção de bronzear
supermarket o supermercado
supper a ceia
supplement o suplemento
to supply abastecer
surcharge a sobretaxa
sure seguro(a)
  I'm sure estou seguro(a)
to surf fazer surfe
  to surf the Net explorar a Internet
surfboard a prancha de surf
surgery (operation) a cirurgia
  (building) o consultório
surname o apelido
  my surname is... o meu apelido é...
surprise a surpresa
surrounded by rodeado(a) por
suspension a suspensão
to survive sobreviver
to swallow engolir
swan o cisne
to swear (bad language) blasfemar; praguejar
  (in court) jurar
to sweat suar
sweater o pulover
sweatshirt a sweatshirt
sweet (not savoury) doce
sweet (dessert) a sobremesa

sweetener o edulcorante
sweets os doces
to swell (injury etc) inchar
to swim nadar
swimming pool a piscina
swimsuit o fato de banho
swing (for children) o baloiço
Swiss suíço(a)
switch o interruptor
to switch off apagar ; desligar
to switch on acender ; ligar
Switzerland a Suíça
swollen (finger, ankle, etc) inchado(a)
swordfish o espadarte
synagogue a sinagoga
syringe a seringa

T

table a mesa
tablecloth a toalha de mesa
tablespoon a colher de sopa
tablet (pill) o comprimido
table tennis o ping-pong
table wine o vinho de mesa
tail o rabo ; a cauda
tailor's a alfaiataria
take (carry) levar ; transportar
  (to grab, seize) agarrar
  (medicine etc) tomar
  (to take someone to) levar
  how long does it take? quanto tempo demora?

T

take-away *(food)* para levar

to take off levantar voo

to take out *(of bag etc)* tirar

talc o talco

to talk to conversar

tall alto(a)

tame *(animal)* manso(a)

tampons os tampões

tangerine a tangerina

tank *(car)* o depósito
(fish) o aquário

tap a torneira

tap water a água da
torneira

tape *(video)* a cassette de
vídeo

tape measure a fita métrica

tape recorder o gravador

target o alvo

tarragon o estragão

tart a tarte

tartar sauce o molho tártaro

taste o sabor

to taste provar
can I taste it? posso provar?

tax o imposto

taxi o táxi

taxi driver o/a taxista

taxi rank a praça de táxis

tea o chá
herbal tea a tisana
lemon tea o chá de limão
strong tea o chá forte
tea with milk o chá com
leite

teabag o saquinho de chá

teapot o bule (de chá)

to teach ensinar

teacher o/a professor(a)

team a equipa

teapot o bule

tear *(in eye)* a lágrima
(in material) o rasgão

teaspoon a colher de chá

teat *(on baby's bottle)* a tetina

tea towel o pano de cozinha

teenager o/a adolescente

teeshirt a camisola de
manga curta

teeth os dentes

teething dentição

telegram o telegrama

telephone o telefone
mobile telephone o
telemóvel

to telephone telefonar

telephone box a cabine
telefónica

telephone call a chamada

telephone card o cartão
telefónico

telephone directory a lista
telefónica

telephone number o
número de telefone

television a televisão

television set o televisor

telex o telex

to tell dizer

temperature a temperatura

to have a temperature ter febre

temple o templo

temporary temporário(a)

tenant o/a inquilino(a)

tendon o tendão

tennis o ténis

tennis ball a bola de ténis

tennis court o campo de ténis

tennis racket a raqueta de ténis

tent a tenda

tent peg a estaca

terminal *(airport)* o terminal

terrace a esplanada

terracotta a terracota; o barro

terrorist o/a terrorista

to test *(try out)* testar

testicles os testículos

tetanus o tétano

than que
  better than melhor do que
  more than you mais do que tu
  more than five mais de cinco

to thank agradecer

thank you/thanks obrigado(a)
  thank you very much muito obrigado(a)
  no thanks não, obrigado(a)

that aquele (aquela)
  that one esse (essa)

the *(sing)* o (a)
  (plural) os (as)

theatre o teatro

theft o roubo

their seu (sua)

them *(direct object)* os (as)
  (indirect object) lhes
  (after preposition) eles (elas)

then então

there *(over there)* ali

there is/there are há

thermometer o termómetro

these estes (estas)
  these ones estes (estas)

they eles (elas) see
  GRAMMAR

thick grosso(a)

thief o/a ladrão (ladra)

thigh a coxa

thin magro(a)

thing a coisa
  my things as minhas coisas

to think pensar
  (to be of opinion) achar

third terceiro(a)

thirsty: I'm thirsty tenho sede

this este (esta)
  this one este (esta)

thorn o espinho

those aqueles (aquelas)
  those ones aqueles (aquelas)

thousand mil

thread a linha

T

thriller *(film)* o filme de
suspense
(book) o livro de suspense

throat a garganta

throat lozenges as pastilhas
para a garganta

through através de

to throw away deitar fora;
descartar

thrush *(candida)* a candidíase
vaginal

thumb o polegar

thunder o trovão

thunderstorm o temporal;
a trovoada

Thursday a quinta-feira

thyme o tomilho

ticket *(bus, train, etc)*
o bilhete
(for cinema, theatre etc)
a entrada
a single ticket um bilhete
de ida
a return ticket um bilhete
de ida e volta
a tourist ticket um bilhete
de turista
a book of tickets uma
caderneta de bilhetes

ticket collector o/a revisor(a)

ticket inspector o/a inspec-
tor(a) de bilhetes

ticket office a bilheteira

tide *(sea)* a maré
low tide a maré baixa
high tide a maré alta

tidy arrumado(a)

to tidy up arrumar

tie a gravata

tight apertado(a)

tights os collants

tile *(floor)* o ladrilho
(wall) o azulejo

till *(cash desk)* a caixa

till *(until)* até
till 2 o'clock até às duas

time o tempo
(clock) as horas
what time is it? que horas
são?
this time esta vez

timetable o horário

tin *(can)* a lata

tinfoil a folha de alumínio

tin-opener o abre-latas

tip a gorjeta

to tip dar uma gorjeta

tipped *(cigarette)* com filtro

Tippex® o fluido corrector

tired cansado(a)

tissues os lenços de papel

to a
to London para Londres
to the airport ao
aeroporto

toadstool o cogumelo
venenoso

toast *(to eat)* a torrada
(raising glass) brindar

tobacco o tabaco

tobacconist's a tabacaria

today hoje

A

albergue *m* hostel
albergue da juventude youth hostel
alcoólico(a) alcoholic
aldeia *f* small village
alegre jolly
Alemanha *f* Germany
alemão (alemã) German
alérgico(a) allergic to
alface *f* lettuce
alfaiate *m* tailor
alfândega *f* customs
alfinete *m* pin
alforreca *f* jellyfish
algodão *m* cotton
algum(a) some ; any
alguns (algumas) a few ; some
mais alguma coisa? anything else?
alho *m* garlic
alhos-porros *mpl* leeks
ali there
alimentação *f* food
alívio *m* relief
almoço *m* lunch
pequeno-almoço breakfast
almofada *f* pillow ; cushion
alojamento *m* accommodation
alpinismo *m* climbing
alto! stop!
alto(a) high ; tall ; loud
a estação alta high season
altura *f* height

204

alugar to hire ; to rent
aluga-se to rent
alugam-se quartos rooms to let
aluguer *m* rental
amanhã tomorrow
amarelo(a) yellow
amargo(a) bitter
ambulância *f* ambulance
amêijoa *f* clam ; cockle
ameixa *f* plum
ameixa seca prune
amêndoa *f* almond
amêndoa amarga bitter almond liqueur
amendoim *m* peanut
amigo(a) *m/f* friend
amora *f* blackberry ; mulberry
amortecedor *m* shock absorber
amostra *f* sample
analgésico *m* painkiller
ananás *m* pineapple
anchovas *fpl* anchovies
andar to walk
andar *m* floor ; storey
o primeiro andar first floor
anel *m* ring
anis *m* aniseed liqueur
aniversário *m* anniversary ; birthday
ano *m* year
Ano Novo New Year
antes de before

A

a to ; the *(feminine)*
abadia f abbey
abaixo down ; below
aberto open
  aberto todo o ano open all year round
abrande slow down
abre-garrafas m bottle-opener
abre-latas m tin/can-opener
Abril m April
abrir to open; to unlock *(door)*
acabar to end ; to finish
acampar to camp
aceitar to accept
acelerador m accelerator
acender to switch/turn on ; to light *(fire, cigarette)*
  acenda as luzes switch on the lights
acepipes m titbit
  acepipes starters
aceso(a) on *(light, etc)*
acesso m access
achar to think ; to find
  acha bem? do you think it's all right?
acidente m accident
acima above
aço m steel
  aço inoxidável stainless steel
açorda f bread-based dish

acordo m agreement
Açores mpl the Azores archipelago
actual present(-day)
actualizar to modernize ; to update
açúcar m sugar
adega f wine cellar
adesivo m plaster *(for cut)*
adeus goodbye
adiantado(a) fast *(watch)* ; early *(train, etc)*
adulto(a) adult
advogado(a) m/f lawyer
aéreo(a): *a linha aérea* airline
  via aérea air mail
aeroporto m airport
agência f agency
  agência de viagens travel agents
agente m/f agent
agora now
Agosto m August
agradável pleasant
agradecer to thank
água f water
  água destilada distilled water
  água potável drinking water
  água com gás fizzy water
  água sem gás still water
aguardente f spirit brandy
agudo(a) sharp *(pain)*
ajudar to help

wrong errado(a)
wrought iron o ferro forjado

X

x-ray a radiografia
to x-ray radiografar

Y

yacht o iate
year o ano
  last year o ano passado
  next year o ano que vem
  this year este ano
yearly: *twice yearly* duas vezes por ano
yellow amarelo(a)
Yellow Pages as Páginas Amarelas
yes sim
yesterday ontem

yet: *not yet* ainda não
yoghurt o iogurte
  plain yoghurt o iogurte natural
yolk a gema
you você/tu/vocês/vós
young novo(a)
  (person) o/a jovem
your teu (tua)
youth hostel o albergue da juventude

Z

zebra crossing a passadeira para peões
zero o zero
zip o fecho éclair
zone a zona
zoo o jardim zoológico
zoom lens o zoom

widow a viúva
widower o viúvo
width a largura
wife a mulher ; a esposa
wig a peruca
to win ganhar
wind o vento
windbreak o guarda-vento
windmill o moínho
window a janela
 (shop) a montra
windscreen o pára-brisas
windscreen wipers o limpa-pára-brisas
to windsurf fazer windsurf
windsurfing o wind-surf
windy: it's windy está vento
wine o vinho
 red wine o vinho tinto
 white wine o vinho branco
 rosé wine o vinho rosé
 dry wine o vinho seco
 sweet wine o vinho doce
 sparkling wine o vinho espumante
 house wine o vinho da casa
 table wine o vinho de mesa
wine list a lista de vinhos
wing a asa
wing mirror o retrovisor exterior
winter o inverno
wire o arame
 (electric) o fio (eléctrico)

with com
 with ice com gelo
 with milk com leite
 with sugar com açúcar
without milk sem leite
 without sugar sem açúcar
witness a testemunha
wolf o lobo
woman a mulher
wonderful maravilhoso(a)
wood (substance) a madeira
woods a floresta
wool a lã
word a palavra
to work (person) trabalhar
 (machine) funcionar
 it doesn't work não está a funcionar; não funciona
work permit a autorização de trabalho
world o mundo
worldwide no mundo inteiro
worried preocupado(a)
worse pior
worth: it's worth... vale...
to wrap (parcel, etc) embrulhar
wrapping paper o papel de embrulho
wrinkles as rugas
wrist o pulso
to write escrever
 please write it down escreve-o, por favor
writing paper o papel de carta

wedding o casamento

wedding anniversary o aniversário de casamento

wedding cake o bolo de noiva

wedding dress o vestido de noiva

wedding present a prenda de casamento

wedding ring a aliança de casamento

Wednesday a quarta-feira

week a semana
last week a semana passada
next week a semana que vem
per week por semana
this week esta semana
during the week durante a semana

weekday o dia útil

weekend o fim-de-semana
next weekend o próximo fim-de-semana
this weekend este fim-de-semana

weekly por semana
weekly ticket o bilhete semana

to weigh pesar

weight o peso

welcome bem-vindo(a)

well bem
he's not well ele não se sente bem

well *(for water)* o poço

well-done *(steak)* bem-passado

wellington boots as galoshas

Welsh galês (galesa) *(language)* o galês

west o oeste

wet molhado(a) *(weather)* chuvoso(a)

wetsuit o fato de mergulhador

what que
what is it? o que é?

wheat o trigo

wheel a roda

wheelchair a cadeira de rodas

wheel clamp o imobilizador

when? quando?

where? onde?

which: which is it? qual é?

while enquanto
in a while dentro de pouco

whipped cream o chantilly

whisky o uísque

white branco(a)

who: who is it? quem é?

whole inteiro(a)

wholemeal bread o pão integral

whose: whose is it? de quem é?

why? porquê?

wide largo(a)

ward *(in hospital)* a enfermaria

wardrobe o guarda-fato

warehouse o armazém

warm quente
I'm warm estou com calor
it's warm (weather) está calor

to warm up aquecer

warning triangle o triângulo de sinalização

wash: to have a wash lavar-se

to wash lavar

wash and blow-dry lavar e secar

washbasin o lavatório

washing machine a máquina de lavar roupa

washing powder o detergente para a roupa

washing-up bowl o lava-louças

washing-up liquid o detergente para a louça

wasp a vespa

waste bin o balde do lixo

watch o relógio

to watch ver ; observar

watchstrap a pulseira de relógio

water a água
bottled water a água mineral (engarrafada)
cold water a água fria
drinking water a água potável

fresh water a água corrente

hot water a água quente

mineral water a água mineral

salt water a água salgada

sparkling water a água com gás

still water a água sem gás

watercress o agrião

waterfall a queda de água

water heater o esquentador

watermelon a melancia

waterproof impermeável

to waterski fazer esqui aquático

water-skiing o esqui aquático

waterwings as braçadeiras

waves as ondas

wax a cera

waxing *(hair removal)* depilação com cera

way *(path)* o caminho *(manner)* a maneira

way in *(entrance)* a entrada

way out *(exit)* a saída

we nós see **GRAMMAR**

weak fraco(a) *(tea, etc)* aguado(a)

to wear vestir

weather o tempo

weather forecast a previsão do tempo

website o website

venereal disease a doença venérea

venison a carne de veado

ventilator o ventilador

very muito

vest a camisola interior

vet o/a veterinário(a)

via por

video o vídeo

to video *(from TV)* gravar

video camera a câmara de vídeo

video cassette a videocassete

video game o jogo de vídeo

video phone o videofone

video recorder o gravador de video

view a vista

village a aldeia

vinaigrette a vinagreta

vinegar o vinagre

vineyard a vinha

violet *(flower)* a violeta

viper a víbora

virus o vírus

visa o visto

visit a visita

to visit visitar

visiting hours *(hospital)* as horas de visita

visitor a visita

vitamin a vitamina

vodka a vodka

voice a voz

volcano o vulcão

volleyball o voleibol

voltage a voltagem

to vomit vomitar

voucher o vale ; o recibo

W

wage o salário

waist a cintura

waistcoat o colete

to wait for esperar por

waiter o empregado de mesa

waiting room a sala de espera

waitress a empregada de mesa

to wake up acordar

Wales o País de Gales

to walk andar

walk o passeio

Walkman® o Walkman®

walking boots as botas de montanha

walking stick a bengala

wall *(inside)* a parede *(outside)* o muro

wallet a carteira

walnut a noz

to want querer
I want... quero...
we want... queremos...

war a guerra

U

unhappy triste; infeliz
to be unhappy with... não estar satisfeito(a) com...

United Kingdom o Reino Unido

United States os Estados Unidos

university a universidade

unleaded petrol a gasolina sem chumbo

unlikely improvável

to unlock destrancar

unlucky infeliz; sem sorte

to unpack *(suitcases)* desfazer as malas

unpleasant desagradável *(person)* antipático(a)

to unplug desligar

to unscrew desaparafusar

until até
until 2 o'clock até às duas

unusual insólito(a)

up: *to get up* levantar-se

upside down invertido(a)

upstairs em cima

urgent urgente

urine a urina

us nos
(after preposition) nós

USA os EUA

to use utilizar

useful útil

usual habitual

usually geralmente

U-turn a meia-volta

V

vacancies *(in hotel etc)* os quartos vagos
(jobs) as vagas

vacant livre
(hotel room) o quarto vago

vacation as férias
on vacation de férias

vaccination a vacinação

vacuum cleaner o aspirador

vagina a vagina

valid válido(a)

valley o vale

valuable valioso(a)

valuables os objetos de valor

value o valor

valve a válvula

van a carrinha

vanilla a baunilha

vase *(for flowers)* a jarra

VAT o IVA

veal a carne de vitela

vegan vegetalista
I'm vegan sou vegetalista

vegetables os legumes; os vegetais

vegetarian vegetariano(a)
I'm vegetarian sou vegetariano(a)

vehicle o veículo

vein a veia

Velcro® o Velcro®

velvet o veludo

vending machine a máquina de venda automática

trout a truta

truck o camião

true verdadeiro(a)

trunk *(luggage)* o baú ;
a mala grande

trunks *(swimming)* os calções
de banho

truth a verdade

to try *(attempt)* tentar

to try on *(clothes, shoes)*
provar

T-shirt a T-shirt

Tuesday a terça-feira

tulip a túlipa

tumble dryer a máquina
de secar roupa

tuna o atum

tunnel o túnel

turkey o peru

to turn voltar ; girar
to turn around voltar-se

to turn off *(light etc)* apagar
(engine) desligar
(tap) fechar

to turn on *(light etc)* acender
(engine) ligar
(tap) abrir

turnip o nabo

turquoise *(colour)* turquesa

tweezers a pinça

twice duas vezes

twin-bedded room o quarto
com duas camas

twins os gémeos
identical twins os gémeos
idênticos

to type escrever à máquina

typical típico

tyre o pneu

tyre pressure a pressão dos
pneus

U

ugly feio(a)

ulcer a úlcera

umbrella o guarda-chuva;
a sombrinha
(sunshade) o guarda-sol

uncle o tio

uncomfortable incómodo(a)

unconscious inconsciente

under debaixo de

undercooked mal cozido(a)

underground *(metro)*
o metropolitano

underpants as cuecas

underpass a passagem
subterrânea

to understand compreender
I don't understand não
percebo
do you understand?
percebe?

underwear a roupa interior

underwater debaixo da
água

undo desfazer

to undress despir-se

unemployed
desempregado(a)

to unfasten desapertar

antiguidades *fpl* antiques

apagado(a) off *(radio, etc)* ; out *(light, etc)*

apagar to switch/turn off *(light, etc)*

aparelho *m* gadget ; machine ; apparatus
aparelho para a surdez hearing aid

apartamento *m* apartment ; flat

apelido *m* surname
apelido de solteira maiden name

apenas only

apertado(a) tight

apetite *m* appetite
bom apetite! enjoy your meal!

apólice de seguro *f* insurance certificate

aquecedor *m* heater ; electric fire

aquecimento *m* heating

aqui here

ar *m* air ; choke *(car)*
ar condicionado air conditioning

arder to burn

areia *f* sand

arenque *m* herring

armário *m* cupboard ; closet

armazém *m* warehouse
grande armazém department store

arrendar to let

arroz *m* rice
arroz doce rice pudding

artesanato *m* handicrafts

artigo *m* item
artigos de ménage household goods
artigos de vime wickerwork

árvore *f* tree

ascensor *m* lift

assado(a) roast ; baked

assinar to sign

assinatura *f* signature

assistência *f* audience ; assistance

atacadores *mpl* laces

até until ; as far as

aterrar to land

atrás behind

atrasado(a) late *(for appointment)*

atrasar to delay

atraso *m* delay

atravessar to cross

atum *m* tuna (fish)

autocarro *m* bus ; coach
a paragem de autocarro bus stop

auto-estrada *f* motorway

automobilista *m/f* driver

automóvel *m* car

autorização *f* licence ; permit

avaria *f* breakdown

A

avariado(a) out of order *(machine)*; broken down *(car)*

ave f bird

avelã f hazelnut

avenida f avenue

avião m plane

aviso m warning

avô m grandfather

avó f grandmother

azedo(a) sour

azeite m olive oil

azeitona f olive

azul blue

azulejo m ornamental tile

B

bacalhau m dried salt cod
bacalhau à Brás dried salt cod with eggs, onion and potatoes

bagaceira f eau de vie

bagaço m eau de vie

bagagem f luggage ; baggage

Bairrada region producing full-bodied red and aromatic white wines

bairro m quarter ; district

Baixa f commercial centre of Lisbon

baixar to lower

baixo: em baixo below

baixo(a) low

balança f scales *(weighing machine)*

balcão m shop counter ; circle in theatre

banco m bank ; seat *(in car, etc)*

bandeira f flag ; banner

bandeja f tray ; salver

bandido m gangster ; robber

banheira f bath-tub

banheiro m lifeguard

banho m bath
a casa de banho bathroom
tomar banho to have a bath

banquete m banquet ; sumptuous dinner

barato(a) cheap

barba f beard
fazer a barba to shave

barbeiro m barber

barco m boat ; ship
barco a remos rowing boat
barco à vela sailing boat

barraca f hut *(shed)*; beach hut

barreira f trench ; obstacle ; barrier

barriga f belly

barro m pottery ; terracotta

barulho m noise

bastante enough

batata f potato
batatas fritas chips ; crisps

bater to beat ; to knock
bata à porta please knock

bateria f battery *(for car)*

PORTUGUESE-ENGLISH

batido de leite *m* milk shake

baunilha *f* vanilla

bebé *m* baby

beber to drink

bebida *f* drink

beco *m* alley

belo(a) beautiful

bem well
  está bem OK
  bem passado well done
  (steak)

bem-vindo(a) welcome

bengaleiro *m* cloakroom (at
  theatre) ; hat and umbrella
  stand

benzer to bless

beringela *f* aubergine

berma *f* hard shoulder
  bermas baixas steep verge
  – no hard shoulder

berço *m* crib; cradle; cot

besugo *m* sea bream

beterraba *f* beetroot

bexiga *f* bladder

bica *f* espresso coffee

bicha *f* queue
  fazer bicha to queue

bicicleta *f* bicycle

bife *m* steak
  bife com batatas fritas
  steak and chips

bifurcação *f* junction

bilhar *m* billiards

bilhete *m* ticket ; fare
  bilhete de entrada
  admission ticket

bilhete de identidade
  identity card

bilheteira *f* ticket office

binóculos *mpl* binoculars

boa *see* bom

boca *f* mouth

bocado: *um bocado* a bit ;
  a portion

boîte *f* nightclub

bola *f* ball
  bola de Berlim doughnut

bolacha *f* biscuit

bolo *m* cake
  bolo-rei ring-shaped fruit
  cake eaten at Christmas

bolsa *f* stock exchange ;
  handbag

bom (boa) good ; fine
  (weather) ; kind
  bom dia good morning
  boa noite good evening ;
  good night
  boa tarde good afternoon

bomba *f* bomb ; pump
  (petrol)

bombeiros *mpl* fire brigade

bondade *f* kindness

boneco(a) doll ; puppet toy

bonito(a) pretty

borbulha *f* spot ; pimple

bordados *mpl* embroidered
  items

borrego *m* lamb

bosque *m* small forest ;
  woodland

bota *f* boot (to wear)

botão m button; bud

braço m arm

branco(a) white
vinho branco white wine

breve brief
em breve soon

brigada de trânsito f traffic police

brincos mpl earrings

brinquedo m toy

britânico(a) British

broa f corn (maize) bread
broas corn (maize) cakes

bronzeador m suntan oil

brushing m blow-dry

bugigangas fpl bric-à-brac

burro(a) m/f ass ; donkey ; stupid person

buscar to look for

bússola f compass

buzinar to toot (car horn)

C

cá here ; in this place

cabana f shack ; hut

cabeça f head

cabedais mpl leather goods

cabeleireiro(a) m/f hairdresser

cabelo m hair

cabide m coat hanger ; peg (for clothes)

cabine f cabin ; booth
cabine telefónica phone box

cabo m knife handle ; electric lead
cabos de emergência jump leads
cabo de reboque tow rope

cabra f goat
queijo de cabra goat's cheese

cabrito m kid (goat)

caça f game (to eat) ; hunting

caçador m hunter

cachorro m hot dog ; puppy

cada each ; every

cadeado m padlock

cadeia f jail ; chain

cadeira f chair
cadeira de bebé high chair ; push chair
cadeira de lona deck chair
cadeira de rodas wheel-chair

cadela f female dog

café m (black) coffee ; café

câimbra f cramp

caír to fall ; to fall over

cais m quay

caixa f cash desk
caixa automática cash machine
caixa do correio letterbox

caixão m coffin

caixote m bin ; wooden box ; container

calar to stop talking ; to keep silent

calçado m footwear

calças *fpl* trousers

calções *mpl* shorts
  calções de banho swimming trunks

calços para travões *mpl* brake pads

calcular to estimate ; to calculate

caldeirada *f* fish stew

caldo *m* stock *(for soup)*
  caldo verde cabbage soup

calor *m* heat

calorífero *m* heater

cama *f* bed
  cama de casal double bed
  cama de bebé cot
  cama de criança child's bed
  cama de solteiro single bed
  a roupa de cama bedding

câmara de ar *f* inner tube

câmara municipal *f* town hall

camarão *m* shrimp

camarote *m* cabin ; box *(theatre)*

cambiar to exchange ; to change money

câmbio *m* exchange rate
  casa de câmbios *f* money exchange shop

camião *m* lorry

caminho *m* path ; way ; route

camioneta *f* coach

camisa *f* shirt
  camisa de noite nightdress

camomila *f* camomile *(tea)*

campainha *f* bell *(on door)*

campismo *m* camping

campo *m* field ; countryside

campo de golfe golf course

camurça *f* suede

cancelar to cancel

canela *f* cinnamon

caneta *f* pen

cano de esgoto *m* drain

canoagem *f* canoeing

cansaço *m* fatigue

cansado(a) tired

cantar to sing

cantina *f* canteen

canto *m* corner

cão *m* dog

capacete *m* crash helmet

capela *f* chapel

capitão *m* captain

capot *m* bonnet *(of car)*

cara *f* face

caracóis *mpl* snails ; curls *(hair)*

caramelos *mpl* toffees

caranguejo *m* crab

carapau *m* horse mackerel

caravana *f* caravan

carburador *m* carburettor

carga *f* refill ; load

caril *m* curry

carioca *m* weak coffee
  carioca de limão lemon infusion

carne *f* meat

carne de borrego spring lamb
carne picada mince
carne de porco pork
carne de vaca beef
carne de vitela veal
carnes frias cold meats
carneiro *m* mutton ; lamb
caro(a) expensive
caro(a) amigo(a) dear friend
caroço *m* kennel ; pip
carregamento *m* cargo ; load
carrinha *f* van
carrinho *m* trolley
carrinho de bebé pram ; carry cot
carro *m* car
carruagem *f* carriage *(railway)*
carruagem-cama sleeper *(railway)*
carruagem-restaurante *f* restaurant car
carta *f* letter
cartão *m* card ; business card
cartão bancário cheque card
cartão de crédito credit card
cartão de embarque boarding card
cartão de felicitações greetings card
cartão garantia cheque card

cartaz *m* poster ; billboard
carteira *f* wallet
carteirista *m* pickpocket
carteiro *m* postman
carvalho *m* oak tree
carvão *m* coal
casa *f* home ; house
casa de banho toilet ; bathroom
casaco *m* jacket ; coat
casado(a) married
casal *m* couple
casamento *m* wedding
caso *m* case
em caso de... in case of...
castanha *f* chestnut
castanhas assadas roast chestnuts
castanhas piladas dried chestnuts
castanho(a) brown
castelo *m* castle
catedral *f* cathedral
causa *f* cause
por causa de because of
cautela take care
cavala *f* mackerel
cavalheiro *m* gentleman
cavalo *m* horse
cave *f* cellar
cebola *f* onion
cedo early
cego(a) *adj* blind
m/f blind man/woman
ceia *f* supper

célebre famous
cem one hundred
cemitério m cemetery
cenoura f carrot
centígrado m centigrade
centímetro m centimetre
cêntimo m cent
cento: *por cento* per cent
centro m centre
  centro da cidade city centre
  centro comercial shopping centre
  centro de saúde health centre
cera f wax
cerâmica f pottery
cérebro m brain
cereja f cherry
certeza f certainty
  ter a certeza to be sure
certificado m certificate
certo(a) right *(correct, accurate)* ; certain
cerveja f beer ; lager
  cerveja preta bitter *(beer)*
cervejaria f beer house
cesto m basket
céu m sky
chá f tea
  chá de limão lemon tea
chamada f telephone call
  chamada gratuita free call
  chamada internacional international call
  chamada pagável no destino reverse charge call

chamar to call
champô m shampoo
chão m floor
chapa de matrícula f number plate
chapéu m hat
  chapéu de sol sunhat
charcutaria f delicatessen
chave f key
  fechar à chave to lock up
chávena f cup
chefe m boss
  chefe de cozinha chef
chega! that's enough!
chegadas fpl arrivals
chegar to arrive
cheio(a) full
cheirar to smell
cheiro m smell
  mau cheiro bad smell
cheque m cheque
  cheque de viagem traveller's cheque
  levantar um cheque to cash a cheque
cherne m black jewfish or grouper
chispalhada f bean stew with pig's trotters
chispe m pig's trotters
chocos mpl cuttlefish
  chocos com tinta cuttlefish cooked in their ink
chouriço m spicy sausage
churrascaria f barbecue restaurant

churrasco *m* barbecue
   no churrasco barbecued
chuva *f* rain
chuveiro *m* shower *(bath)*
Cia. see companhia
cidadão (cidadã) *m/f* citizen
cidade *f* town ; city
cigarro *m* cigarette
cima: em cima de on (top of)
cinco five
cinto *m* belt
   cinto de salvação lifebelt
   cinto de segurança seat belt
cinzento(a) grey
circuito *m* circuit
circular *f* roundabout *(for traffic)*
cirurgia *f* surgery *(operation)*
claro(a) light *(colour)* ; bright
classe *f* class
cliente *m/f* client
clínica *f* clinic
clube *m* club
cobertor *m* blanket
cobrar to cash
cobrir to cover
código *m* code ; dialling code
   código postal postcode
codorniz *f* quail
coelho *m* rabbit
coentro *m* coriander
cofre *m* safe

cogumelo *m* mushroom
coisa *f* thing
cola *f* glue
colar *n* necklace
colar *vb* to stick
colcha *f* bedspread
colchão *m* mattress
colecção *f* collection *(of stamps etc)*
colégio *m* (secondary) school
colete de salvação *m* life jacket
colher *f* spoon
colina *f* hill
collants *mpl* tights
colorau *m* paprika
coluna *f* pillar
   coluna vertebral spine
com with
comandos *mpl* controls
comboio *m* train
combustível *m* fuel
começar to begin ; to start
comer to eat
comida *f* food
comissário de bordo *m* steward ; purser
como as ; how
   como disse? I beg your pardon?
   como está? how are you?
comodidade *f* comfort
companheiro(a) *m/f* live-in partner
companhia (Cia.) *f* company

compartimento m compartment

completar to complete

completo no vacancies *(sign in hotel etc)*

compota f jam

compra f purchase
ir às compras to go shopping

comprar to buy

compreender to understand

comprido(a) long

comprimento m length

comprimido m pill ; tablet

computador m computer

concelho m council

concordar to agree

concorrente m/f candidate

concurso m competition

condução f driving
a carta de condução driving licence

condutor m driver ; chauffeur

conduzir to drive

conferência f conference

conferir to check

congelado(a) frozen *(food)*

congelar to freeze
não congelar do not freeze

conhaque m cognac

conhecer to know *(person, place)*

conselho m advice

consertos mpl repairs

conservar to keep ; to preserve
conservar no frio store in a cold place

constipação f cold *(illness)*

consulado m consulate

consulta f consultation ; appointment

consultório m surgery

consumir antes de... best before... *(label on food)*

conta f account; bill

contador m meter *(electricity, water)*

conter to contain
não contem... does not contain...

contra against

contraceptivo m contraceptive

contrato m contract

convidado(a) m/f guest

convidar to invite ; to ask *(invite)*

convite m invitation

copo m glass *(container)*

cor f colour

coração m heart

cordeiro m lamb

cor-de-laranja orange *(colour)*

cor-de-rosa pink

corpo m body

correia f strap
correia de ventoinha fan belt

correio m post office

C

pelo correio by post
corrente f chain ; current
correr to flow ; to run
(person)
correspondência f mail
corrida f race
corrida de touros bullfight
corridas de cavalos races
cortar to cut ; to cut off
cortar e fazer brushing
to cut and blow-dry
corte m cut
cortiça f cork
costa f shore ; coastline
costela f rib
costeleta f chop *(meat)* ; cutlet
cotovelo m elbow
couro m leather
couve f cabbage
couves-de-Bruxelas
Brussels sprouts
couve-flor f cauliflower
couvert m cover charge
coxia f aisle
cozer to boil
cozido(a) boiled
mal cozido underdone
cozinha f kitchen
cozinhar to cook
cozinheiro(a) m/f cook
cravinhos mpl cloves
cravo m carnation
creme m custard
creme de barbear shaving
cream

creme para bronzear
suntan cream
creme hidratante
moisturizer
creme de limpeza cleansing
cream
criança f child
cru(a) raw
cruz f cross
cruzamento m junction
(crossroads)
cruzar to cross
cruzeiro m cruise
cuecas fpl briefs ; pants
cuidado m care *(caution)*
cumprimento m greeting
cumprimentos regards
cunhado(a) m/f brother-in-
law/sister-in-law
curso m course
curto(a) short
curva f bend ; turning ; curve
curva perigosa dangerous
bend
custar to cost
custo m charge ; cost

D

damasco m apricot
dança f dance
dano m damage
Dão fruity red and white
wines from the north of
Portugal
dar to give

dar prioridade to give way
data f date
  data de nascimento date
  of birth
de of ; from
debaixo de under
decidir to decide
dedo m finger
dedo do pé toe
defeito m flaw
deficiente disabled
degrau m step *(stair)*
deitar-se to lie down
deixar to let *(allow)* ; to leave
  behind
delito m crime
demais too much ; too many
demasia f change *(money)* ;
  excess
demorado(a) late
demorar to delay
dente m tooth
dentes teeth
dentes postiços false teeth
dentista m dentist
dentro inside
depois after(wards)
depósito m deposit *(in bank)*
  depósito de bagagens
  left-luggage
  depósito da gasolina
  petrol tank
depressa quickly
desafio m match ; game
  (sport) ; challenge

desaparecido(a) missing
desapertar to loosen
descafeinado m decaffeinated
descansar to rest
descartável throw-away ;
  disposable
descer to go down
descoberta f discovery
descongelar to defrost
  (food) ; to de-ice
desconhecido(a) m/f
  stranger
desconhecido(a) adj
  unknown
desconto m discount ;
  reduction
desculpe excuse me ; sorry
desejar to desire ; to wish
desembarcar to disembark
desempregado(a)
  unemployed
desenho m design ; drawing
desinchar to go down
  (swelling)
desinfectante m disinfectant
desligado(a) off *(engine, gas)*
desligar to hang up *(phone)* ;
  to switch off *(engine, radio)*
desligue o motor switch off
  your engine
desmaiar to faint
desodorizante m deodorant
despachante m shipper ;
  transport agent
despesa f expense

desporto m sport

destinatário m addressee

desvio m bypass ; detour ; diversion

detergente m detergent

detergente para a louça washing-up liquid

detergente para a roupa washing powder

devagar slowly ; slow down *(sign)*

dever: eu devo I must

deve-me... you owe me...

devolver to give back ; to return

Dezembro m December

dia m day
  dias da semana weekdays
  dia útil working day
  dia de anos birthday

diabético(a) diabetic

diante de in front of *(place)*

diário daily

diarreia f diarrhoea

dieta f diet ; special diet

diferença f difference

difícil difficult

digestão f digestion

diluir to dilute

diminuir to reduce

dínamo m dynamo

dinheiro m money ; cash

direcção f direction ; address ; steering

directo(a) direct

direita f right(-hand side)
  à direita on the right
  para a direita to the right

direito(a) straight ; right(-hand)
  Dto. on right-hand side *(address)*

direitos mpl duty *(tax)* ; rights

dirigir to direct

disco m record *(music, etc)*
  disco de estacionamento parking disk

disponível available

dissolver to dissolve

distância f distance

distrito m district

divã-cama m bed settee

diversões fpl entertainment

divertir-se to enjoy oneself ; to have fun

dívida f debt

divisas fpl foreign currency

dizer to say

dobrada f tripe

dobrado(a) bent

dobro m double

doce adj sweet *(taste)*

doce m dessert ; jam

documentos mpl documents

doente ill ; sick

doer to ache ; to hurt

dólar m dollar

domicílio m residence

domingo m Sunday

dono(a) m/f owner

dona de casa housewife
dor f ache ; pain
dormir to sleep
Douro region producing port
Dto. *see* direito(a)
duche m shower
duplo(a) double
durante during
durar to last
duro(a) hard ; stiff ; tough *(meat)*
dúzia f dozen

E

e and
é he/she/it is ; you are
economizar to save
écrã m screen
edifício m building
edredão m duvet ; quilt
educado(a) polite
eixo de roda m axle
ela she ; her ; it
elas they *(feminine)*
elástico m elastic band
ele he ; him ; it
eles they *(masculine)*
electricista m electrician
eléctrico m tram
electrodomésticos mpl electrical appliances
elevador m lift
em at ; in *(with towns, countries)* ; into

embaixada f embassy
embarcar to board *(ship, plane)*
embarque m embarkation ; time of sailing
embraiagem f clutch
ementa f menu
ementa fixa set menu
emergência f emergency
empregado(a) m/f waiter(ess) ; maid ; attendant *(at petrol station)* ; assistant *(in shop)* ; office worker
emprego m job ; employment
empurrar to push
empurre push *(sign)*
EN *see* estrada
encaracolado(a) curly
encarnado(a) red
encerrado(a) closed
encher to fill up ; to pump up *(tyre)*
enchidos mpl processed meats ; sausages
encomenda f parcel
encontrar to meet ; to find
encontro m date ; meeting
encosta f hill *(slope)*
endereço m address
energia f energy
o corte de energia power cut
enfermeiro(a) m/f nurse
enganar-se to make a mistake

E

engano m mistake
engolir to swallow
   não engolir do not swallow
engraxar to polish (shoes)
enguia f eel
enjoar to be sick
ensinar to teach
ensopado m stew served on slice of bread
enorme big ; huge
entender to understand
entorse f sprain
entrada f entrance ; starter (in meal)
   entrada livre admission free
entrar to go in ; to come in ; to get into (car, etc)
entre among ; between
entregar to deliver
entrevista f interview
enviar to send
enxaqueca f migraine
época f period
equipamento m equipment
equitação f horse riding
erro m mistake
erva f grass ; herb
ervilhas fpl peas
esc. see escudo
escada f ladder ; stairs
escada rolante escalator
escalfado(a) poached (egg)
escape m exhaust
escocês (escocesa) Scottish

Escócia f Scotland
escola f school
escova f brush
escova de dentes toothbrush
escrever to write
escrito: por escrito in writing
escritório m office
escudo (esc.) m escudo (former Portuguese currency)
escuro(a) dark (colour)
escutar to listen to
esferográfica f ballpoint pen
esgotado(a) sold out (tickets) ; exhausted
esgoto m drain
esmalte m enamel
espaço m space
espadarte m swordfish
espalhar to scatter
Espanha f Spain
espanhol m Spanish (language)
espanhol(a) Spanish
espargo m asparagus
esparguete m spaghetti
esparregado m puréed spinach
especialidade f speciality
especiarias fpl spices
espectáculo m show (in theatre etc)
espelho m mirror
   espelho retrovisor driving mirror
esperar to expect ; to hope

esperar por to wait for

espetada *f* kebab

espinafre *m* spinach

esplanada *f* terrace

esposa *f* wife

espumante *m* sparkling wine

espumoso(a) sparkling *(wine)*

Esq. *see* esquerda

esquadra *f* police station

esquentador *m* water heater

esquerda *f* left(-hand side)
à esquerda on the left
Esq. on left(-hand) side
(address)

esqui *m* ski

esquina *f* corner *(outside)*

está he/she/it is ; you are

estação *f* station
estação alta high season
estação baixa low season
estação do ano season
estação de autocarros bus
station
estação de serviço service
station
estação do comboio railway
station

estacionamento *m* parking

estacionar to park *(car)*

estádio *m* stadium

estado *m* state
estado civil marital status

Estados Unidos (EUA) *mpl*
United States

estalagem *f* inn

estância termal *f* spa

estar to be

este/esta *m/f* this
estes/estas *m/f* these

estômago *m* stomach
o mal-estar de estômago
stomach upset

estores *mpl* blinds

estrada *f* road
estrada em mau estado
uneven road surface
estrada nacional (EN)
major road ; national highway
estrada sem saída no
through road
estrada secundária minor
road

estrangeiro(a) *m/f* foreigner

estranho(a) strange

estreito(a) narrow

estudante *m/f* student

estufado(a) braised

etiqueta *f* ticket ; label ;
etiquette

eu I

EUA *see* Estados Unidos

euro *m* euro

europeu (europeia)
European

evitar to avoid

excepto except
excepto aos domingos
Sundays excepted

excesso de bagagem *m*
excess luggage ; excess
baggage

E excursão f excursion ; tour
excursão guiada guided tour

exemplo m example
por exemplo for example

expirar to expire

explicar to explain

exportação f exportation

exportar to export

exposição f exhibition

extintor m fire extinguisher

extremidade f edge ; extremity

F

fábrica f factory

fabricado(a) em ... made in ...

faca f knife

fácil easy

facilidade f facility ; ease

factura f invoice

fado m traditional Portuguese song

faiança f pottery

faisão m pheasant

faixa f lane *(in road)*

falar to speak

falecido(a) deceased

falésias fpl cliffs

falta f lack
falta de corrente power cut

família f family

farinha f flour

farinheira f sausage made with pork fat and flour

farmácia f chemist's
farmácia permanente duty chemist
farmácias de serviço emergency chemists'

faróis mpl headlights

farol m headlight ; light-house

farolim m sidelight

fatia f slice

fato m suit *(man's)*
fato de banho swimsuit
fato de treino tracksuit

favas fpl broad beans

favor m favour
faz favor please
por favor please

fazer to do ; to make

febras de porco fpl thin slices of roast pork

febre f fever
febre dos fenos hay fever
ter febre to have a temperature

fechado closed
fechado Domingos e Feriados closed Sundays and Bank holidays

fechar to shut ; to close

feijão m beans

feijão-verde m French beans

feijoada f bean stew with pork and spicy sausage

feio(a) awful ; ugly

feira f fair *(commercial)* ; market

feito(a) à mão handmade

feliz happy

feriado m public holiday
feriado nacional bank holiday

férias fpl holidays

ferido(a) injured

ferragens fpl ironware

ferro m iron
ferro de engomar iron *(for clothes)*

ferver to boil

festa f party *(celebration)*

Fevereiro m February

fiambre m ham

ficar to stay ; to be ; to remain
ficar bem to suit

ficha f plug *(electrical)* ; registration card *(in hotel, clinic)*
ficha dupla/tripla adaptor *(electrical)*

fígado m liver

figo m fig
figos secos dried figs

fila f row *(line)* ; queue

filete m fillet steak ; tenderloin

filha f daughter

filho m son

filial f branch *(of bank, etc)*

filigranas fpl filigree work

fim m end
fim-de-semana weekend

fio m wire

fita f tape ; ribbon
fita métrica tape measure

flor f flower

floresta f forest

florista f florist

fogão m cooker

fogo m fire
fogos de artifício fireworks

folha f leaf
folha de alumínio aluminium foil
folha de estanho tinfoil

folhados mpl puff pastries

folheto m leaflet

fome f hunger
tenho fome I'm hungry

fonte f fountain ; source

fora out ; outside

força f power *(strength)* ; force

formiga f ant

fornecer to supply

forno m oven

fortaleza f fortress

forte strong

forte f fortress

fósforo m match

fotografia f photograph ; print

fraco(a) weak

fralda f nappy

framboesa f raspberry

F

França f France
francês m French (language)
francês (francesa) French
frango m chicken (young and tender)
  frango assado roast chicken
frase f sentence
freguês (freguesa) m/f customer
frente f front
  em frente de in front of ; opposite
fresco(a) fresh ; cool ; crisp
  sirva fresco serve cool
frigorífico m fridge
frio(a) cold
fritar to fry
frito(a) fried
fronha f pillow case
fronteira f border (frontier)
fruta f fruit
frutaria f fruit shop
fruto m fruit
fuga f leak ; escape
fugir to run away
fumadores mpl smokers
  para não fumadores non-smoking (compartment, etc)
fumar to smoke
  não fumar no smoking
fumo m smoke
funcionar to work (machine)
  não funciona out of order (sign)
funcionário(a) m/f employee ; civil servant

fundo m bottom
fundo(a) deep
furar to pierce
furnas fpl caverns
furto m theft
fusível m fuse
futebol m football

G

gabinete de provas m changing room
gado m cattle
  gado bravo beware – unfenced bulls
gaivota f seagull ; pedal boat
galão m large white coffee ; gallon
galeria f gallery
Gales: o País de Gales Wales
galês (galesa) Welsh
galinha f hen ; chicken
gamba f prawn
ganhar to earn ; to win
ganso m goose
garagem f garage
garantia f guarantee
gare f platform
garfo m fork
garganta f throat
garoto m boy ; small white coffee
garrafa f bottle

garrafão m two or five-litre bottle

gás m gas
  a botija de gás gas cylinder

gasóleo m diesel

gasolina f petrol

gasosa f fizzy sweetened water

gastar to spend

gaveta f drawer

gelado m ice cream ; ice lolly

gelar to freeze

gelataria f ice cream parlour

geleia f jelly

gelo m ice

gémeo(a) m/f twin

género m kind ; type
  o meu género de filme my kind of film

gengibre m ginger

gengivas fpl gums

genro m son-in-law

gente f people
  toda a gente everybody

geral f gallery (in theatre)

geral adj general
  em geral generally

geralmente usually

gerente m manager

ginjinha f morello cherry liqueur

gira-discos m record player

girassol m sunflower

gola f collar

golfe m golf

o taco de golfe golf club (stick)

gordo(a) fat

gorjeta f tip (to waiter, etc)

gostar de to like

gosto m taste

governo m government

Grã-Bretanha f Britain

grama m gramme

grande big ; large ; great

grão m chickpeas

grátis free (costing nothing)

gravador m tape recorder

gravata f tie

grávida pregnant

gravura f print (picture)

grelhado(a) grilled

greve f strike (industrial)
  em greve on strike

gripe f flu

groselha f (red)currant

grosso(a) thick

grupo m group ; party (group)
  grupo sanguíneo blood group

grutas fpl caves

guarda m/f police officer

guarda-chuva m umbrella

guarda-lamas m mudguard

guardanapo m napkin

guardar to keep ; to watch over

guarda-sol m sunshade

guia m/f guide

guiché m window (at post office, bank)

guisado m stew

guitarra f guitar

há there is ; there are

habitação f residence ; home

habitar to reside

história f history ; story

hoje today

homem m man
o wc dos Homens gents' toilet

hora f hour ; time (by the clock)
hora de chegada time of arrival
hora de partida departure time
hora de ponta rush hour

horário m timetable

hortelã f mint (herb)

hortelã-pimenta f peppermint

hóspede m/f guest

hospedeira f hostess
hospedeira de bordo flight attendant

iate m yacht

icterícia f jaundice

ida f visit ; trip
ida e volta return trip

idade f age

identificação f identification

idosos mpl the elderly ; old people

ignição f ignition ; starter (in car)

igreja f church

igual equal ; the same as

ilha f island

impedir to prevent

impedido(a) engaged (phone)

imperial m draught beer

impermeável m raincoat
adj waterproof

importação f importation

importância f importance ; amount (money)

importante important

imposto m tax ; duty
impostos duty ; tax

impressão digital f fingerprint

impresso m form (to fill in)

imprevisto(a) unexpected

impulso m unit of charge (for phone) ; impulse

incêndio m fire

inchado(a) swollen

incluído(a) included

incomodar to disturb
não incomodar do not disturb

indicativo m dialling code

indigestão f indigestion

infecção f infection
infeccioso(a) infectious *(illness)*
inflamação f inflammation
informação f information
infracção f offence
Inglaterra f England
inglês m English *(language)*
inglês (inglesa) English
iniciais fpl initials
iniciar to begin
início m beginning
inquilino m tenant
inscrever to register
insecto m insect
insolação f heatstroke ; sunstroke
instalações fpl facilities
instituto m institute
insuflável inflatable
inteiro(a) whole
interdito(a) forbidden
interessante interesting
interior inside
interno(a) internal
intérprete m/f interpreter
interruptor m switch
intervalo m interval *(in theatre)*
intestinos mpl bowels
intoxicação f food poisoning
introduzir to introduce
inundação f flood
inverno m winter

iogurte m yoghurt
ir to go
Irlanda f Ireland
  a Irlanda do Norte Northern Ireland
irlandês (irlandesa) Irish
irmã f sister
irmão m brother
iscas fpl marinated pig's liver with potatoes
isqueiro m lighter
isso that
isto this
Itália f Italy
italiano(a) Italian
itinerário m route ; itinerary
IVA m VAT

J

já already ; now
jamais never
Janeiro m January
janela f window
jantar m dinner ; evening meal
jardim m garden
joalharia f jeweller's ; jewellery
joelho m knee
jogar to play
jogo m match ; game; play
jóia f jewel
jornal m newspaper
jovem young

J

judeu (judia) *m/f* Jew ; Jewish
juiz(a) *m/f* judge
julgamento *m* verdict ; sentence
Julho *m* July
Junho *m* June
juntar to join
junto near
justiça *f* justice
juventude *f* youth

K

kg. *see* quilo(grama)

L

lã *f* wool
lábio *m* lip
laço *m* bow (ribbon, string) ; bow-tie
lado *m* side
ao lado de next to
ladrão (ladra) *m/f* thief
lagarto *m* lizard
lago *m* lake
lagosta *f* lobster
lagostim *m* king prawn
lâminas de barbear *fpl* razor blades
lâmpada *f* light bulb
lampreia *f* lamprey
lançar to throw
lanchar to go for a snack

lanche *m* light mid-afternoon snack
lápis *m* pencil
lápis de cera crayons *(wax)*
lar *m* home
laranja *f* orange
o doce de laranja marmalade
largo *m* small square
largo(a) broad ; loose *(clothes)* ; wide
largura *f* width
lata *f* tin ; can *(of food)*
latão *m* brass
lavabo *m* lavatory ; toilet
lava-louça *m* sink
lavandaria *f* laundry
lavandaria automática launderette
lavandaria a seco dry-cleaner's
lavar to wash *(clothes, etc)*
lavar a louça to wash up
lavar à mão to handwash
lavável washable
lebre *f* hare
legumes *mpl* vegetables
lei *f* law
leilão *m* auction
leitão *m* sucking pig
leite *m* milk
com leite white *(coffee)*
leite desnatado skimmed milk
leite evaporado evaporated milk

leite gordo full-cream milk
leite magro skimmed milk
leite meio-gordo semi-skimmed milk
lembranças *fpl* souvenirs
lembrar-se to remember
leme *m* rudder ; helm
lenço *m* handkerchief ; tissue
lençol *m* sheet
lente *f* lens
lentes de contacto contact lenses
lento(a) slow
leque *m* fan (hand-held)
ler to read
leste *m* east
letra *f* letter (of alphabet)
letra maiúscula capital letter
levantar to draw (money) ; to lift
levantar-se to stand up ; get up (from bed)
levar to take ; to carry
leve light (not heavy)
libra *f* pound
libras esterlinas pounds sterling
lição *f* lesson
licença *f* permit
liceu *m* secondary school
licor *m* liqueur
ligação *f* connection (trains, etc)
ligado(a) on (engine, gas, etc)
ligeiro(a) light

lima *f* lime (fruit)
lima *f* file
lima das unhas nail file
limão *m* lemon
limite *m* limit
limite de velocidade speed limit
limonada *f* lemonade
limpar to wipe ; to clean
limpeza *f* cleaning
limpeza a seco dry-cleaning
limpo(a) clean
língua *f* language ; tongue
linguado *m* sole (fish)
linguiça *f* narrow spicy pork sausage
linha *f* line ; thread ; platform (railway)
linho *m* linen
liquidação *f* (clearance) sale
Lisboa (Lx) Lisbon
liso(a) smooth ; straight
lista *f* list
lista de preços price list
lista telefónica telephone directory
litro *m* litre
livraria *f* bookshop
livre free ; vacant ; for hire
livro *m* book
lixívia *f* bleach
lixo *m* rubbish
loção *f* lotion
loja *f* shop
lombo *m* loin (cut of meat)

Londres London
longe far
  é longe? is it far?
longo(a) long
lotaria f lottery
louça f dishes ; crockery
louro(a) fair (hair)
louro m bay leaf (herb)
lua f moon
lua-de-mel f honeymoon
lugar m seat (theatre) ; place
lulas fpl squid
luvas fpl gloves
luxo m luxury
luz f light
  luzes de presença side-
  lights
  luzes de perigo hazard
  lights
Lx see Lisboa

M. underground (metro)
má see mau
maçã f apple
maçaroca f corn on the cob
macho m male (animal)
macio(a) soft ; smooth
maço m packet (of cigarettes)
Madeira f Madeira
madeira f wood
Madeira m Madeira wine
madrugada f early morning
maduro(a) ripe

mãe f mother
magro(a) thin
Maio m May
maior larger
  a maior parte de the
  majority of
mais more
  o/a mais the most
mal wrong ; evil
mala f suitcase ; bag ; trunk
malagueta f chilli
mal-entendido m misunderstanding
mal-estar m discomfort
mancha f stain
mandar to send ; to order
maneira f way (method)
manga f sleeve ; mango
manhã f morning
manteiga f butter
manter to keep ; to maintain
mão f hand
mapa m map
  mapa das estradas road
  map
  mapa das ruas street plan
máquina f machine
  máquina fotográfica
  camera
mar m sea
maracujá m passion fruit
marca f brand ; mark
marcação f booking ; dialling
marcar to dial (phone) ;
  to mark

marcha-atrás f reverse (gear)

Março m March

marco do correio m pillar box

maré f tide
maré alta high tide
maré baixa low tide

marfim m ivory

marido m husband

marisco m seafood ; shellfish

marmelada f quince jam

marmelo m quince

mármore m marble (substance)

Marrocos Morocco

marroquinaria f leather goods

mas but

massa f dough
massas pasta
massa folhada puff pastry

matrícula f number plate

mau (má) bad ; evil

máximo(a) maximum

mazagrã m iced coffee and lemon

me me

mecânico m mechanic

média f average

medicamento m medicine

médico(a) m/f doctor

medida f measure ; size

médio(a) medium

medusa f jellyfish

meia f stocking ; half

meia-hora f half-hour

meia-noite f midnight

meio m middle
no meio de in the middle of

meio(a) half
meia garrafa a half bottle
meia de leite cup of milky coffee (half milk, half coffee)
meia pensão half board

meio-dia m midday ; noon

meio-seco medium sweet (wine)

mel m honey

melancia f watermelon

melão m melon

melhor better
o/a melhor the best

meloa f small round melon

menina f Miss ; girl

menino m boy

menor smaller ; minor (underage)

menos least ; less

mensagem f message

mensal monthly

menstruação f period (menstruation)

mercado m market

mercearia f grocer's

merengue m meringue

mês m month

mesa f table

mesmo(a) same

mesquita f mosque

metade f half
  pela metade do preço
  half-price
meter to put in
metro m metre ; underground
  (rail)
metropolitano m tube
  (underground)
meu (minha) my ; mine
mexer to move
  não mexer do not touch
mexilhão m mussel
migas à alentejana bread
  dish with pork meats
mil thousand
milhão m million
milho m maize ; corn
mim me
minha see meu
mínimo(a) minimum
minúsculo(a) tiny
missa f Mass (church service)
mobília f furniture
mochila f backpack ; rucksack
moda f fashion
moeda f coin ; currency
moído(a) ground (coffee, etc)
moinho m windmill
  moinho de café coffee
  grinder
mola f peg ; spring (coiled
  metal)
molhado(a) wet
molho m sauce ; gravy
momento m moment

montanha f mountain
montante m amount (total)
montra f shop window
morada f address
moradia f villa
morango m strawberry
morar to live ; to reside
morcela f black pudding
mordedura f bite (animal)
morder to bite
  fui mordido(a) por um cão
  I was bitten by a dog
moreno(a) tanned ; dark-
  skinned
morrer to die
mortadela f cold meat
mosaicos mpl mosaic tiles
mosca f fly (insect)
mostarda f mustard
mosteiro m monastery
mostrador m dial ; glass
  counter
mostrar to show
motocicleta f motorbike
motor m engine ; motor
  motor de arranque starter
  motor
motorista m driver
motorizada f motorbike
muçulmano(a) m/f Muslim
mudar to change
  mudar-se to move house
muito very ; much ; quite
  (rather)

muitos(as) a lot (of) ; many ; plenty (of)
mulher *f* female ; woman ; wife
multa *f* fine
multidão *f* crowd
mundial worldwide
mundo *m* world
muralhas *fpl* ramparts
muro *m* wall
museu *m* museum
música *f* music

N

nabo *m* turnip
nacional national
nacionalidade *f* nationality ; citizenship
nada nothing
 nada a declarar nothing to declare
nadar to swim
namorada *f* girlfriend
namorado *m* boyfriend
não no ; not
nariz *m* nose
nascer to be born
nascimento *m* birth
nata *f* cream
natação *f* swimming
Natal *m* Christmas
naturalidade *f* place of birth
natureza *f* nature
navio *m* ship

neblina *f* mist
negar to refuse
negativo(a) negative
negócios *mpl* business
negro(a) black
nem: *nem... nem...* neither... nor...
nenhum(a) none
neta *f* granddaughter
neto *m* grandson
neve *f* snow
nevoeiro *m* fog
ninguém nobody
nível *m* level
nó *m* knot
 nó rodoviário motorway junction
No. see número
nocivo(a) harmful
nódoa *f* stain
noite *f* evening ; night
 à noite in the evening/ at night
 boa noite good evening/night
noivo(a) *adj* engaged (to be married)
 m/f bride/groom; fiancé(e)
nome *m* name
 nome próprio first name
nora *f* daughter-in-law
nordeste *m* north east
normalmente usually
noroeste *m* north west
norte *m* north

nós we ; us
nosso(a) our
nota f note ; banknote
notar to notice
notícia f piece of news
Nova Zelândia f New Zealand
Novembro m November
novo(a) new ; young ; recent
noz f nut ; walnut
noz-moscada f nutmeg
nu(a) naked
nublado(a) dull *(weather)* ; cloudy
número (No.) m number ; size *(of clothes, shoes)*
nunca never
nuvem f cloud

O

o the *(masculine)*
objeto m object
  objetos perdidos lost property
obra-prima f masterpiece
obras fpl roadworks ; repairs
obrigado(a) thank you
oceano m ocean
ocidental western
oculista m optician
óculos mpl glasses
  óculos de sol sunglasses
ocupado(a) engaged *(phone, toilet)*
oeste m west

oferecer to offer ; to give something
  ofereço este livro I give this book
oferta f offer ; gift
olá hello
olaria f pottery
óleo m oil
  óleo dos travões brake fluid
oleoso(a) greasy ; oily
olhar para/por to look at/after
olho m eye
onda f wave *(on sea)*
onde where
ontem yesterday
óptimo(a) excellent
ora now ; well now
orçamento m budget
ordem f order
ordenado m wage
orelha f ear
organizado(a) organized
orquídea f orchid
osso m bone
ostra f oyster
ou or
ourivesaria e joalharia goldsmith's and jeweller's
ouro m gold
  de ouro gold *(made of gold)*
outono m autumn
outro(a) other
  outra vez again
Outubro m October

ouvido m ear
ouvir to hear ; to listen (to)
ovelha f sheep
ovo m egg
oxigénio m oxygen

P

padaria f baker's
pagamento m payment
  pagamento a pronto cash payment
pagar to pay
página f page
  páginas amarelas Yellow Pages
pago(a) paid
pai m father
  pais parents
país m country
palácio m palace
palavra f word
pálido(a) pale
palito m toothpick
panado(a) fried in egg and breadcrumbs
pane f breakdown (car)
panela f pan ; pot
pano m cloth
pão m bread ; loaf
  pão de centeio rye bread
  pão integral wholemeal bread
  pão de ló sponge cake
  pão de milho maize bread
  pão torrado toasted bread

pão de trigo wheat bread
papel m paper
  papel de carta writing paper
  papel de embrulho wrapping paper
  papel higiénico toilet paper
papelaria f stationer's
papo-seco m roll (of bread)
par m pair ; couple
para for ; towards ; to
parabéns mpl congratulations ; happy birthday
pára-brisas f windscreen
pára-choques m bumper
parafuso m screw
paragem f stop (for bus, etc)
parar to stop
pare stop (sign)
  pare ao sinal vermelho stop when lights are red
parede f wall
parente m/f relation (family)
pargo m sea bream
parque m park
parquímetro m parking meter
parte f part
  parte de frente front
  parte de trás back
particular private
partidas fpl departures
partir to break ; to leave
  a partir de... from...
Páscoa f Easter
passa f raisin

passadeira f zebra crossing

passado m the past

passado(a): *mal passado(a)* rare (steak)

bem passado(a) well done (steak)

passageiro m passenger

passagem f fare ; crossing
passagem de nível level-crossing
passagem de peões pedestrian crossing
passagem proibida no right of way
passagem subterrânea underpass

passaporte m passport

passar to pass ; to go by

pássaro m bird

passatempos mpl hobbies

passe m season ticket

passe go (when crossing road) ; walk

passear to go for a walk

passeio m walk ; pavement

pasta f paste
pasta dentífrica toothpaste

pastéis mpl pastries

pastel m pie ; pastry (cake)
pastel folhado puff pastry

pastelaria f pastries ; café ; cake shop

pastilha f pastille
pastilha elástica chewing gum
pastilhas para a garganta throat lozenges

pataniscas fpl salted cod fritters

patinagem f skating (ice) ; roller-skating

patinar to skate

pátio m courtyard

pato m duck

pau m stick

pé m foot
a pé on foot

peão m pedestrian

peça f part ; play
peças e acessórios spares and accessories

peça... ask for...

pediatra m/f paediatrician

pedir to ask
pedir alguma coisa to ask for something
pedir emprestado(a) to borrow

peito m breast ; chest

peixaria f fishmonger's

peixe m fish
peixe congelado frozen fish

peixe-espada m scabbard fish

pele f fur ; skin

película f film (for camera)

pensão m guesthouse
pensão completa full board
pensão residencial boarding house
meia pensão half board

pensar to think

penso m sticking plaster
  penso higiénico sanitary
  towel
pente m comb
peões mpl pedestrians
pepino m cucumber
  pepino de conserva
  gherkin
pequeno(a) little ; small
  pequeno-almoço breakfast
pera f pear
  pera abacate avocado pear
percebes mpl edible
  barnacles
percurso m route
perdão I beg your pardon ;
  I'm sorry
perder to lose ; to miss
  (train, etc)
perdido(a) lost
  perdidos e achados lost
  and found ; lost property
perdiz f partridge
pergunta f question
  fazer uma pergunta to ask
  a question
perigo m danger
  perigo de incêndio fire
  hazard
perigoso(a) dangerous
permitir to allow
perna f leg
pérola f pearl
pertencer: *pertencer a*
  to belong to
perto de near

perú m turkey
pesado(a) heavy
pêsames mpl condolences
pesar to weigh
pesca f fishing
pescada f hake
pescadinhas fpl whiting
pescar to fish
peso m weight
pêssego m peach
pessoa f person
pessoal adj personal
pessoal m staff ; personnel
petiscos mpl snacks ; titbits
petróleo m oil
peúgas fpl socks
picada f sting
picado(a) chopped ; minced
picante spicy
picar to sting
  uma picada de mosquito
  a mosquito bite
pilha f pile ; battery *(for torch)*
pílula f the pill
pimenta f pepper
pimento m pepper *(vegetable)*
pintar to paint
pintura f painting
pior worse
piripiri m hot chilli dressing
pisca-pisca m indicator *(on
  car)*
piscina f swimming pool
  piscina aberta outdoor
  swimming pool

piscina para crianças paddling pool

piso m floor ; level ; surface
piso escorregadio slippery surface

pista f track ; runway

planta f plant ; map

plataforma f platform

plateia f stalls *(in theatre)*

platinados fpl points *(in car)*

pneu m tyre
a pressão dos pneus tyre pressure

pó m dust ; powder
pó de talco talcum powder

poço m well

poder to be able

polegar m thumb

polícia f police

polícia m policeman ; police officer
mulher-polícia f police-woman

poluição f pollution

polvo m octopus

pomada f ointment
pomada para o calçado shoe polish

pomar m orchard

pombo m pigeon

ponte f bridge

população f population

por by *(through)*
por aqui/por ali this/that way
por hora per hour

por pessoa per person

pôr to put

porção f portion

porco m pig ; pork

por favor please

pormenores mpl details

porque because

porquê why

porta f door
a porta No. ... gate number ...

porta-bagagens m boot *(of car)* ; luggage rack

porta-chaves m key ring

portagem f motorway toll

porta-moedas m purse

porteiro m porter

porto m harbour

Porto : *o Porto* Oporto
o vinho do Porto Port wine

português m Portuguese *(language)*

português (portuguesa) Portuguese

posologia f dose *(medicine)*

postal m postcard

posto m post ; job
posto clínico first aid post
posto de socorros first aid centre

pouco(a) little

pousada f state-run hotel ; inn

povo m people

povoação f small village

praça f square *(in town)* ; market

236

praça de táxis taxi rank
praça de touros bullring
praia f beach ; seaside
prata f silver
prateleira f shelf
praticar to practise
prato m dish ; plate ; course of meal
prato da casa speciality of the house
prato do dia today's special
prazer m pleasure
prazer em conhecê-lo pleased to meet you
precipício m cliff ; precipice
precisar to need
preciso(a): *é preciso* it is necessary
preço m price
preços de ocasião bargain prices
preços reduzidos reduced prices
preencher to fill in
preferir to prefer
prejuízo m damage
prémio m prize
prenda f gift
preocupado(a) worried
preparado(a) ready
presente m gift ; present
preservativo m condom
pressão f pressure
pressão dos pneus tyre pressure
presunto m cured ham

preto(a) black
primavera f spring *(season)*
primeiro(a) first
primeiro andar first floor
de primeira classe first-class
primo(a) m/f cousin
princípio m beginning
prioridade f priority
prioridade à direita give way to the right
prisão f prison
ter prisão de ventre to be constipated
privado(a) *adj* private
procurar to look for
produto m product ; proceeds
produtos alimentares foodstuffs
professor(a) m/f teacher
profissão f profession
profissão, idade, nome profession, age and name
profundidade f depth
profundo(a) deep
proibido(a) forbidden
proibida a entrada no entry
proibido estacionar no parking
proibido fumar no smoking
proibida a paragem no stopping
proibida a passagem no access
proibido pisar a relva do not walk on the grass

proibido tomar banho no bathing
promoção f special offer ; promotion *(at work)*
pronto(a) ready
propriedade f estate *(property)*
proprietário(a) m/f owner
prospecto m pamphlet
prótese dentária f dental fittings
provar to taste ; to try on
provisório(a) temporary
próximo(a) near ; next
público m audience ; public
pudim m pudding
pulmão m lung
pulseira f bracelet ; wrist strap
pulso m wrist
pura lã f pure wool
purificador do ar m air freshener
puxar to pull
puxe pull *(sign)*

quadro m picture ; painting
qual which
qualidade f quality
quando when
quantidade f quantity
quanto(a) how much
quantos(as)? how many?
quanto tempo? how long? *(time)*

quarta-feira f Wednesday
quarto m room ; bedroom
quarto de banho bathroom
quarto com duas camas twin-bedded room
quarto de casal double room
quarto individual single room
quarto fourth ; quarter
um quarto de hora a quarter of an hour
que what
o que é? what is it?
quebra-mar m pier
quebrar to break
queda f fall
queijada f cheesecake
queijo m cheese
queimadura f burn
queimadura do sol sunburn *(painful)*
queixa f complaint
quero apresentar uma queixa I want to make a complaint
quem who
quente *adj* hot
querer to want ; to wish
quilo(grama) (kg.) m kilo
quilómetro m kilometre
quinta f farm
quinta-feira f Thursday
quiosque m kiosk ; news-stand
quotidiano(a) daily

R

R. *see* rua
rã *f* frog
rabanete *m* radish
rádio *m* radio
radiografia *f* X-ray
raia *f* skate *(fish)*
raiva *f* rabies
raíz *f* root
rapariga *f* girl
rapaz *m* boy
rápido *m* express *(train)*
rápido(a) fast
raposa *f* fox
raqueta *f* racquet ; bat
(for table tennis)
rasgar to tear
ratazana *f* rat
rato *m* mouse
R/C *see* rés-do-chão
real real ; royal
reboques *mpl* breakdown
service
rebuçado *m* boiled sweet
recado *m* message
dar um recado to give a
message
receber to receive
receita *f* recipe
receita médica prescription
recepção *f* reception
recibo *m* receipt
reclamação *f* protest ; official
complaint

recolher to collect
recolha de bagagem
baggage reclaim
recomendar to recommend
recompensa *f* reward
reconhecer to recognize
recordação *f* souvenir
recordar-se to remember
rede *f* net
redução *f* reduction ; discount
reembolsar to reimburse
refeição *f* meal
reformado(a) *m/f* senior
citizen ; retired
região *f* area *(region)*
região demarcada official
wine-producing region
registar to register
regulamentos *mpl* regulations
Reino Unido *m* United
Kingdom
relógio *m* watch ; clock
relva *f* grass
não pisar a relva keep off
grass
remédio *m* medicine ; remedy
remetente *m* sender
renda *f* lace ; rent
rendas de bilros hand-
woven lacework
reparação *f* repair
reparar to fix ; to repair
repartição *f* state department
repetir to repeat
rés-do-chão (R/C) *m* ground
floor

reserva de lugar seat reservation
reservado(a) reserved
reservar to book ; to reserve
residência f boarding house ; residence
residir to live
respirar to breathe
responder to answer ; to reply
resposta f answer
restaurante m restaurant
retalho m oddment
retrosaria f haberdashery
reunião f meeting
revelar to develop (photos) ; to reveal
revisor(a) m/f ticket collector
revista f magazine
ribeiro m stream
rins mpl kidneys
rio m river
rissol m rissole
rochas fpl rocks
roda f wheel
rodovia f highway
rolha f cork
rolo m cartridge (for camera) ; roll
rosé adj rosé (wine)
rosto m face
roteiro m guidebook
roubar to steal ; to rob
roupa f clothes

roupa de cama bedding
roupa interior underwear
roxo(a) purple
rua (R.) f street
rubéola f German measles
ruído m noise
ruptura f break

S

S. see São
sábado m Saturday
sabão m soap
sabão em flocos soapflakes
sabão em pó soap powder
saber to know (fact)
sabonete m toilet soap
sabor m flavour ; taste
saca-rolhas m corkscrew
saco m bag ; handbag
saco cama sleeping bag
saco do lixo bin bag
safio m sea eel
saia f skirt
saída f exit ; way out
saídas departures
sair to go out ; to come out
sal m salt
sala f room
sala de chá tea room ; café
sala de embarque airport lounge
sala de espera waiting room
sala de estar living room ; lounge

sala de jantar dining room
salada f salad
salão m hall (for concerts, etc)
salário m wage ; salary
saldo m sale
salgado(a) salty
salmão m salmon
  salmão fumado smoked salmon
salmonete m red mullet
salpicão m spicy sausage
salsa f parsley
salsicha f sausage
salsicharia f delicatessen
salteado(a) sautéed
salvar to rescue ; to save (rescue)
sandálias fpl sandals
sandes f sandwich
  sandes de fiambre ham sandwich
sanduíche f sandwich
sangue m blood
sanitários mpl toilets
Santo(a) (Sto./Sta.) m/f saint
santo(a) holy
santola f spider crab
São (S.) m Saint
sapataria f shoe shop
sapateira f type of crab
sapateiro m shoemaker ; cobbler
sapato m shoe
saquinhos de chá mpl tea bags

sarampo m measles
sardinha f sardine
satisfeito(a) happy ; satisfied
saudação f greeting
saudável healthy
saúde f health
  saúde! cheers!
se if ; whether
  se faz favor (SFF) please
sé f cathedral
secador m dryer
secar to dry ; to drain (tank)
secção f department
seco(a) dry
secretária f desk
secretário(a) m/f secretary
século m century
seda f silk
sede f thirst
  ter sede to be thirsty
segredo m secret
seguinte following
seguir to follow
  seguir pela direita keep to your right
  seguir pela esquerda keep to your left
segunda-feira f Monday
segundo m second (time)
segundo(a) second
  segundo andar second floor
  de segunda classe second-class
  em segunda mão second-hand

segurança *f* safety
segurar to hold
seguro *m* insurance
  seguro contra terceiros third party insurance
  seguro contra todos os riscos comprehensive insurance
seguro de viagem travel insurance
seguro(a) safe ; reliable
seio *m* breast
selecção *f* selection
selo *m* stamp
selvagem wild
sem without
semáforos *mpl* traffic lights
semana *f* week
  para a semana next week
  na semana passada last week
  por semana weekly (rate, etc)
semanal weekly
sempre always
senhor *m* sir ; gentleman ; you
  Senhor Mr
senhora *f* lady ; madam ; you
  Senhora Mrs, Ms
  a casa de banho das Senhoras ladies' toilet
senhorio(a) *m/f* landlord/lady
sentar-se to sit (down)
sentido *m* sense ; meaning
  sentido único one-way street
sentir to feel

ser to be
serviço *m* service ; cover charge
  serviço de quartos room service
  serviço (não) incluído service (not) included
  serviço permanente 24-hour service
servir to serve
  pode servir? can you serve?
sessão *f* session ; performance
Setembro *m* September
seu (sua) his ; her ; your
sexta-feira *f* Friday
SFF *see* se faz favor
shampô *m* shampoo
significar to mean
sim yes
simpático(a) nice ; friendly
sinal *m* signal ; deposit (part payment)
  sinal de impedido engaged tone
  sinal de marcação dialling tone
  sinal de trânsito road sign
sino *m* bell
sítio *m* place ; spot
situado(a) situated
só only ; alone
sobre over ; on top of
  sobre o mar overlooking the sea
sobrecarga *f* excess load ; surcharge

sobremesa f dessert
sobressalente spare
  a roda sobressalente spare
  wheel
sobretudo m overcoat *(man's)*
sócio m member ; partner
socorro m help ; assistance
  socorro 115 emergency
  service 999
  socorros e sinistrados
  accidents and emergencies
sogro(a) m/f father-in-law/
  mother-in-law
sol m sun
solteiro(a) single *(not married)*
solúvel soluble
som m sound
soma f amount *(sum)*
sombra f shadow *(in sun)*
sono m sleep
sopa f soup
  sopa à alentejana garlic,
  coriander and bread soup
  topped with poached egg
sorte f luck ; fortune
  boa sorte good luck
sorvete m water ice ; sorbet
sótão m attic
soutien m bra
sua see seu
subida f rise ; ascent
subir to go up
sudeste m south east
sudoeste m south west
suficiente enough

sujo(a) dirty
sul m south
sumo m juice
suor m sweat
supermercado m super-
  market
supositório m suppository
surdo(a) deaf
surf m surfing

T

tabacaria f tobacconist's ;
  newsagent
tabaco m tobacco
tabela f list ; table
taberna f wine bar
tabuleiro m tray
taça f cup
tacão m heel
talão m voucher
talco m talc
talheres mpl cutlery
talho m butcher's
talvez perhaps
tamanho m size
também also ; too
tamboril m monkfish
tampa f lid ; cover ; top ; cap
tampões mpl tampons
tanto(a) so much
tão so
  isto é tão bonito this is so
  beautiful
tapete m carpet ; rug

tapetes e carpetes rugs and carpets

tarde f afternoon
  boa tarde good afternoon

tarde adverb late *(in the day)*

tarifa f charge ; rate
  tarifas de portagem toll charges

tarte f tart
  tarte de amêndoa almond tart

tasca f tavern ; wine bar ; restaurant

taxa f fee ; rate
  taxa de juro interest rate
  taxa normal peak-time rate
  taxa reduzida off-peak rate

teatro m theatre

tecido m fabric ; tissue ; cloth

tejadilho m roof rack

telecomandado(a) remote-controlled

teleférico m cable car

telefone m telephone

telefonista f operator

televisão f television

televisor m television set

telhado m roof

temperatura f temperature

tempero m dressing *(for salad)* ; seasoning

tempestade f storm

tempo m weather ; time *(duration)*
  tempo inteiro full-time
  tempo parcial part-time

temporada f season

temporário(a) temporary

tenda f tent

ténis m tennis

tenro(a) tender *(meat)*

tensão f tension
  tensão arterial alta/baixa high/low blood pressure

tentar to try

ter to have

terça-feira f Tuesday

terceiro(a) third
  terceiro andar third floor
  para a terceira idade for the elderly

termas fpl spa

termo m (vacuum) flask

termómetro m thermometer

terra f earth ; ground

terraço m veranda ; balcony

terramoto m earthquake

terreno m ground ; land

tesoura f scissors

tesouro m treasure

testemunha f witness

tímido(a) shy

tingir to dye

tinta f ink ; paint

tinturaria f dry-cleaner's

tio(a) m/f uncle/aunt

tipo m sort ; kind

tira-nódoas m stain remover

tirar to remove ; to take out

tiro m shot

toalha f towel

toalhete de rosto m face cloth ; flannel (for washing)

toalhetes refrescantes mpl baby wipes

tocar to touch ; to ring ; to play
tocar piano to play the piano

todo(a) all ; the whole
toda a gente everyone
todas as coisas everything
em toda a parte everywhere

toldo f sunshade (on beach)

tomada f socket ; power point

tomar to take
tomar banho to bathe ;
to have a bath
tomar antes de se deitar take before going to bed
tomar em jejum take on an empty stomach
tomar... vezes ao dia take... times a day

tomate m tomato

tonelada f ton

toranja f grapefruit

torcer to twist ; to turn

torneio m tournament

torneira f tap

tornozelo m ankle

torrada f toast

torre f tower

torto(a) twisted

tosse f cough

tosta f toasted sandwich
tosta de queijo toasted cheese sandwich

totobola m football pools

totoloto m lottery

toucinho m bacon

tourada f bullfight

touro m bull

tóxico(a) poisonous ; toxic

trabalhar to work (person)

trabalho m work
trabalhos na estrada roadworks

tradução f translation

traduzir to translate

tráfego m traffic

tranquilo(a) calm ; quiet

transferir to transfer

trânsito m traffic
trânsito condicionado restricted traffic
trânsito proibido no entry

transpiração f perspiration ; sweat

transportar to transport ; to carry

transtorno m upset ; inconvenience

trás: *para trás* backwards
no banco de trás on the back seat (car)
a parte de trás the back

tratamento m treatment

tratar de to treat ; to deal with

travar to brake

travessa f lane (in town) ;
serving dish

travessia f crossing (voyage)

travões mpl brakes

trazer to bring ; to carry

triângulo m warning triangle

tribunal m court

trigo m wheat

triste sad

trocar to exchange ;
to change

troco m change (money)
trocos small change

trovoada f thunderstorm

truta f trout

tu you (informal)

tubo m exhaust pipe ; tube ;
hose

tudo everything ; all

turista m/f tourist

U

úlcera f ulcer

ultimamente lately ; recently

último(a) last ; latest

ultrapassar to overtake ;
to pass

um(a) a ; an ; one

unha f nail (on finger, toe)

único(a) single ; unique

unidade f unit (hi-fi, etc) ; unity

unir to join

universidade f university ;
college

urgência f urgency

urtiga f nettle

urze f heather

urso(a) m/f bear

usado(a) used (car, etc)

usar to use ; to wear

uso m use
uso externo for external use

útil useful

utilização f use

utilizar to use

uva f grape

V

vaca f cow

vacina f vaccination

vagão m railway carriage ;
coach

vagão-restaurante m buffet
car

vagar to be vacant

vagas vacancies

vale m valley

valer to be worth

validação: *validação de
bilhetes* validate tickets

válido(a) valid
válido(a) até... valid until...

valor m value

válvula f valve ; tap

vapor m steam

varanda f veranda ; balcony

variado(a) varied

varicela f chickenpox

vários(as) several

vazio(a) empty

vegetal *m* vegetable
  vegetais congelados frozen vegetables

vegetariano(a) vegetarian

veículo *m* vehicle
  veículos pesados heavy goods vehicles

vela *f* sail ; sailing

vela *f* spark plug ; candle

velho(a) old

velocidade *f* gear ; speed
  velocidade limitada speed limit in force

velocímetro *m* speedometer

vencimento *m* wage ; expiry date

venda *f* sale *(in general)*
  venda proibida not for public sale
  vendas e reparações sales and repairs

vender to sell
  vende-se for sale

veneno *m* poison

vento *m* wind

ventoinha *f* fan *(electric)*

ver to see ; to look at

verão *m* summer

verdade *f* truth
  não é verdade? isn't it?

verdadeiro(a) true

verde green

vergas *fpl* wicker goods

verificar to check

vermelho(a) red

verniz *m* varnish

vertigem *f* dizziness ; vertigo

vespa *f* wasp

véspera *f* the day before ; the eve

vestiário *m* cloakroom ; changing room

vestido *m* dress

vestir to dress ; to wear
  vestir-se to get dressed

vestuário *m* clothes

veterinário(a) *m/f* vet

vez *f* time ; turn
  às vezes occasionally ; sometimes
  uma vez once
  duas vezes twice
  muitas vezes often
  é a sua vez it's your turn

via *f* lane

via via
  via aérea by air mail
  via nasal to be inhaled
  via oral orally

viaduto *m* viaduct ; flyover

viagem *f* trip ; journey
  viagem de negócios business trip

viajante *m/f* traveller

viajar to travel

vida *f* life

vidros *mpl* glassware

vila *f* small town

vinagre *m* vinegar

vindima *f* harvest *(of grapes)*

V

vinho *m* wine
 vinho branco white wine
 vinho da casa house wine
 vinho de mesa table wine
 vinho doce sweet wine
 vinho espumante sparkling
 wine
 vinho rosé rosé wine
 vinho seco dry wine
 vinho tinto red wine
 vinho verde young white
 wine
vir to come
virar to turn
 vire à direita turn right
 vire à esquerda turn left
vírgula *f* comma
visitar to visit
vista *f* view
 com linda vista with a
 beautiful view
visto *m* visa
vitela *f* veal
viúvo(a) *m/f* widower/widow
vivenda *f* chalet ; villa
viver to live
vivo(a) alive
vizinho(a) *m/f* neighbour
você(s) you
volante *m* steering wheel
volta *f* turn
 à volta de about
 em volta de around
 dar uma volta to go for a
 short walk/ride
voltagem *f* voltage

voltar to return *(go/come back)*
 volto já I'll be back in a
 minute
vomitar to vomit
voo *m* flight
 voo fretado charter flight
 voo normal scheduled
 flight
vos you ; to you
vós you
vosso yours
voz *f* voice
vulcão *m* volcano

W

WC toilet
wind-surf *m* windsurfing

X

xadrez *m* chess
xarope *m* syrup
 xarope para a tosse cough
 syrup
xerez *m* sherry

Z

zero zero ; nought
zona *f* zone
 zona azul permitted parking zone
 zona de banhos swimming
 area
 zona interdita no thorough-
 fare

GRAMMAR

NOUNS

Portuguese nouns are *masculine* or *feminine*, and their gender is shown by the words for **the (o/a)** and **a (um/uma)** used before them (the 'article'):

masculine	*feminine*
o/um castelo the/a castle	**a/uma mesa the/a table**
os castelos/(uns) castelos	**as mesas/(umas) mesas**
the castles/(some) castles	**the tables/(some) tables**

It is usually possible to tell whether a noun is *masculine* or *feminine* by its ending: nouns ending in **-o** or **-or** are usually *masculine*, while those ending in **-a**, **-agem**, **-dade** and **-tude** tend to be *feminine*. There are exceptions, however, and it's best to learn the noun and the article together.

PLURAL

Nouns ending in a vowel form the plural by adding **-s**, while those ending in a consonant usually add **-es**. The exceptions to this are words ending in an **-m** which change to **-ns** in the plural and words ending in **-l** which change to **-is** in the plural: e.g. **hotel – hotéis**.

NOTE: When used after the words **a to**, **de of**, **em in** and **por by**, the articles (and many other words) contract:

a + as = às *ash*	**to the**
de + um = dum *dooñ*	**of a**
em + uma = numa *noomuh*	**to a**
por + os = pelos *peloosh*	**by the**

'This', 'That', 'These', 'Those'

These depend on the gender and number of the noun they represent:

este rapaz	**this boy**	esta rapariga	**this girl**
estes rapazes	**these boys**	estas raparigas	**these girls**
esse rapaz	**that boy**	essa rapariga	**that girl**
esses rapazes	**those boys**	essas raparigas	**those girls**
aquele rapaz	**that boy** (over there)	aquela rapariga	**that girl** (over there)
aqueles rapazes	**those boys** (over there)	aquelas raparigas	**those girls** (over there)

ADJECTIVES

Adjectives normally follow the nouns they describe in Portuguese, e.g. **a maçã verde the green apple**. Some exceptions which precede the noun are: **muito much, many**; **pouco little, not much**; **tanto so much, so many**; **primeiro first**; **último last**; **bom good**; **nenhum no, not any**; **grande great, big**.

Portuguese adjectives have to reflect the gender of the noun they describe. To make an adjective feminine, **-o** endings change to **-a**, and **-or** and **-ês** change to **-ora** and **-esa**. Otherwise they generally have the same form for both genders. Thus:

masculine	feminine
o livro vermelho	a saia vermelha
the red book	**the red skirt**
o homem falador	a mulher faladora
the talkative man	**the talkative woman**

To make adjectives plural, follow the general rules given for nouns.

'My', 'Your', 'His', 'Her'

These words also depend on the gender and number of the following noun and not on the sex of the 'owner'.

	with masc. / with fem.	with plural nouns
my	o meu / a minha	os meus / as minhas
his/her/its/your	o seu / a sua	os seus / as suas
our	o nosso / a nossa	os nossos / as nossas
their/your	o seu / a sua	os seus / as suas

NOTE: Since **o seu, a sua,** etc can mean **his, her, your,** etc, Portuguese will often replace them with the words for **of him, of her, of you,** etc (**dele** , **dela** , **de você** , etc) in order to avoid confusion:

os livros *dela*	**her books**
os livros *de você*	**your books**
os livros *deles*	**their books**

PRONOUNS

SUBJECT		OBJECT	
I	eu *ay-oo*	**me**	me *muh*
you (informal)	tu *too*	**you** (informal)	te *teh*
you	você *voh-se*	**you**	o/a *oo/uh*
he	ele *ayl*	**him**	o *oo*
she	ela *eluh*	**her**	a *uh*
it	ele/ela *ayl/eluh*	**it**	o/a *oo/uh*
we	nós *nosh*	**us**	nos *noosh*
you (informal)	vocês *voh-sesh*	**you** (informal)	os/as *oosh/ush*
you	vós *vosh*	**you**	vos *voosh*
they (masc.)	eles *aylush*	**them** (masc.)	os *oosh*
they (fem.)	elas *elush*	**them** (fem.)	as *ush*

NOTES

1. **YOU** The polite form of addressing someone would be with **o Senhor** or a **Senhora** using the **(s)he** form or the verb and the object pronoun **o/a**. The semi-formal **you** is **você** and the informal **you** is **tu** (like French and Spanish).

2. Subject pronouns are normally not used except for emphasis or to avoid confusion:

> *eu* vou para Lisboa e *ele* vai para Coimbra
> **I'm going to Lisbon and *he*'s going to Coimbra**

3. Object pronouns are usually placed after the verb and joined with a hyphen:

> vejo-*o*   **I see him**

However, in sentences beginning with a 'question word' or a 'negative word' the pronoun goes in front of the verb:

> quando *o* viu?   **when did you see him?**
> não *o* vi   **I did not see him**

Also, in sentences beginning with **that** and **who**, etc ('subordinate clauses') the pronoun precedes the verb:

> sei que *o* viu   **I know that you saw him**
> o homem que *o* viu   **the man who saw him**

4. **Me** also = **to me** and **nos** = **to us**, but **lhe** = **to him/to her/to it/to you** *(formal)*, **te** = **to you** *(informal)* and **lhes** = **to them/to you**.

5. When two pronouns are used together they are often shortened. The verb will also change spelling if it ends in **-r**, **-s**, **-z** or a nasal sound:

dá-mo (= dá + me + o)	**he gives me it**
dê-lho (= dê + lhe + o)	**give him it**
fá-lo (= faz + o)	**he does it**
dão-nos (= dão + os or dão + nos)	**they give them** or **they give us**

6. The pronoun following a preposition has the same form as the subject pronoun, except for **mim** (**me**), **si** (**you** – *formal*), **ti** (**you** – *informal*).

VERBS

There are three main patterns of endings for verbs in Portuguese – those ending -**ar**, -**er** and -**ir** in the dictionary.

CANT<u>AR</u>	TO SING	COM<u>ER</u>	TO EAT
canto	I sing	como	I eat
cantas	you sing	comes	you eat
canta	(s)he/it sings/ you sing	come	(s)he/it eats/ you eat
cantamos	we sing	comemos	we eat
cantais	you sing	comeis	you eat
cantam	they/you sing	comem	they/you eat

PART<u>IR</u>	TO LEAVE
parto	I leave
partes	you leave
parte	(s)he/it leaves/you leave
partimos	we leave
partis	you leave
partem	they/you leave

And in the past tense:

cantei	I sang	comi	I ate
cantaste	you sang	comeste	you ate
cantou	(s)he/it/you sang	comeu	(s)he/it/you ate
cantámos	we sang	comemos	we ate
cantastes	you sang	comestes	you ate
cantaram	they/you sang	comeram	they/you ate

parti	I left
partiste	you left
partiu	(s)he/it/you left
partimos	we left
partistes	you left
partiram	they/you left

Four of the most common verbs are irregular:

SER	TO BE		ESTAR	TO BE
sou	I am		estou	I am
és	you are		estás	you are
é	(s)he/it is/you are		está	(s)he/it is/you are
somos	we are		estamos	we are
sois	you are		estais	you are
são	they/you are		estão	they/you are

TER	TO HAVE		IR	TO GO
tenho	I have		vou	I go
tens	you have		vais	you go
tem	(s)he/it has/you have		vai	(s)he/it goes/you go
temos	we have		vamos	we go
tendes	you have		ides	you go
têm	they/you have		vão	they/you go

NOTE: **Ser** and **Estar** both mean **to be**.
Ser is used to describe a permanent place or state:

> sou inglês   I am English
> é uma praia   it is a beach

Estar is used to describe a temporary state or where something is located:

> como está?   how are you?
> onde está a praia?   where is the beach?